Popular Conceptions

of Mental Health

Popular Conceptions
of Mental Health

THEIR

DEVELOPMENT

AND

CHANGE

JUM C. NUNNALLY, JR.

Professor of Psychology
Vanderbilt University

Holt, Rinehart and Winston, Inc.

New York

To SARAH

Preface

THIS BOOK SUMMARIZES the results of six years of research by a team of investigators. It is intended to serve three purposes: (1) to report basic research findings relating to opinion-attitude investigation, (2) to serve as an adjunct to graduate courses in clinical psychology and related subjects, and (3) to provide a practical guide to psychiatrists, psychological counselors, social workers, physicians, nurses, and all those who are involved in mental-health education.

The research was conducted by members of the Institute of Communications Research, University of Illinois, supported by a series of special grants from the National Institute of Mental Health, United States Public Health Service. The work began in January 1954 and was terminated in August 1959. Initiated and directed by Wilbur Schramm during its first two years, the project has since been under the joint direction of Dr. Charles E. Osgood and myself. It has been a joint effort of the Institute staff from its inception, and many people have contributed to its various phases: George Gerbner, Theodore R. Husek, George J. Suci, Percy H. Tannenbaum, Wilson L. Taylor, Edward Ware, and Robert Wolff on the Institute staff; Howard M. Bobren, Gerald Cashman, Evelyn Walker Katz, John M. Kittross, Patricia V. Klein, Jack Schwartz, Robert Severson, Donald Smith, Mary Snowden, Yasumasa Tanaka, Carol Tucker, and Sharon Wolfe who served as research assistants. In addition, many faculty members of the University of Illinois and other schools have given their advice and assistance most generously. We owe a special word of appreciation to Mrs. Freda Pierce, who has served as secretary to the project.

The author owes a special debt of gratitude to Dr. Osgood. Without his constant encouragement, advice, and hard work the project would have been far less fruitful, and this book would not be in print.

Some sections of the book, including some tables and figures, were adapted from articles submitted to professional journals by members of the project staff. For permission to use these materials, thanks are expressed to the editors of the following journals: *American Psychologist, Behavioral Science, Journal of Consulting Psychology, Journal of Personality,* and *Public Opinion Quarterly.*

The project included a very satisfying set of ingredients. It was focused on a problem of national concern, and, at the same time, it permitted us to explore some basic issues in psychology. Also, our relationship with the staff of the National Institute of Mental Health has been a pleasant and fruitful feature of the work. They offered many ideas and helped us to evaluate the merits of various approaches. We are particularly grateful to Joseph M. Bobbitt, assistant director of NIMH, for his active assistance and encouragement. While our sponsors helped us in many ways, they permitted us complete freedom in the exercise of our own judgment as to what to do and how to do it; this made for a very healthy research climate.

The nature of the research problems has interested people from different disciplines, and the plan and scope of the project has not only permitted but encouraged them to work together toward their solution. We use the phrase ". . . *toward* their solution" deliberately. We are painfully aware of the fact that our research over the past six years, as diversified as it has been, has only daubed here and there on the immense canvas of communication problems in the area of mental health and illness. Nevertheless, we think that what we have done provides at least a few solid answers, and we hope that it poses more clearly some important questions.

J. C. N.

Nashville, Tenn.
September 1960

Contents

APPENDIX   239

INDEX   309

1

Introduction

THE FOLLOWING CHAPTERS will report a wide range of studies, varying from experimental investigations of attitude change to content analyses of radio programs. Each of the investigations was intended to fill in one piece in a puzzle, or, perhaps using a more appropriate metaphor, to light one more candle in a rather large and dark forest. In addition to having a common purpose, the investigations were mainly concerned with different aspects of the same psychological variables.

THE PROBLEM

For centuries man has been concerned with disorders of an immediate, visible kind—the physical diseases that pain, debilitate, and kill. At the present rate of progress, the not-too-distant future should see man living in a world relatively free from major physical disorders and diseases. As this gradually comes about, attention is shifting to the least-understood human malfunctions—the mental disorders—and to mental health generally—human happiness and social effectiveness.

The fledgling fields of psychology and psychiatry are trying to develop a firm factual basis for mental-health programs. Progress has been relatively slow because of the intrinsic complexities of the problems and the meager support that has been given to the research. Regardless of how little is known or how slowly progress is made, the research effort is crucially important and will probably receive increasing support.

Careful plans should be drawn now for putting to use the results of research in the mental-health field. At first thought this seems like a relatively simple matter, as it is in some research areas. For example, as new information about cancer is discovered, preventatives and methods of treatment are communicated to physicians, who then apply them. In contrast, much of what we know about human adjustment cannot be applied so directly. Although some of it can be put to use directly by psychologists, psychiatrists, and kindred professionals, much of the information is of value only if effectively communicated to the general public.

The effectiveness of cancer treatment will depend only slightly on what the patient knows about the treatment, what he thinks about the ailment, and what his family and friends do. Just the opposite is true of the effective prevention and treatment of human maladjustment. In this area desirable changes in attitudes and outlooks depend, in large part, on effective methods of communicating with individuals about their ailments and with family, friends, and community agencies in order to promote healthy environments. Families need to know how to help in rehabilitation. Teachers need to be able to recognize the signs of mental disorder in children and to know what can be done in the classroom and elsewhere to help them. Civic agencies need to know how to promote favorable community attitudes toward treatment facilities. Thus the effective prevention and treatment of mental illness depends in large measure on knowing how to communicate the information.

One approach to communicating with the public is to have mental-health professionals (psychologists, psychiatrists, social workers, and others) work directly with the people who need information and advice. However, there are not now, and may never be, enough professionals to do the job. Consequently, we must depend on less-direct methods of communication: presentations in the media of mass communication, in pamphlets, in special films, in classrooms, in group discussions, and so on.

Communicating mental-health information may, on first thought, seem to be a relatively straightforward task—merely presenting facts in a clear and interesting manner. Unfortunately, the problem is much more complicated than that, and there are many stumbling blocks in the communication process. For example, the attitudes that people have toward mental disorders and afflicted individuals make them resistant to certain kinds of new ideas and to some types of communications. Because the direct approach often fails to change people's attitudes and opinions in desired directions, new appeals and communication strategies must be found. Research on these and other problems involved in communicating mental-health information will be discussed in this book.

THE RESEARCH AREA

"Mental health" is a rather global concept, and even such seemingly tangential matters as recreation and entertainment may be relevant. In planning the project it was necessary to choose some smaller portion of the whole mental-health field in which to work. We decided to study public reactions to mental illness—psychoses, neuroses, and lesser disturbances. The plan was to study popular concepts of mental illness and how those conceptions develop and change, both naturally and as a function of outside influences. Our research did not specifically deal with the nature of mental health itself but rather with what people think and feel about mental-health phenomena—popular ideas about the causes, symptoms, treatment, and social effects of mental disorder. Although mental illness was our primary focus, some of the research touched on broader issues of human adjustment.

The research was intended to provide some partial answers to two very large questions: (1) What are the existing conceptions of mental health? (2) How can the existing conceptions be changed for the better? The first question involves "descriptive," or measurement and survey studies; the second, experimental studies which measure the differential effectiveness of various communication methods and strategies. The descriptive studies are reported in Chapters 2 through 8; the experimental studies, in Chapters 9 through 17. In addition, we conducted a number of studies which do not fall neatly into either of these categories—content analyses of the mass media, interview studies of media personnel, analyses of terminology, a factor analysis of the stylistic features of written messages, and so forth. These studies are scattered throughout the text at the places where they are most relevant.

The project period is divided roughly in half, the first half being devoted mainly to the study of public conceptions and the second half, to experimental studies of attitude change. We measured the attitudes and information held by three sources: the general public, the experts (psychologists and psychiatrists), and the mass media. To clarify some of the results, we conducted two special studies: a study of the views of general medical practitioners (Ch. 8) and an analysis of the internal processes of the mass-communications media (Ch. 7).

As we were sure they would, the descriptive studies of existing conceptions furnished many leads to important variables for consideration in the experimental studies of information transmission and attitude change. Some of these variables are the relative public interest in different kinds of mental-health topics, the amount of anxiety generated by messages, the "certainty" with which messages are phrased, and the degree to which messages provide solutions to problems (see Chs. 9 through 17).

Information and Attitudes

In our research the distinction between *information* and *attitudes* has been very important. The term *information* is used here to refer to verifiable statements such as "There are more men than women in mental hospitals." In contrast, a statement such as "I am afraid to be around anyone who has had a mental disorder" concerns an *attitude*, or feeling, in which no question of truth or falsity is at issue. The terms *opinion* and *knowledge* will be used synonymously with information.

Although it is often difficult to distinguish between information and attitudes, and the two often interact in popular beliefs, it is important to separate them as clearly as possible in research work. In the following chapters it will be shown that very different principles apply to the two kinds of "conceptions." Apparent contradictions in research findings are often explainable by the fact that one investigator who purports to study mental-health "beliefs" is dealing with informational types of responses, and another investigator, also purporting to study mental-health "beliefs," is dealing with attitudinal types of responses.

RESEARCH METHODS

The studies which will be reported here are not only diverse in terms of content, they are also diverse in terms of design and method. They range from the "hard" to the "soft," the "macro" to the "micro," and the "basic" to the "applied." The research methods range from those typical of journalistic studies to those typical of experimental psychology studies, from controlled experiments to descriptive field explorations. In some cases only our judgment and subjective analysis are cited as "evidence."

The amount of energy devoted to each study was metered by the importance of the study to the over-all research project. For the same reason that a micrometer is not used to measure lumber, refined methods of investigation were not used to measure gross distinctions. In some cases it was more economical to tap the large differences that occur in small studies rather than to expend a disproportionate amount of energy in documenting finer results.

Sample-survey Methods

The first part of the book is largely concerned with popular information about and attitudes toward mental-health phenomena. Ideally, large national samples should be used for such studies. In no case was such a sample used. Instead, the survey studies are based on relatively small samples (100 to 700 persons), which in most cases could be better described as "collections" rather than as samples. In these studies an effort was made to construct a group of respondents which generally resembled the country as a whole in terms of a number of demographic characteristics.

Most of our survey studies were conducted with an "opinion panel" which was organized for the particular purpose. Except for the fact that the majority of the 400 respondents live in central Illinois, the panel is an approximate miniature of the United States population in terms of education, sex ratio, income, religious affiliation, and age.

Of course, when anything other than a carefully drawn national sample is used, survey results are somewhat equivocal. For many of our studies, however, moderate-sized, quasi-representative groups were probably adequate. Carefully drawn large samples are needed most when the purpose is to finely measure central tendencies. For example, in a pre-election poll, where fine differences are important, it makes a great deal of difference whether the prospective vote for a candidate is 49 or 51 percent. In our studies we were concerned only with much more gross distinctions. That is, if 80 percent of the subjects in one of our quasi-representative groups held an opinion, we felt safe in saying that the predominate tendency is for people in general to hold that opinion.

A second reason why more extensive samples were not needed is because many of our findings are concerned with correlations rather than central tendencies. For example, we found that years of schooling correlates with the tendency to agree with certain kinds of opinion statements. Correlations usually persist over samples drawn by different methods even if their sizes fluctuate.

A third reason why more extensive samples were not required is that in many cases we were interested in *relative* responses rather than absolute responses. For example, we compared public attitudes toward psychotics and neurotics. Whereas we do find differences in the central tendency with respect to these attitudes which vary somewhat with the age, education, and other demographic characteristics of respondents, the relative responses are the same for all groups. For example, both high- and low-education respondents and young and old respondents regard psychotics as more dangerous and unpredictable than neurotics.

Now that the research is completed, we realize that in some areas even our quasi-representative samples were more elaborate than had been needed. Many of the findings are the same when only women are studied, when only people over 70 years of age are studied, or when only college freshmen are studied. However, we know this only from hindsight.

Generally then, we metered the size and accuracy of our "samples" by the precision required of the results. In a number of instances, only 100 respondents were used in the first part of a study. If the results looked promising, we gathered a larger and more representative collection of respondents. In one instance early results led us to make an area sampling of Knoxville, Tennessee. In other instances early results indicated that more extensive sampling would not yield important results.

Communication-effect Experiments

The typical approach to studying the effects of communications variables is the before-after design. Prior to receiving the communication, experimental subjects respond to an attitude or information questionnaire. After receiving the communication, the same subjects again respond to the same instrument or instruments. The advantage of this design is that each subject acts as his "own control," and consequently, the power of statistical tests is high.

For a number of reasons, however, we have generally not used the before-after design in our experiments. One reason why we generally have not used the before-after design is that it probably sensitizes the subjects to certain features of the communication. For example, if one of the "before" questions is, "Can mental illness be treated effectively with drugs?," subjects will probably look for material relating to this question in the communication. A second weakness of the before-after design is that subjects are probably influenced on the "after" measure by the way in which they responded on the "before" measure. If subjects remember their "before" answers, they may repeat them on the "after" form in order not to appear inconsistent. The before-after design has a third weakness. The subject may become aware of the fact that an experiment is being conducted. For example, if the subject responds to a questionnaire about mental illness and subsequently is shown a film on mental illness, it is easy for him to conclude that the communication is meant to change him in some way. In such a case, the subject may change his responses on the "after" questionnaire just to help the experimenter, or, if he is recalcitrant, he may not change his responses even if the communication was effective.

Instead of using the before-after technique, we generally compared an experimental group or groups with a control group or groups. In a typical experiment four groups of college students received one of four different kinds of messages about mental illness. After the groups had read the messages, attitude and information measures were applied. In addition, two control groups read one of two "control" messages which had nothing to do with mental health, and then responded to the same attitude and information measures. The over-all and differential effectiveness of the four experimental messages was determined by comparing them statistically with the control messages. Occasionally we used as a second control group people who received no messages.

Although more powerful statistical tests can be applied to the before-after design, the experimental-control design is logically better. In the experimental-control design there is no "before" measure. Subjects are not sensitized to look for particular features of the communication, nor are they necessarily aware that they are participating in an experiment, at least until the "after" measure is applied. Since there is no "before" measure, the responses on the "after" measure are unaffected by the memory of "before" responses. In other words, we have been more concerned with the validity of our results than with the power of statistical designs per se. Our decision to use the experimental-control design rather than the before-after design for most studies was justified later by some of the research results (see Ch. 15).

Measuring Instruments

As is so often the case in psychological investigations, one of our biggest hurdles was the construction of adequate measuring instruments. In most cases it was necessary to develop our own instruments instead of using existing measures. We relied heavily on questionnaire-type measuring instruments. In using instruments of this kind, the validity of the responses is always questionable. It is well known that people often distort their "real" feelings in order to give socially acceptable responses. Even if the subject tries to cooperate, he may not have insight into his "real" feelings. The problems of faking, or the attempt to give socially acceptable responses, are different for information instruments than for attitude instruments. Because information instruments are concerned mainly with verifiable statements, they are much like tests of ability. Faking is a minor problem on tests of ability since people usually try to earn the best possible score. But it is a matter of concern on attitude instruments.

There is some evidence to indicate that our major attitude-measuring instrument, the Semantic Differential (Osgood, Suci, & Tannenbaum, 1957), is not entirely fakable. We were often able to offset the tendency of respondents to give socially acceptable answers by statistical methods —for example, we analyzed the relative attitudes toward concepts. In our study of public attitudes toward psychiatrists, the results indicate that psychiatrists are held in high public esteem. However, when public attitudes toward psychiatrists are compared with public attitudes toward physicians in general, psychiatrists are viewed, relatively speaking, as less valuable and effective than other physicians.

As another precaution against faking we tried to protect the anonymity of respondents as much as possible. We stressed that frankness was essential, that we wanted to know what they really felt, regardless of what they thought was a "good" attitude. In most cases, attitude-survey forms were filled out in privacy, and respondents were asked not to write their names on the forms.

A principle which guided us in interpreting attitude-measurement results is that usually there is less reason to suspect socially unacceptable and negative responses than socially acceptable and positive responses. To the extent that "acceptability" can influence responses, "nice" attitudes are suspect. In spite of our best efforts, some of the attitude studies were probably influenced (to some unknown extent) by the respondents' desire to give socially acceptable answers. When respondents rate psychotics as dangerous, dirty, and ignorant, however, it is unlikely that they are being influenced by the desire to respond in a socially acceptable manner.

In only a few instances do we have information about how people actually behave toward mental-health phenomena; we only know what they say they think and feel. While it is worthwhile to investigate how people behave toward these phenomena, this type of study was beyond the resources available to our project. It should not be assumed, however, that expressed attitudes are unimportant or less important than what people "really" feel. What people say and are willing to stand on publicly is perhaps a more important determiner of action than what people may "really" feel in some other sense.

Studies of the Mass Media

An important phase of our investigations was to learn some of the ways that the media of mass communication influence popular conceptions of mental health and mental illness. Our primary efforts were directed toward (1) an analysis of the content in the media pertaining to mental health and (2) a study of the internal processes of the media which select and mold material relevant to mental health.

In many ways our content analysis of the mass media utilized traditional procedures. It differed, however, in one important respect from traditional approaches. Whereas content analyses usually depend on a priori, or "rational," content categories, our categories were derived empirically in such a way to insure a broad coverage of important content characteristics. How this advantage was obtained will be discussed in Chapters 2 and 6.

In studying the internal processes of the mass media, we sometimes found it necessary to rely on the judgments of expert observers. This was the case in analyzing the results of personal interviews with writers, directors, and others who influence the content of mass-media presentations. Although it is generally preferable to use objective methods of analysis, if possible, more impressionistic investigation may also serve a useful purpose. In the present case, our analysis of mass-media processes proved to be a valuable addition to our more objective investigations.

Related Basic Research

One of the important side effects of the project was that it encouraged members of the staff to investigate a number of basic research issues. For example, in one of the studies it was necessary to measure the influence of various response-set tendencies in a questionnaire. Because no satisfactory measure of response-set tendencies was available, members of the staff developed a new instrument and subsequently used it in several studies (see Nunnally & Husek, 1958a). Several members of the research team also developed a promising instrument designed to measure anxiety and performed a number of validation studies with it.

THE STRUCTURE OF THE BOOK

The book will be structured in terms of a list of propositions, each of which represents a general conclusion from our studies. The term *proposition* will be used in a general sense to refer to tested hypotheses, generalizations, and recommendations for communication programs. Each proposition will be accompanied by a description of the supporting evidence. The most pertinent statistical results, tables, and graphs will be presented in the body of the text. Other findings and a number of questionnaire instruments will be presented in the Appendix. To keep the book from becoming unmanageably bulky, in some places we will cite references to evidence presented in duplicated project reports and professional journals.

PART
I

Studies of Existing States

of Information

and Attitudes

2

What the Public Knows

THE OBVIOUS FIRST STEP in a program of research concerning public information about mental health is to learn what the public currently knows and thinks. For this reason, the first year of our research (1954) was devoted in large measure to surveying the information held by the general public. In order to view the studies discussed in this chapter in the proper perspective, it is important to keep in mind the distinction between information and attitudes. By information we mean the tendency to agree or disagree with factual, or potentially factual, statements, regardless of whether such information is correct or not.

In addition to measuring the current level of public information, we compared the information held by the public with that held by psychologists and psychiatrists and with that expressed in the media of mass communication. Such a three-way comparison imposes formidable methodological problems. Before the information in the three sources could be compared directly, comparable "yardsticks," or measuring instruments, had to be devised. The section below will describe the instrument-making phase of the study of public information, and the sections to follow will describe the results obtained when the instruments were applied.

CONSTRUCTING THE INSTRUMENTS

In order to insure comparability for the three information sources, the information measure was based on what was *currently* being said by members of the public, by experts, and in the mass media. Therefore, a preliminary search of the three sources was made to determine the content coverage needed in our measures of information.

Collecting Items

The first step in constructing an instrument was to gather a large number (over 3,000) of opinion statements from the three sources. This is much like what a naturalist would do in studying the flora of a particular region: he would first gather a wide sample of plants and then study his collection in detail.

Samples of expert opinions were gathered from mental-hygiene books, professional publications, and over 200 public-information pamphlets. Samples of public opinions were taken from the protocols of 200 detailed personal interviews, eight interviews with mothers of children in psycho therapy, and 12 interviews with the wives of men who were in mental hospitals.[1] Opinions expressed in the interviews ranged from a belief that the blood of the insane is blue to a belief that mental illness is not a hopeless condition. For the media, small samples of the content of newspapers, magazines, and radio and television programs were examined. For example, when the "psychiatrist" in a daytime "soap opera" advised his patient to take a long vacation, this was recorded as an opinion about methods of treatment.

We obtained over 3,000 statements related to the causes, symptoms, prognosis, treatment, incidence, and social significance of mental-health problems. The next step in constructing an instrument was the reduction of the large number of opinion statements to a number that could be used in questionnaire studies. By removing apparent duplicates in meaning, the larger collection was reduced to 240.

Pretesting the Questionnaire

Before the final questionnaire could be formulated, it was necessary to take several precautions. First the effect of response-set tendencies in the form had to be minimized. One type of response set is the tendency of some people to agree and other people to disagree with questionnaire items regardless of what the items say. To offset this tendency we randomly determined the direction of each item. A table of random numbers was used to decide whether each item would be left as it was or reversed in meaning. For example, the item "A vacation will help cure a nervous breakdown" could be reversed to "A vacation will not help cure a nervous breakdown," and the item "There are more men than women in mental hospitals," could be reversed to "There are more women than men in mental hospitals." Sometimes it was difficult to reverse statements, and some of the reversals read a bit strangely. Even with these difficulties, the randomization of directions was a good precaution. It had the interesting effect of making items randomly either true of false, even if their

[1] For the use of material employed in the sampling of items, we would like to thank, among others, Drs. A. Campbell, J. Clausen, E. Freidson, and Shirley Star.

truth or falsity is not presently known. The procedure also insured that true and false items would not be lumped together in the questionnaire and that about half of all of the items would be true.

As a second precaution in constructing the questionnaire, a study was made of the bias inherent in various kinds of item forms. There is usually more than one way to phrase an item, and the phrasing that is chosen may influence the responses obtained. Members of the project staff invented a technique for measuring the bias of item forms (Nunnally & Husek, 1958a). This permitted us to pretest the item forms to be used in questionnaire studies.

In addition to the major pilot studies described above, several smaller studies were carried out to test the clarity of the questionnaire instructions and rating procedure. The results of the pilot studies guided us in composing the questionnaire. Each of the 240 opinion statements was presented with a seven-step rating scale, some examples of which are as follows (see Appendix 1 for the complete questionnaire):

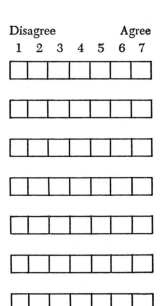

	Disagree					Agree	
	1	2	3	4	5	6	7

1. A person can avoid worry by keeping busy.

2. The eyes of the insane are glassy.

3. X-rays of the head will tell whether or not a person is likely to develop insanity.

4. Most of the people in mental hospitals speak in words that can be understood.

5. Books on "peace of mind" prevent many persons from developing nervous breakdowns.

6. Early training will not make the child's brain grow faster.

7. A change of climate seldom helps an emotional disorder.

The Champaign Sample

For the pretest, we planned to administer the 240-item form to a group of subjects and to make a factor analysis of the responses. From the analysis we hoped to uncover some major dimensions of public information about mental-health phenomena. The obtained factors could subsequently be used in more extensive surveys of public information and to measure the opinions of experts and the viewpoints portrayed in the media of mass communication. In this way, the measurements would be comparable for the three information sources.

The 240-item questionnaire was administered to 349 persons living in the vicinity of Champaign-Urbana, Illinois (see Appendix 1 for complete results); 100 of the subjects had previously participated in a study of attitudes toward political concepts. This group of 100, which had been obtained by an area sampling of the twin cities, was augmented by 249 subjects living in and around Champaign-Urbana. No subjects younger than 15 years of age were sought for the sample.

The Champaign-Urbana group is more appropriately regarded as a diverse collection of persons rather than as a sample in the strict meaning of the term. Because we intended to make a factor analysis of the responses, the major requirement for our group was that it vary widely in terms of education, age, occupation, and other demographic characteristics. Some demographic characteristics of the group are shown in Table 2.1

TABLE 2.1. Demographic Characteristics of the
Champaign-Urbana Sample (N = 349) *

Characteristic	Frequency	Characteristic	Frequency
Age		*Annual income*	
15–19	38	under $1,200	20
20–29	43	$1,200–3,600	77
30–39	77	$3,600–6,000	109
40–49	79	$6,000–8,400	61
50–59	49	$8,400–10,800	34
60–69	39	$10,800 and over	41
70–79	16		
80–89	4	*Marital status*	
90–99	1	Married	245
		Single	68
Years of education		Widowed/divorced	34
2–3	0		
4–5	1	*Religious preference*	
6–7	6	Protestant	250
8–9	30	Catholic	32
10–11	43	Jewish	15
12–13	92	None of these	50
14–15	40		
16–17	83	*Sex*	
18–19	48	Male	188
		Female	158

* Because a few respondents failed to supply all the information, the frequencies do not add up to 349.

Analyzing the Responses

Almost everyone either agreed strongly or disagreed strongly with 60 of the 240 statements. These statements were not included in the subsequent factor analysis, and the questionnaire was immediately reduced to 180 items.

The responses obtained from the Champaign sample were factor analyzed.[2] (For the reader who is unfamiliar with the technical details, factor analysis is a mathematical procedure for grouping items so that the items in each group show a relatively high correlation with one another and a relatively low correlation with items in other groups. Each such group contains items that tend to measure the same thing and is referred to as a factor.) The purpose of the factor analysis was to "boil down" the remaining 180 questionnaire items to a relatively small number of general dimensions of public information. Ten factors, listed below,[3] were obtained from the analysis. Under each factor name is summarized the content of those items belonging to it. (See Nunnally, 1957, for a more detailed discussion of the factor-analysis procedures and results.)

Information Factors

I. LOOK AND ACT DIFFERENT (SUBMAN). The mentally ill are recognizably different in manner and appearance from normal persons. They have glassy eyes and small brains, laugh more than normal people, and pay little attention to their personal appearance.

II. WILL POWER. Will power is the basis of personal adjustment. Once adjustment is lost, the psychiatrist exercises his own will power to bolster the patient's failing will. Persons who remain mentally ill do not "try" to get better. Most of the people who seek treatment do not need it, and those who do are not very worthwhile persons.

III. SEX DISTINCTION. Women are more prone to mental disorder than men are. Women worry more than men and more often have "nervous breakdowns."

IV. AVOIDANCE OF MORBID THOUGHTS. Preoccupation with pleasant thoughts is the basis of mental health. Mental disturbances can be avoided by keeping busy, reading books on "peace of mind," and not discussing troublesome topics. Psychiatrists must have a good sense of humor. The psychiatrist recommends hobbies and other ways for the patient to occupy himself.

V. GUIDANCE AND SUPPORT. Mental health can be maintained by de-

[2] This work would not have been possible without the help of the Digital Computer Laboratory at the University of Illinois.
[3] Members of the project staff devised a technique for measuring the interpretability of factors and subsequently applied the technique to three widely used multifactor personality inventories (Nunnally & Husek, 1958b).

pending on strong persons in the environment. The therapist explains to the patient the origin of his troubles and tells the patient where his ideas are incorrect. The mentally ill are persons who lacked affection in child-hood.

VI. HOPELESSNESS. There is little that can be done to cure a mental disorder. Few of the inmates of mental hospitals return to work in society. Psychiatrists cannot tell whether a condition is curable.

VII. IMMEDIATE EXTERNAL ENVIRONMENT VERSUS PERSONALITY DY-NAMICS. The individual's state of mental health is dependent on the pressures in his immediate environment. Mental troubles are caused by physical exhaustion, financial and social problems. A cure can be effected by a vacation or change of scenery. The opposite point of view is that the individual's state of well-being is dependent on his personal history, espe-cially his childhood.

VIII. NONSERIOUSNESS. Emotional difficulties are relatively unimportant problems that cause little damage to the individual. Good emotional habits are easy to develop and maintain. (This factor differs from the *hopeless-ness* factor in that *hopelessness* is concerned with the likelihood of re-covery and the value of treatment, regardless of the extent to which the problems are damaging. To illustrate, an individual may have a disorder, such as an allergy, which would be hopeless in the sense of being in-curable, but not serious in the sense of being debilitating.)

IX. AGE FUNCTION. Persons become more susceptible to emotional dis-orders as they grow older—an apparent analogy with the increasing susceptibility to some of the "physical" disorders. Children are less af-fected by frightening experiences. Older persons are more prone to insanity and recover more slowly from "nervous breakdowns."

X. ORGANIC CAUSES. Mental disorder is brought on by organic factors like poor diet and diseases of the nervous system. It is associated with physical symptoms like brain damage and can be cured by "physical" means.

As the factors are described, they sound like popular misconceptions. As in all factor analyses, there was a choice as to which pole of each factor to use in the interpretation. The wording above was selected merely to simplify later analyses. It would have been just as easy to reverse most of the interpretations, for example, *nonseriousness* to *seriousness*. Then the factors would tend to sound more like "correct" opinions.

It should be remembered that all of the research described up to this point was preparatory to the actual studies of public information. The ten factors served as the yardsticks by which comparisons were made of the viewpoints expressed by the general public, by psychiatrists and psy-chologists, and in the mass media of communications. The application of the ten factors to the three information sources is described in the follow-ing sections.

APPLICATION OF THE INFORMATION FACTORS

The Public

The sample of responses obtained from the Champaign-Urbana area was rescored in terms of the ten factors by finding the mean score for each person on the several items which best represented each factor. In addition, a revised form of the information questionnaire was constructed containing only the items which characterized the factors. The new form,[4] containing 50 items, was administered to a sample of 201 respondents in Knoxville, Tennessee. An area sampling of that city was used to obtain an approximately representative cross-section of the population.[5] Some demographic characteristics of the sample are shown in Table 2.2. A third sample of 150 subjects was obtained in Eugene, Oregon.[6] These subjects were restricted in age range, consisting mostly of couples with young children. Otherwise, they were spread broadly across the demographic parameters. Some population characteristics of the three samples combined are listed in Table 2.3. The intercorrelations of four of the demographic variables are shown in Table 2.4. Note that, with the reasonable exception of income and education, these variables are essentially independent.

TABLE 2.2. Demographic Characteristics of the Knoxville Sample (*N* = 201)

Characteristic	Frequency	Characteristic	Frequency
Age		*Years of education*	
15–19	13	2–3	1
20–29	48	4–5	10
30–39	67	6–7	7
40–49	33	8–9	30
50–59	25	10–11	27
60–69	9	12–13	57
70–79	6	14–15	20
		16–17	41
Marital status		18–19	8
Married	156		
Single	30	*Sex*	
Widowed/divorced	15	Male	79
		Female	122

[4] After using the 50-item form in research for two years, a revised 60-item form was constructed. The 60-item form is described and presented in Appendix 2, which also gives the rationale for this modification.

[5] We would like to thank Dr. William Coleman, University of Tennessee, for directing the sampling of subjects in Knoxville.

[6] Dr. Richard Littman, University of Oregon, was kind enough to administer our questionnaire while pursuing his own studies of parental attitudes and opinions.

TABLE 2.3. Demographic Characteristics of Combined Samples
of the Public (N = 700)

Characteristic	Percent	Characteristic	Percent
Age		Annual income	
15–19	7.3	under $1,200	7.1
20–29	20.1	$1,200–3,600	18.5
30–39	30.9	$3,600–6,000	38.2
40–49	20.1	$6,000–8,400	17.0
50–59	10.7	$8,400–10,800	7.8
60–69	6.9	$10,800 and over	11.4
70–99	4.0		
		Marital status	
Years of education		Married	79.0
2–3	.3	Single	14.0
4–5	1.6	Widowed/divorced	7.0
6–7	2.0		
8–9	10.4	Religious preference	
10–11	11.9	Protestant	79.9
12–13	31.1	Catholic	7.3
14–15	10.6	Jewish	2.7
16–17	22.7	None of these	10.1
18–19	9.4		
		Sex	
		Male	47.8
		Female	52.2

Experts

A revised form of the 50-item questionnaire was used to study the opinions of mental-health experts. It contained the same items as the questionnaire used for the public, but instead of asking the expert what he personally believed, he was asked to indicate what he thought the public *should* be told. Consequently, the rating scale for each item was as follows:

```
                                    Repudiate        Support
                                    1  2  3  4  5  6  7
The good psychiatrist acts          ┌──┬──┬──┬──┬──┬──┬──┐
like a father to his patients.      └──┴──┴──┴──┴──┴──┴──┘
```

Our expert sample was drawn from psychologists and psychiatrists in the United States. Questionnaires were mailed to 150 psychologists who are members of the American Psychological Association and have been awarded diplomas by the American Board of Examiners in Professional Psychology. Half of the sample were diplomates in clinical psychology and the remainder were diplomates in counseling and guidance. Questionnaires were also mailed to 150 psychiatrists, drawn from the Group for the Advancement of Psychiatry. Thus the expert sample consisted of what most mental-health professionals would consider "qualified" persons.

TABLE 2.4. Intercorrelations of Four Demographic Variables
for Combined Samples (N = 700)

	Education	Age	Sex	Income
Education	—			
Age	.06	—		
Sex *	−.16	.02	—	
Income	.29	.04	−.09	—

* A positive correlation means that women are higher than men; a negative correlation means that men are higher than women. For example, in our sample, men as a group were slightly higher in education than women.

The study of experts will be described in detail in Chapter 3. The study is mentioned here because some of the results are needed in order to discuss the findings from the general public.

Mass Media

The questionnaire form used with the general public and the experts could not be used for the media. Instead, the ten factors were used as *coding categories* in a content analysis of the media. For example, if an individual's psychotic behavior is explained in a comic strip as having resulted from a "bump on the head," this would be coded as an instance of the *organic-causes* factor. This empirical derivation of a set of coding categories is a departure from traditional approaches to content analyses, where categories are usually established on an a priori basis. The content analysis procedure and results will be discussed in detail in Chapter 6.

WHAT THE PUBLIC THINKS

PROPOSITION 2.1: **Public information is not highly structured.**

The major evidence for this proposition comes from the factor analysis described previously. Correlations among the items were generally low. The average correlation, disregarding sign, was about .25. The factors which were derived were not statistically strong. Few of the loadings were above .40, and the first ten centroid factors explained less than 25 percent of the total item variance. These facts indicate that the information statements do not fall into neat groups.

The mental-health area can be contrasted with a domain of opinions like economic beliefs. We would expect that people who believe that periodic depressions inevitably occur would also have a number of related opinions. There is only a relatively weak tendency for such patterns of opinions to exist in the mental-health area.

PROPOSITION 2.2: Mental-health information is not highly crystallized.

People are unsure of the correctness of their information and will change their opinions readily. The lack of *structure* described in the first proposition offers circumstantial evidence for this proposition. It is possible that even if individual differences in opinions are not highly structured (in the sense described previously), individuals will have highly crystallized opinions. In other words, even if his opinion patterns tend to be idiosyncratic, the individual may feel relatively sure of his particular set of beliefs and will resist change. This is seldom the case, however. More often a lack of structure accompanies a lack of crystallization. One reason why this is so is that a lack of crystallization implies a lack of reliability, in the statistical sense, which depresses correlations among questionnaire items.

More evidence for the lack of crystallization is that people often agree with inconsistent opinion statements or fail to agree with apparently consistent statements. For example, if an individual agrees with the statement "More women than men have nervous breakdowns," it is expected that he will disagree with the statement "Women have no more emotional problems than men do." There should be strong negative correlations between inconsistent statements and strong positive correlations between consistent statements. Typically, the correlations should be at least $-.50$ in the former case and $.50$ in the latter case. The correlations that we found between apparently inconsistent items and between apparently consistent items were nearer to zero than was anticipated.

Another source of "evidence" for the proposition is our impression that people are uncertain of the opinions that they hold. In studying 200 personal interviews with members of the general public about mental-health phenomena (mentioned on p. 14 in connection with the gathering of questionnaire items), we found that the respondents seemed to be unsure of their opinions. They expressed themselves tentatively and seemed apologetic about their opinions.

A more direct type of evidence for the proposition will be described in detail in later chapters where it will be shown that people change their opinions markedly after rather light doses of persuasion.

PROPOSITION 2.3: The average man is not grossly misinformed.

Our research design permitted a direct comparison of popular opinion with expert opinion. The comparison can be made either in terms of the ten factors or in terms of individual questionnaire items. (Mean responses for the Knoxville sample on the 50 items are shown in Table 2.5; for the experts, in Ch. 3.) Regardless of which way comparisons are made, the same conclusion is reached: mean responses for the public are not markedly different in most cases from mean responses for experts. The

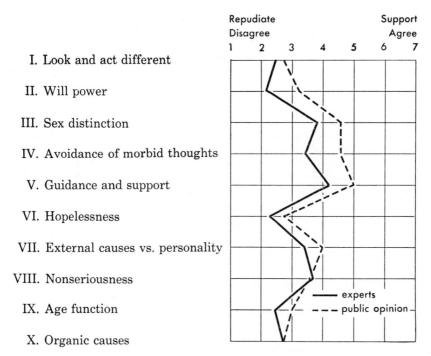

I. Look and act different

II. Will power

III. Sex distinction

IV. Avoidance of morbid thoughts

V. Guidance and support

VI. Hopelessness

VII. External causes vs. personality

VIII. Nonseriousness

IX. Age function

X. Organic causes

Repudiate / Disagree ... Support / Agree

1 2 3 4 5 6 7

——— experts
– – – public opinion

FIGURE 2.1. Comparison of Experts and the Public on Ten Information Factors

general similarity for the information factors can be seen in Figure 2.1. Illustrating the similarity with specific items, experts and laymen (the arithmetic means of both samples) *agree* with the following information statements:

1. Early training will *not* make the child's brain grow faster.
2. Most of the people in mental hospitals speak in words that can be understood.
3. Children usually do *not* forget about frightening experiences in a short time.
4. X-rays of the head will *not* tell whether a person is likely to develop insanity.

Laymen, along with the experts, preponderantly *disagree* with statements like the following:

1. There is not much that can be done for a person who develops a mental disorder.
2. Most people who "go crazy" try to kill themselves.
3. If a child is jealous of a younger brother, it is best not to let him show it in any way.
4. Almost any disease that attacks the nervous system is likely to bring on insanity.

TABLE 2.5. Means and Standard Deviations for the Knoxville Sample
on the 50-item Information Questionnaire

Item	Means [*]	Standard deviations
1. Most of the people in mental hospitals speak in words that can be understood.	5.49	1.93
2. More women than men have nervous breakdowns.	4.92	2.05
3. Books on "peace of mind" prevent many people from developing nervous breakdowns.	4.14	2.01
4. Men worry more than women.	3.28	2.13
5. Most clergymen will encourage a person with a mental disorder to see a psychiatrist.	5.30	1.92
6. If a person concentrates on happy memories he will not be bothered by unpleasant things in the present.	4.24	2.26
7. Physical exhaustion does not lead to a nervous breakdown.	3.72	2.29
8. The adult who needs a great deal of affection is likely to have had little affection in childhood.	5.32	2.01
9. Feeble-minded children are less obedient than normal children.	3.66	2.30
10. Physical rest will not prevent a mental disorder.	4.42	2.16
11. The brains of the feeble-minded are smaller than those of normals.	3.08	2.22
12. The main job of the psychiatrist is to recommend hobbies and other ways for the mental patient to occupy his mind.	4.42	2.34
13. There is not much that can be done for a person who develops a mental disorder.	1.96	1.75
14. Adult problems are less important in causing emotional disorders than the individual's childhood experiences.	3.40	2.16
15. Most people who "go crazy" try to kill themselves.	2.73	2.07
16. Few of the people who seek psychiatric help need the treatment.	3.60	2.24
17. Most people can recognize the type of person who is likely to have a nervous breakdown.	3.17	2.20
18. If a child is jealous of a younger brother, it is best not to let him show it in any way.	3.45	2.40
19. The main job of the psychiatrist is to explain to the patient the origin of his troubles.	4.98	2.25
20. Psychiatrists have to have a good sense of humor in order to help their patients.	5.33	1.99
21. Psychiatrists try to show the mental patient where his ideas are incorrect.	4.86	2.21
22. Early training will not make the child's brain grow faster.	4.67	2.43
23. Most suicides occur because of rejection in love.	3.10	2.22
24. People who are likely to have a nervous breakdown pay little attention to their personal appearance.	3.43	2.35
25. Many of the people who go to mental hospitals are able to return to work in society again.	5.70	1.93
26. Almost any disease that attacks the nervous system is likely to bring on insanity.	3.37	2.29
27. Older people have a less difficult time recovering from a nervous breakdown.	3.25	2.27

Item	Means *	Standard deviations
28. Mental illness is one of the most damaging disorders that a person can have.	4.93	2.29
29. Women have no more emotional problems than men do.	4.09	2.34
30. Most of the time psychiatrists have difficulty in telling whether or not a patient's mental disorder is curable.	3.79	1.96
31. Children usually do not forget about frightening experiences in a short time.	5.69	1.95
32. Disappointments do not affect children as much as they do adults.	3.54	2.43
33. People who have little sexual desire are less likely to have a "nervous breakdown" than are other people.	3.21	1.95
34. A person can avoid worry by keeping busy.	5.80	1.60
35. A poor diet does not lead to feeblemindedness.	4.76	2.30
36. Most social workers go into their field because of their own misfortunes in life.	2.47	1.98
37. The insane laugh more than normals.	3.82	2.28
38. Helping the mentally ill person with his financial and social problems will not cure his disorder.	4.57	2.11
39. Emotionally upset persons are often found in important positions in business.	4.97	2.11
40. Most of the insanity cases are found in people over fifty years of age.	2.85	1.93
41. Mental health is largely a matter of trying hard to control the emotions.	4.31	2.08
42. The good psychiatrist acts like a father to his patients.	5.11	1.92
43. Good emotional habits cannot be taught to children in school as easily as spelling can.	4.45	2.31
44. The eyes of the insane are glassy.	3.67	2.11
45. When a person is recovering from a mental illness, it is best not to discuss the treatment that he has had.	5.09	2.12
46. Psychiatrists try to teach mental patients to hold in their strong emotions.	3.64	2.16
47. A change of climate seldom helps an emotional disorder.	4.49	2.12
48. People who go from doctor to doctor with many complaints know that there is nothing really wrong with them.	3.83	2.32
49. A person cannot rid himself of unpleasant memories by trying hard to forget them.	4.75	2.08
50. X-rays of the head will not tell whether a person is likely to develop insanity.	5.41	2.00

* Ratings were made on a seven-step scale. A mean of 7.00 would indicate an average complete agreement with a statement. A mean of 1.00 would indicate an average complete disagreement with a statement. A mean of 4.00 would indicate an average "neutrality." The larger the standard deviation, the more disagreement among members of the public about the truth and falsity of a statement.

The average man and the average expert disagree most on some of the techniques required to maintain personal adjustment and to restore personal adjustment once it is lost. In terms of particular items, the most pronounced differences are as follows:

1. Books on "peace of mind" prevent many persons from developing nervous breakdowns. [Experts repudiate, public agrees.]
2. If a person concentrates on happy memories, he will not be bothered by unpleasant things in the present. [Experts repudiate, public agrees.]
3. The main job of the psychiatrist is to explain to the patient the origin of his troubles. [Experts repudiate, public agrees.]
4. Good emotional habits *cannot* be taught to children in school as easily as spelling can. [Experts support, public disagrees.]
5. When a person is recovering from a mental illness, it is best not to discuss the treatment he has had. [Experts repudiate, public agrees.]
6. A person *cannot* rid himself of unpleasant memories by trying hard to forget them. [Experts support, public disagrees.]

Another source of support for the proposition is that, as was mentioned previously, the public either highly agreed or highly disagreed with 60 items on the original 240-item questionnaire. These 60 items concern what most professionals would regard as nearly obvious truths or falsities, such as the following:

1. An excess of sexual intercourse leads to insanity. [Public disagrees.]
2. A change of diet will help a nervous breakdown. [Public disagrees.]
3. Good schooling can make a feebleminded child as smart as any other. [Public disagrees.]
4. Telling a child that you don't love him is usually more disturbing than giving him a spanking. [Public agrees.]
5. It is not likely that a person will recover from a nervous breakdown overnight. [Public agrees.]

We were not sure that the public would overwhelmingly accept or reject even those items on which the experts showed high agreement. We included in the 240-item form only statements that we thought would receive a wide range of public response. Many of the 180 items which we retained for the factor analysis had variance only on the "agree" or the "disagree" pole of the seven-step continuum. In constructing the questionnaire, we had anticipated a more misinformed public than we found.

PROPOSITION 2.4: **Some groups in the population are misinformed.**

Whereas, on the average, the members of the public generally agree with experts, there are two groups in the population whose knowledge is apparently inaccurate. These are people with less than a high-school education and people over fifty years of age. Positive correlations were found between correctness of information as judged by experts and years of formal schooling (see Table 2.6). That is, in general, people with more education tend to have more correct information. Negative correlations were found between correctness of information and age. In other words, older people as a group hold less accurate information than younger adults. The relationship still holds when statistical adjustments are made to discount the differences in years of education of older and younger adults: older people and younger adults with the same number of years of formal schooling have different ideas about mental health.

The finding that correctness of information correlates with amount of formal education supports the contention that relatively straightforward communications programs, such as occur in school classrooms, can be used to some extent to increase public knowledge of mental-health issues. There are at least two feasible explanations of the tendency for older people to hold less correct information. First, it is possible that the aging process and the personality changes which occur affect beliefs about mental health. Second—and we think this is a more plausible explanation —older people and younger adults with the same years of education have received different kinds of education. The social studies are emphasized more now, and it is also likely that younger people discuss matters related to mental health more than older people do.

We also found some significant correlations between sex (men versus women) and our information factors and between income and our information factors (see Table 2.6). The correlations with sex are too large to be easily ascribed to chance and too small to be of much importance. There is a slight tendency for women as a group to reject *organic causes* in favor of explanations in terms of the *immediate external environment,* and for men as a group to react in the opposite direction. *Avoidance of morbid thoughts* and *guidance and support of others* are accepted as factors by women more often than by men.

TABLE 2.6. Correlation of Information Factors with Four
Demographic Variables (N = 700) *

Factor	Education	Age	Sex †	Income
I. Look and act different	—.40	.16	.08	—.21
II. Will power	—.35	.18	—.03	—.28
III. Sex distinction	—.05	.06	.06	.01
IV. Avoidance of morbid thoughts	—.24	.38	.10	—.17
V. Guidance and support	—.15	.09	.18	—.09
VI. Hopelessness	—.27	.22	—.03	—.20
VII. Immediate external environment versus personality dynamics	.02	.16	.10	—.01
VIII. Nonseriousness	—.30	.30	.08	—.14
IX. Age function	—.31	.18	—.05	—.22
X. Organic causes	—.21	—.02	—.11	—.16

* The standard error of the correlation coefficient with an N of 700 is .038. Correlations as large as .10 are beyond the .01 level of significance.

† Point-biserial correlations were computed between sex and information factors. A positive correlation means that women are more prone to believe the particular factor.

When the correlation between income and education is partialed, the remaining correlations between income and the information factors are too small to be of practical significance, although they are statistically significant in several instances. People of higher income tend to reject the will-power factor and the age-function factor. They are also more prone to regard the outlook for the mentally ill as "hopeful."

No significant differences were found on the information factors for rural versus urban dwellers. Also no significant differences were found among Protestants, Catholics, and Jews.

PROPOSITION 2.5: **The public is uninformed about many issues.**

A careful distinction should be made between misinformation and lack of information. An earlier proposition stated that at present the public's information is not grossly erroneous. If we examine what people say about mental-health phenomena, the picture is not black. This does not mean, however, that people know a great deal, or that they know enough to handle everyday problems. By these standards, the average man probably is very much *uninformed*. Our evidence for the proposition is largely circumstantial.

As we said previously, in constructing questionnaire items we used only terms that the population at large understands. Consequently, it was not feasible to use terms like "Oedipus complex," "oral compulsiveness," and "positive transference." Without using these terms, it was not possible (for us) to express a large number of the experts' ideas in a form suitable for use with the general public. Rather than being misinformed about some of the complexities with which the experts deal, the public probably has no information, correct or incorrect.

Another bit of circumstantial evidence for the proposition is that many of the things which the average man might want to learn about mental-health phenomena are not presently known. Since the experts do not know many of the answers, it is only to be expected that the average man will have even larger gaps in his storehouse of information.

The lack of structure and the uncrystallized state of opinions also add circumstantial evidence to the proposition. One reason for the lack of structure may be that people do not know enough to form schools of thought about the issues.

It is encouraging to see that the average man rejects the superstitions and obvious misconceptions about mental health. If, as our results indicate, the problem is mainly that of filling in the near-voids where people are uninformed, this gives us a clear idea about the communication problem ahead. It is usually easier to supply people with new information when they hold few competing opinions initially than to convert well-established opinions. This assumption accords with other research findings (to be described in later chapters), which indicate that public knowledge can be effectively increased by relatively straightforward information programs in schools, the mass media, and group discussions. In contrast to these relatively encouraging findings about public *information,* a darker and more complicated set of findings is obtained in relation to public *attitudes* (see Ch. 4 and subsequent chapters).

It would be a great mistake if the distinction between *misinformation* and *lack of information* were passed over as mere hair-splitting. As will be shown in the following chapters, the distinction is one of the important keys to understanding the public reaction to mental-health phenomena.

3

What the Experts Think

OUR PRIMARY REASON for studying the opinions of experts was to establish a basis for measuring the accuracy of information held by members of the general public. Some aspects of this study were mentioned in Chapter 2. Here the study of experts will be described in greater detail. In addition to serving as a basis of comparison for the opinions of the "average man," the study of experts shows a number of interesting things about professional schools of thought.

The Expert Questionnaire

If the opinions of the general public were to be compared with the opinions of experts, it was necessary for the two groups to respond to the same items. Consequently, the expert form contained the same 50 items used in the questionnaire administered to the general public. To review: After 180 items in the original 240-item form had been factor analyzed (60 items were not analyzed because their variances were too small), a new 50-item form was constructed, containing those items most representative of our ten information factors.

The 50-item expert form differed from the form used with the public in only two ways: the rating scales and the instructions were different. The experts were asked to rate the extent to which each opinion statement should be repudiated or supported in public-information programs. The items on the expert form appeared as follows:

	Repudiate	Omit	Support
	1 2 3	4 5	6 7
If a child is jealous of a younger brother, it is best not to let him show it in any way.			
The main job of the psychiatrist is to explain to the patient the origin of his troubles.			

The instructions explained that the middle of the continuum should be used to indicate that a particular idea should be ignored in public-information programs.

Besides the difference in rating scales, the only other difference between the public and expert forms was in the questionnaire instructions. In the questionnaire used with the public, the purpose of the study was intentionally left vague (the instructions for the public are given in Appendix 1; the instructions for the experts are given in Appendix 3). The public was told only that the questionnaire concerned "what people thought about health problems." The experts were told directly what the study was about. The instructions explained that the items were expressed in nonprofessional language and that some of them might seem trivial. It was further explained that the opinion statements and the wording were used to allow us to make comparisons with the responses of the general public.

The Expert Sample

We confined our study of experts to psychologists and psychiatrists in the United States. There are, of course, other professional experts in the mental-health field, but our resources did not permit an extensive sampling of social workers, social anthropologists, sociologists, and others.

In studying experts we were not interested in obtaining either a representative sample or even a diverse collection of psychologists and psychiatrists. We wanted to obtain groups comprized of respected authorities on mental-health problems. Psychiatrists were drawn from the Group for Advancement of Psychiatry. All 150 members were mailed questionnaires. The psychologists were randomly selected from the diplomates in clinical psychology ($N = 75$) and in counseling and guidance ($N = 75$) of the American Psychological Association.

Of the 300 questionnaires mailed out, 201 were returned, 176 in time for our analysis. The group which was analyzed contained the responses of 86 psychologists and 90 psychiatrists.

Analysis of Data

A number of different statistical analyses were made of the experts' responses. Percentages of responses to each item are shown in Table 3.1. Mean factor scores for experts are shown in Figure 3.1 (they were also shown in Fig. 2.1). An analysis was made of the over-all agreement among experts, and comparisons were made of the amount of agreement on specific items. Finally a factor analysis was performed on some of the items in the expert questionnaire.

An Exploratory Comparison

Before continuing with the results from the main study of experts, it is necessary to describe a small side study. The experts were asked what

TABLE 3.1. Responses by the Expert Sample on the Information Questionnaire

Item	Percentages						
	Repudiate			Omit		Support	
	1	2	3	4	5	6	7
1. Most of the people in mental hospitals speak in words that can be understood.	1	1	1	10	20	29	37
2. More women than men have nervous breakdowns.	17	12	19	42	7	2	1
3. Books on "peace of mind" prevent many people from developing nervous breakdowns.	6	15	25	31	21	1	1
4. Men worry more than women.	14	11	27	46	2	0	0
5. Most clergymen will encourage a person with a mental disorder to see a psychiatrist.	1	6	7	17	29	27	12
6. If a person concentrates on happy memories, he will not be bothered by unpleasant things in the present.	20	27	29	13	10	1	0
7. Physical exhaustion does not lead to a nervous breakdown.	4	12	17	7	24	25	10
8. The adult who needs a great deal of affection is likely to have had little affection in childhood.	2	2	11	21	30	24	10
9. Feeble-minded children are less obedient than normal children.	23	24	25	22	2	2	1
10. Physical rest will not prevent a mental disorder.	2	7	16	14	24	24	13
11. The brains of the feeble-minded are smaller than those of normals.	21	14	18	37	6	2	1
12. The main job of the psychiatrist is to recommend hobbies and other ways for the mental patient to occupy his mind.	40	24	20	9	6	1	0
13. There is not much that can be done for a person who develops a mental disorder.	84	11	4	1	1	0	1
14. Adult problems are less important in causing emotional disorders than the individual's childhood experiences.	11	20	10	17	20	12	9
15. Most people who "go crazy" try to kill themselves.	64	24	7	4	1	0	1
16. Few of the people who seek psychiatric help need the treatment.	63	27	6	4	0	0	0
17. Most people can recognize the type of person who is likely to have a nervous breakdown.	47	30	12	9	0	1	1

Item		Percentages					
	Repudiate		Omit			Support	
	1	2	3	4	5	6	7
18. If a child is jealous of a younger brother it is best not to let him show it in any way.	45	38	11	3	1	1	0
19. The main job of the psychiatrist is to explain to the patient the origin of his troubles.	17	17	18	12	20	9	7
20. Psychiatrists have to have a good sense of humor in order to help their patients.	2	4	11	45	23	11	4
21. Psychiatrists try to show the mental patient where his ideas are incorrect.	9	12	12	17	34	12	4
22. Early training will not make the child's brain grow faster.	7	4	7	22	15	14	31
23. Most suicides occur because of rejection in love.	29	26	18	17	7	3	0
24. People who are likely to have a nervous breakdown pay little attention to their personal appearance.	25	20	23	25	5	1	0
25. Many of the people who go to mental hospitals are able to return to work in society again.	1	2	0	1	6	17	73
26. Almost any disease that attacks the nervous system is likely to bring on insanity.	47	20	11	15	4	2	1
27. Older people have a less difficult time recovering from a nervous breakdown.	15	24	26	28	6	1	1
28. Mental illness is one of the most damaging disorders that a person can have.	17	16	10	22	11	12	12
29. Women have no more emotional problems than men do.	4	7	9	30	21	14	16
30. Most of the time psychiatrists have difficulty in telling whether or not a patient's mental disorder is curable.	12	25	22	25	9	3	2
31. Children usually do not forget about frightening experiences in a short time.	2	4	9	11	30	30	14
32. Disappointments do not affect children as much as they do adults.	32	31	20	9	2	6	1
33. People who have little sexual desire are less likely to have a "nervous breakdown" than are other people.	26	23	24	25	2	0	0
34. A person can avoid worry by keeping busy.	12	15	15	14	28	14	2
35. A poor diet does not lead to feeble-mindedness.	4	6	8	23	20	16	23

TABLE 3.1. Responses by the Expert Sample on the Information Questionnaire
(*continued*)

Item	Percentages						
	Repudiate			Omit		Support	
	1	2	3	4	5	6	7
36. Most social workers go into their field because of their own misfortunes in life.	21	19	13	42	4	1	1
37. The insane laugh more than normals.	35	19	16	29	0	1	0
38. Helping the mentally ill person with his financial and social problems will not cure his disorder.	5	1	21	12	37	15	9
39. Emotionally upset persons are often found in important positions in business.	2	4	2	18	37	18	19
40. Most of the insanity cases are found in people over fifty years of age.	34	27	22	13	3	1	0
41. Mental health is largely a matter of trying hard to control the emotions.	34	31	16	9	4	4	1
42. The good psychiatrist acts like a father to his patients.	9	12	16	35	23	4	1
43. Good emotional habits cannot be taught to children in school as easily as spelling can.	9	7	7	6	27	25	17
44. The eyes of the insane are glassy.	48	14	17	21	0	0	0
45. When a person is recovering from a mental illness it is best not to discuss the treatment that he has had.	10	15	29	15	17	10	5
46. Psychiatrists try to teach mental patients to hold in their strong emotions.	20	31	16	19	11	1	1
47. A change of climate seldom helps an emotional disorder.	4	5	9	12	25	22	23
48. People who go from doctor to doctor with many complaints know that there is nothing really wrong with them.	38	34	19	6	2	0	0
49. A person cannot rid himself of unpleasant memories by trying hard to forget them.	0	3	6	7	25	34	25
50. X-rays of the head will not tell whether a person is likely to develop insanity.	2	2	1	11	16	23	45

messages should be conveyed to the public. In the strictest sense, then, the results of the study do not show what the experts believe, but, more precisely, what they think the public should be told. A small study was done to help clarify the "repudiate-support" ratings.

In this study we used 35 psychologists and psychiatrists, a catch-as-catch-can group of "competent" (we thought) professionals whom we knew personally or whose names were familiar to us. Each of these was mailed the "agree-disagree" form which had been used to study the responses of the general public. The instruction was to "rate what you believe to be the opinions of the average person in your profession." In other words, we asked the 35 professionals to judge the beliefs of their colleagues. Because of the selectiveness of the respondents and the subjectivity of what they were asked to do, the results should not be taken very seriously. However, the mean "repudiate-support" responses obtained from our main study were quite similar to the "agree-disagree" responses obtained from our special group of 35 (comparisons are shown in Fig. 3.1). This offers some evidence that the experts who responded to the "repudiate-support" form did so largely in terms of what they personally believed. None of the conclusions in Chapters 2, 3, and 6 would be changed materially if we substituted the responses from the special group of 35 to the "agree-disagree" form for the responses of the 176 to the "repudiate-support" form.

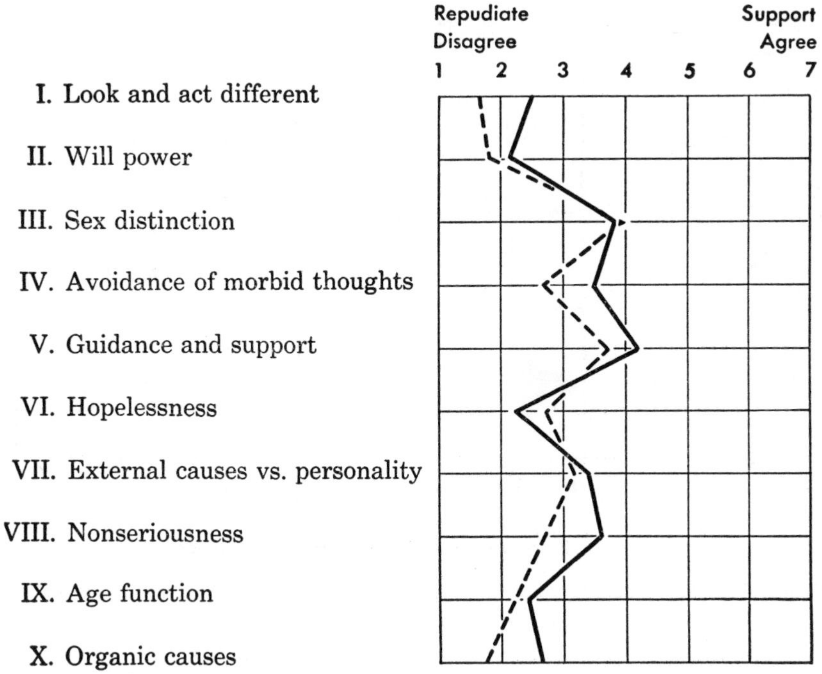

FIGURE 3.1. Mean Factor Profiles for Experts' Recommendations (————) and for Judgments about the Beliefs of Experts (— — —)

PROPOSITION 3.1: **Experts are in reasonable agreement about some aspects of a public-information program.**

Our worst fear was that the experts would show themselves no more in agreement on the questionnaire items than members of the general public. This proved not to be the case. The item variances of the experts were in all cases lower than those of the lay public and generally tended to be less than one half [1] as large. Another way of looking at the amount of agreement among experts is in terms of the percentage of persons who disagreed with the majority decision on each item. If more than 50 percent of the respondents indicate that a particular item should be advocated to the public, then the percentage of persons who mark one of the "repudiate" categories, positions 1, 2, and 3 on the scale, indicates the percentage of disagreement with the majority decision. Whereas on half of the 50 items the experts show less than 10-percent disagreement with the ma-

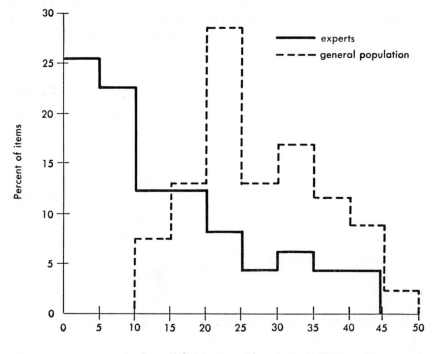

FIGURE 3.2. Percentages of Disagreement with Majority Opinion for Experts and for the General Public

[1] Variances were averaged over the 50 items for experts and the lay population separately. The average variance for the lay population was found to be 2.3 times as large as that for the experts.

jority decision, on none of the items does the general population show such a small amount of disagreement. In Figure 3.2 a graphic comparison is made of the relative amount of disagreement among experts and among members of the general public.

The next concern was whether systematic differences would be found between psychologists and psychiatrists, or between the two groups of psychologists. The average responses of psychologists and psychiatrists proved to be very much alike, although some small differences between professions will be shown in the factor-analysis study. Likewise, the average responses of the clinical and counseling psychologists were very much alike, with none of the differences approaching statistical significance.

The "reasonably good" agreement can be examined from a number of standpoints. Because the language of the questionnaire was restricted to that which the public understands and because it is usually easier to represent simple rather than complicated ideas, our questionnaire does not touch on many of the fine points of theory and technique with which the experts are concerned. We might find less agreement (or, perhaps, more) in a study specifically oriented toward the views of experts, without the accompanying restriction that the items be understandable to the public at large. Even with these restrictions to our findings, it is comforting to know that the experts agree about some of the points of view to advocate to the public.

FACTOR ANALYSIS OF EXPERTS' RESPONSES

The final analysis performed on the responses of experts was to determine whether or not there are schools of thought evidenced in the data. It was doubtful that many of our ten factors would appear prominently in the responses of experts. Because the factors correlate with years of schooling and because all of the experts have had many years of schooling, we expected to find relatively little variance on some factors. Also, we might expect that the professional training of experts would tend to decrease the variance on the ten factors. However, even if the experts did not vary substantially on the same dimensions as the public, they still might exhibit dimensions of their own.

The 22 items which showed the largest variance were intercorrelated and factor analyzed (see Table 3.2).[2] The product-moment correlation formula was used for all coefficients.

The profession of each subject was included as the twenty-third

[2] The correlation matrix was factor analyzed by the principal axes method (see Thomson, 1951), sometimes called the principal components method. Communality estimates were used to fill the diagonal elements of the matrix. These were estimated by selecting the highest correlation coefficient, regardless of sign, in each column of the matrix. The five factors with the largest variance were placed through a series of rotations to achieve the orthogonal solution in Table 3.2.

TABLE 3.2. Rotated Orthogonal Factors for Experts' Responses

Item [*]	I	II	Factor III	IV	V
3	.24	.29	.00	−.15	.03
7	.01	.14	.35	−.23	−.18
8	.10	.27	−.02	.11	.12
10	−.22	.48	.03	−.10	−.17
11	−.03	.00	−.09	.35	−.20
14	.18	.37	.00	.22	.05
19	.57	−.03	.16	−.04	−.05
20	.40	.08	.07	.00	.43
21	.60	.03	−.12	.03	.05
22	.02	.34	−.10	−.14	.25
28	.10	.20	.08	.39	.02
30	−.10	−.12	.30	.26	.01
31	.05	.30	.17	−.09	.04
34	.22	−.23	.21	.25	.07
35	−.07	.08	.35	−.17	.29
36	.04	−.28	.10	.38	.01
38	−.23	.35	.20	.09	−.01
42	.43	−.22	.00	.10	−.10
43	.01	.33	.18	.04	−.06
45	.31	−.04	−.03	−.35	.22
46	.42	−.20	−.11	.07	−.37
47	−.19	.46	−.05	−.02	.00
51	.03	.23	.42	−.01	.00

[*] The item numbers here are consistent with the item numbers in Table 3.1.

variable in the correlation matrix and the factor analysis. A score of 1 indicated that the subject was a psychiatrist and a score of 2 indicated that the subject was a psychologist.[3] The professional-status variable was then factored in with the 22 items. The loadings of the twenty-third variable (item 51) indicate the extent to which one profession is more inclined to believe a factor than is the other. A positive loading for that variable means that the factor is held more highly by psychologists than by psychiatrists. The most highly loaded items on Factor 1 are listed on the opposite page.

Factor I concerns the psychiatrist's [4] role, and, probably, the role of psychotherapists generally. More particularly, the factor appears to concern the degree of "directiveness" that is thought to characterize the ef-

[3] When the product-moment correlation formula is applied to the relationship between one discrete and one continuous variable, the obtained coefficient is the same as the point biserial coefficient.

[4] The term "psychiatrist" was used throughout the questionnaire to refer to an expert in the mental-health field. We would have preferred to use different titles, like psychiatrist, psychologist, and psychoanalyst, but this would have increased the items

FACTOR I

Item	Loading	
Psychiatrists try to show the mental patient where his ideas are incorrect.	.60	(21) *
The main job of the psychiatrist is to explain to the patient the origin of his troubles.	.57	(19)
The good psychiatrist acts like a father to his patients.	.43	(42)
Psychiatrists try to teach mental patients to hold in their strong emotions.	.42	(46)
Psychiatrists have to have a good sense of humor in order to help their patients.	.40	(20)

* The numbers in parentheses refer to the item numbers in the analyses and are consistent with the numbers in Tables 3.1 and 3.2.

fective therapist. The items picture the effective therapist as teaching, correcting, and explaining. The factor illustrates the well-known professional controversy between those who advocate a more directive, interventionist role for the therapist as opposed to those who advocate the more passive role of listening and understanding. Factor I is not more characteristic of psychiatrists than psychologists (see Table 3.2). Item 51, professional affiliation, has a loading of only .03 on the first factor. Instead, Factor I demonstrates that there is a division of opinion within both professions concerning the extent to which the therapist should direct and control the therapy situation.

FACTOR II

Item	Loading	
Physical rest will not prevent a mental disorder.	.48	(10)
A change of climate seldom helps an emotional disorder.	.46	(47)
Adult problems are less important in causing emotional disorders than the individual's childhood experience.	.37	(14)
Helping the mentally ill person with his financial and social problems will not cure his disorder.	.35	(38)

Factor II concerns the causes of mental disorders and the influences that make for better or worse emotional adjustment. Persons who agree strongly with these items would seem to explain mental disorder in terms of the individual's childhood and the history of his personal experience.

---

beyond the number that could be used in survey work. In scanning numerous personal interviews, we found that the psychiatrist is the person most often mentioned by members of the public as a person who deals with mental-health problems. Also, we found that the public makes little distinction between the subprofessions in the mental-health field (see Ch. 5).

The extreme point of view would be that the immediate environmental pressures are of no importance in explaining the individual's adjustment status. A person who held the opposite point of view, one who would disagree with the items above, would look for causal factors in the pressures in the individual's immediate environment. The extreme of the opposite point of view would be that the individual's emotional adjustment is a function only of contemporary external influences. Factor II in the experts study is very similar to Factor VII in the study of the public ("immediate external environment versus personality dynamics").

Item 51, professional affiliation, has a small loading of .23 on Factor II. If this loading is not due to chance,[5] there is a slight tendency for psychologists to endorse Factor II more than psychiatrists. Even if the difference between professions is real, however, the difference within professions is the far larger consideration.

FACTOR III

Item	Loading	
Professional affiliation (Item 51 in Table 3.2).	.42	(51)
A poor diet does not lead to feeblemindedness.	.35	(35)
Physical exhaustion does not lead to a nervous breakdown.	.35	(7)
Most of the time psychiatrists have difficulty in telling whether or not a patient's mental disorder is curable.	.30	(30)

Factor III contains most of the common variance for the variable of professional affiliation. Rather than being a content factor, in which there should be some centralness of meaning, the factor contains an array of the items that psychologists tend to endorse more strongly than do psychiatrists. As mentioned previously, there are few items that differentiate the professions; and the differences, as evidenced in the loadings above, are small. The factor shows that psychologists are more skeptical of organic and "physical" explanations of mental disorder (for example, diet and physical exhaustion) than are psychiatrists. The last listed item in Factor III, that concerning the psychiatrist's difficulties in prognosis, perhaps reflects more enthusiasm by some psychiatrists about their clinical prowess than would be granted by some psychologists.

No sensible interpretation could be found for Factor IV. It is submitted to the reader for his inspection.

The loadings on Factor V are too small to be considered without additional evidence for the statistical stability of the factor. Of the common

[5] There are no exact error formulas that can be applied to rotated factor loadings. An analogous error term can be obtained from the standard error of the correlation coefficient. With an N of 176 in this case, the standard error would be .076, with a coefficient of .19 being significant at the .01 level. By this very approximate standard, the loading of .23 would be indicative of a real difference between the two professions.

FACTOR IV

Item	Loading	
Mental illness is one of the most damaging disorders that a person can have.	.39	(28)
Most social workers go into their field because of their own misfortunes in life.	.38	(36)
The brains of the feebleminded are smaller than those of normals.	.35	(11)
When a person is recovering from a mental illness, it is best not to discuss the treatment that he has had.	−.35	(45)

variance explained by the five factors, the percentages of variance for each were, respectively, 29.8, 28.0, 13.7, 16.6, and 12.1.

SUMMARY

The primary purpose of the study of experts was to provide a basis of comparison for the information held by the public and that portrayed in the mass media. In addition to obtaining a basis of comparison, we learned about some divisions of opinion among the experts.

The results are generally encouraging. Although the information statements used in the survey mainly concerned the "simpler" notions about mental health and mental illness, they served to demonstrate that the experts can agree moderately well about some aspects of public-information programs.

Although on most items disagreement among experts was not large, enough disagreement was found on some items to permit a factor analysis. The main findings were two factors, which indicate schools of thought about (1) the best methods of psychotherapy and (2) the causes of mental disorder.

Whereas it might have been anticipated that the study would show marked differences of opinion between psychiatrists and psychologists, such was not the case. Instead, it was found that on the average psychologists and psychiatrists are in good agreement. What the factor analysis shows is that there are at least two dimensions of disagreement *within* both professions.

4

Public Attitudes toward

the Mentally Ill

PEOPLE IN THE MENTAL-HEALTH-EDUCATION FIELD commonly say that one of the most difficult problems to overcome is the *stigma* attached to the mentally ill. This assumes that the public holds negative attitudes toward the mentally ill. We performed a series of studies to determine (1) to what extent the mentally ill are held in low esteem, (2) whether the public holds different kinds of attitudes toward different kinds of mental illness, and (3) whether attitudes toward the mentally ill correlate with demographic characteristics such as education, age, and the like.

MEASURING INSTRUMENTS

To measure public attitudes toward mental-health phenomena, we relied heavily on an instrument called the Semantic Differential (see Osgood, Suci, & Tannenbaum, 1957, for a detailed description of the measurement method). In essence, the Semantic Differential requires a subject to rate a concept on sets of bipolar adjectives. An illustration follows:

Psychiatrist

```
Ignorant____:____:____:____:____:____:____Intelligent
Effective____:____:____:____:____:____:____Ineffective
    Weak____:____:____:____:____:____:____Strong
 Anxious____:____:____:____:____:____:____Calm
    Ugly____:____:____:____:____:____:____Handsome
  Simple____:____:____:____:____:____:____Complicated
 Strange____:____:____:____:____:____:____Familiar
```

The concept in the example above is *psychiatrist*. Almost anything can be used as a concept, for example, peach ice cream, Marilyn Monroe, United Nations, Communist, shock treatment, or Cadillac. In our studies we were interested in ratings of concepts related to mental health, such as a mentally ill person, insane man, nervous breakdown, neurotic woman, mental hospital, psychologist, nurse, psychotherapy, and related role concepts such as my father, my mother, me (the self-concept), marriage, old man, and child. (See Appendix 4 for the instruction sheet and sample pages of the Semantic Differential.)

The seven-point rating continuum used for each pair of bipolar adjectives is called a *scale*. Scales were chosen to incorporate the factors which have been found in previous studies. There are three well-known factors: (1) *evaluation*, defined by scales like good-bad, valuable-worthless, and kind-cruel; (2) *potency*, defined by scales like strong-weak, large-small, and rugged-delicate; and (3) *activity*, defined by scales like active-passive, fast-slow, and sharp-dull. A fourth factor, *understandability*, occurs prominently in our studies of mental-health concepts. It is defined by scales like understandable-mysterious, familiar-strange, simple-complicated, and predictable-unpredictable.

One of the advantages of the Semantic Differential is that it provides not only an over-all index of attitude but different facets of meaning as well. The *evaluative* factor appears to measure *attitude* as it is conventionally thought of, and high correlations have been found between the factor and conventional attitude-measuring instruments (see Osgood, Suci, & Tannenbaum, 1957). Two concepts that have the same *evaluative* meaning may be given different *potency* and *activity* ratings, and these differences help explain the differential meanings of concepts to the public. The finding of *understandability* as a factor in ratings of mental-health concepts was an important development in our studies. *Understandability*, or rather the lack of it, is a very important component of public reaction to the mentally ill.

In addition to the Semantic Differential, a number of other instruments were used to study public attitudes and meanings. One of these was a "free-association" test in which subjects were asked to provide associations to terms like psychiatrist, emotion, mental hospital, neurotic mother, and mental patient. (This instrument was applied only to college students.) Another instrument which we used was a multiple-choice association form. A sample item follows:

When I think of a neurotic person, I also think of
    a. Selfishness   _____
    b. Physical weakness   _____
    c. Fear of something   _____
    d. Wild sex life   _____
    e. Being lonesome
       and unloved   _____
    f. Paying for misdeeds _____

A fourth instrument which we used was a "pair-comparison" technique in which, for example, subjects were asked whether they would seek help for a mentally ill family member from a psychiatrist or a psychologist, a psychiatrist or a minister, a psychiatrist or a family doctor, and so on for all possible comparisons. The pair-comparison technique was used mainly to study public attitudes toward treatment sources (see Ch. 5). In addition to the four types of instruments described above, on occasion we employed ranking methods and conventional rating scales.

THE POPULATION SAMPLES

Our attitude-measuring instruments were administered to several broad segments of the general population as well as to numerous special groups. In the early studies we were primarily concerned with measuring typical public feelings (attitudes) about mental illness, the mentally ill, and the persons who treat the mentally ill. We speak of these as our survey studies. Attitudes were also measured incidentally in a number of our experimental studies. Since the experimental studies were primarily concerned with changing attitudes toward concepts like *psychiatrist* and *mental patient,* attitudes had to be measured. In sum, we administered a variety of measuring instruments, concerning a variety of concepts, to a variety of groups. The data that will be cited in this chapter illustrate the general attitude trends found in all of our studies. Confirming evidence and supplementary findings are scattered throughout the book.

The first major study of public attitudes was performed on our opinion panel. As was mentioned in Chapter 1, the panel is a group of about 400 persons, most of whom live in central Illinois. Except for its geographic bias, the panel approximates the country as a whole in terms of sex ratio, age, education, income, and other demographic characteristics. A Semantic Differential form was applied to 270 panel members who had not been contacted for any of our studies during the prior ten months (a precaution against "panel effect"). A self-explanatory Semantic Differential form was mailed to each subject with an addressed return envelope. Subjects were routinely mailed one-dollar checks for their participation in each study. A follow-up "prod" was mailed two weeks after the form was sent to obtain a maximum of returns. Of the 270 forms mailed out, 257 were returned. Seven of the 257 returns had errors of one kind or another, leaving 250 to be analyzed.

RESULTS

The 250 Semantic Differential replies from the opinion panel were analyzed in various ways. First, we computed mean responses for all subjects on all concepts and on all scales (see Table 4.1). Next, the total sample was broken into a "high-education" and a "low-education" group (see Table 4.2). Subsequently, breakdowns were made for other demographic characteristics, such as sex and age. Because these comparisons

TABLE 4.1. Mean Scale Positions * on the Seven-step Semantic Differential Scales
(Responses by 250 Members of the Illinois Opinion Panel)

Concepts

Scales	Neurotic man	Average man	Insane woman	Average woman	Old man	Psychiatrist	Neurotic woman	Insane man	Child	Me	Mother	Father	
Foolish	3.00	5.19	2.64	5.00	5.11	5.98	2.75	2.79	4.77	4.94	5.93	5.71	Wise
Ignorant	4.10	5.48	3.45	5.44	5.31	6.42	3.98	3.43	5.38	5.52	5.98	5.80	Intelligent
Sad	2.61	5.76	1.77	5.65	4.94	5.16	2.64	2.96	6.35	6.00	5.67	5.69	Happy
Passive	3.92	5.93	3.40	5.80	3.70	5.80	3.92	3.55	6.56	6.12	6.04	5.91	Active
Insincere	3.80	5.77	3.17	5.78	5.60	6.08	3.66	3.16	5.86	6.26	6.41	6.21	Sincere
Poor	3.83	4.03	3.70	4.04	4.06	5.05	3.94	3.75	4.04	3.78	4.08	4.02	Rich
Unpredictable	3.64	5.24	1.69	5.45	4.20	5.27	2.54	1.73	3.02	5.24	5.72	5.46	Predictable
Weak	2.82	5.37	3.22	4.79	3.40	5.45	2.75	3.27	5.01	5.26	5.44	5.62	Strong
Slow	3.75	5.01	3.80	4.84	2.53	4.80	3.90	3.77	5.60	5.09	5.05	5.04	Fast
Delicate	3.60	5.46	3.72	4.20	3.67	4.82	3.20	4.04	4.74	5.02	4.38	5.45	Rugged
Cold	3.60	5.42	3.69	5.41	4.87	5.08	3.38	3.48	6.08	5.68	5.92	5.74	Warm
Dirty	4.63	5.84	3.96	6.13	4.83	6.20	4.80	3.74	5.10	6.35	6.42	6.19	Clean
Dangerous	3.43	5.99	2.78	6.08	5.46	6.04	3.46	1.94	5.60	6.34	6.46	6.33	Safe
Tense	1.98	5.26	1.96	4.80	5.20	5.41	1.98	1.96	5.22	4.76	4.69	5.18	Relaxed
Worthless	4.03	5.94	3.32	5.90	5.38	6.28	4.03	3.18	6.37	5.64	6.47	6.31	Valuable
Sick	2.32	5.56	1.77	5.35	3.90	5.70	2.32	1.66	5.84	5.91	5.24	5.33	Healthy
Bad	4.21	5.81	3.85	5.93	5.65	5.94	4.25	3.55	5.96	5.88	6.42	6.30	Good

* The means are restricted to the range of 1 to 7. A mean of 1.00 indicates an average scale position at the extreme left of the bipolar continuum. For example, a mean of 1.00 on the foolish-wise scale would indicate an average rating of completely "foolish." A mean of 7.00 indicates an average reaction at the extreme right, in the example above, extremely "wise." The middle of the continuum, 4.00, can be regarded either as "don't know" or "neutral"—using the above example again, "neither foolish nor wise."

produced no striking findings, the results will not be given in this chapter. (Breakdowns for men versus women and for older versus younger adults are given in Appendices 6 and 7.) In addition to the results from the 250 panel members, the results from some of our other studies will be cited at points to help complete the picture of public attitudes toward the mentally ill.

PROPOSITION 4.1: Public attitudes are relatively negative toward persons with mental-health problems.

As is commonly suspected, the mentally ill are regarded with fear, distrust, and dislike by the general public (see Table 4.1). Comparing public attitudes toward the mentally ill (concepts like mental patient, insane woman, neurotic woman, and neurotic man) with public attitudes toward "normal" persons (concepts like average man, me, my father), the mentally ill are regarded as relatively worthless, dirty, dangerous, cold, unpredictable, insincere, and so on. This proposition is supported by a number of other Semantic Differential studies reported in following chapters (see particularly Table 5.2 for mean scale ratings of the concept mental patient and Appendix 5).

The two scales which most clearly distinguish the "normal" concepts from the mental disorders are predictable-unpredictable and tense-relaxed. Evidently, erratic behavior and anxiety were regarded by the public as the key signs of mental disorder.

PROPOSITION 4.2: Public attitudes are different toward neurotic and psychotic disorders.

Although neurotic concepts (neurotic man, neurotic woman, person with a nervous breakdown, and so forth) and psychotic concepts (insane man, insane woman, mental patient, and so forth) are both regarded with fear and distrust, some distinctions are made between the two (see Tables 4.1 and 4.2). Psychotics are generally held in lower esteem than neurotics, being rated as more bad, worthless, dirty, and so on. Neurotics are viewed as being less potent than psychotics, being rated as more weak and delicate. The scale that best differentiates the two kinds of disorders is "predictable," the psychotics being rated as much more unpredictable. In subsequent studies it was found that the scale predictable-unpredictable is one of the primary elements of a new factor, called *understandability*. In addition to predictable-unpredictable, it contains scales like understandable-mysterious, simple-complicated, and familiar-strange.

Lack of predictability seems to be a cornerstone of public attitudes toward psychotics. Because unpredictable behavior is frightening and disruptive, much societal machinery is devoted to making the behavior of individuals predictable to others. For example, if you are being introduced to someone and you say, "I am pleased to meet you," you can usually predict that the other individual will respond in kind. If he replies with

"Fish for sale" or "I hate you," it is, to say the least, disturbing. Much of the dread of the mentally ill might be removed if the public could learn some meaningful patterns and consistencies in psychotic behavior, so that it is more understandable and more predictable.

A study employing a multiple-choice association test (of the kind illustrated previously) supports the results described above and adds some more information about the difference in public attitudes toward psychotic and neurotic disorders (see Appendix 9 for a copy of the form and the results). The term "neurotic" is associated with women rather than men (the Semantic Differential studies also show that the characteristics attributed to the neurotic are generally feminine) and intelligent rather than ignorant persons. The term "insane person" is associated with an older and more ignorant individual.

PROPOSITION 4.3: **Subgroups in the population have slightly different attitudes toward the mentally ill.**

Whereas there are marked differences in the kinds of *information* held by old as compared with young people and by more educated as compared with less educated people, differences in *attitudes* of these and other subgroups are relatively small. There is a small, but statistically significant, tendency for more-educated people to hold less derogatory attitudes toward the mentally ill (see Table 4.2). Even in the better educated group, however, there is a marked tendency to isolate the mentally ill as relatively bad, dirty, dangerous, and so on.

None of the other demographic breakdowns produced more than a few clear-cut differences. For example, we found some significant differences (by *t*-test) between the mean responses of women and men (see Appendix 6). The differences formed no clearly interpretable pattern, however, and differences in one study sometimes were not found in other studies. As was said in Chapter 1, the nature and size of our samples prevented us from interpreting small differences.

The finding that subgroups in the population do not differ substantially in their attitudes toward the mentally ill relates to a point which was made in Chapter 1. There it was said that our moderately representative, moderately sized population samples were more than adequate to document some of the findings. Most of the conclusions about public attitudes in this chapter would have been the same if we had dealt only with male high-school students in a middle-class neighborhood (whose responses will be described in Ch. 10).

Incidental Findings

The major aim of our studies of attitudes was to learn the public feeling toward different kinds of mental disturbances. In order to do this, it was necessary to compare the meaning of mental disorders with the

TABLE 4.2. Mean * Scale Positions on the Semantic Differential for a High-education Group (upper figure) and a Low-education Group (lower figure)

Concepts

Scales	Neurotic man	Average man	Insane woman	Average woman	Old man	Psychia-trist	Neurotic woman	Insane man	Child	Me	Mother	Father	
Foolish	3.22 / 2.81	4.56 / 5.39	2.69 / 2.54	4.49 / 5.20	4.96 / 5.29	5.82 / 5.94	2.75 / 2.78	2.87 / 2.62	3.91 / 5.09	5.22 / 4.94	5.69 / 6.23	5.62 / 5.78	Wise
Ignorant	4.47 / 3.93	4.65 / 5.64	3.85 / 3.07	4.76 / 5.78	4.78 / 5.35	6.44 / 6.35	4.34 / 3.94	3.84 / 3.07	4.76 / 5.52	5.78 / 5.54	5.55 / 6.30	5.64 / 5.78	Intelligent
Sad	2.64 / 2.88	5.18 / 5.93	2.80 / 2.93	5.04 / 5.83	4.14 / 5.16	4.75 / 5.20	2.66 / 2.90	2.81 / 2.90	5.82 / 6.51	5.67 / 6.14	5.16 / 6.01	5.29 / 5.90	Happy
Passive	4.46 / 3.75	5.13 / 6.13	3.82 / 3.29	5.22 / 5.84	3.73 / 3.78	5.38 / 6.17	4.22 / 3.95	4.00 / 3.42	6.27 / 6.67	5.80 / 6.32	5.71 / 6.33	5.58 / 6.25	Active
Insincere	3.85 / 3.78	5.02 / 5.83	3.82 / 2.64	5.11 / 5.93	5.16 / 5.45	5.71 / 6.10	3.73 / 3.93	3.03 / 2.64	5.62 / 5.68	6.31 / 6.29	6.16 / 6.42	5.95 / 6.23	Sincere
Poor	4.07 / 3.59	4.00 / 3.81	3.84 / 3.72	3.96 / 3.88	3.89 / 4.15	5.33 / 4.84	4.07 / 3.78	4.02 / 3.81	4.00 / 3.90	3.82 / 3.30	4.18 / 3.84	4.25 / 3.65	Rich
Unpredictable	4.64 / 2.87	4.93 / 5.42	1.80 / 1.84	4.11 / 4.78	4.16 / 4.10	5.09 / 5.33	2.58 / 2.78	1.89 / 1.68	2.87 / 3.12	5.31 / 5.36	5.44 / 5.88	5.18 / 5.43	Predictable
Weak	3.33 / 3.04	4.73 / 5.52	3.33 / 3.00	4.40 / 4.94	3.36 / 3.51	5.25 / 5.57	2.95 / 2.86	3.82 / 3.35	4.45 / 4.96	5.04 / 5.23	5.46 / 5.67	5.40 / 5.90	Strong

Slow	4.20	4.67	4.15	4.47	2.84	4.64	4.33	5.53	4.33	5.06	5.27	4.96	Fast
	3.54	5.25	3.54	4.97	2.54	4.77	3.86	3.78	5.28	5.00	4.91	5.20	
Delicate	3.65	4.84	3.71	4.00	3.45	4.49	3.29	4.25	4.69	4.91	4.56	5.00	Rugged
	3.87	5.48	3.88	4.52	3.62	5.00	3.26	4.33	4.67	5.00	4.33	5.67	
Cold	3.40	4.85	3.64	5.05	4.44	4.80	3.45	3.56	5.82	5.45	5.78	5.40	Warm
	3.62	5.70	3.71	5.61	4.90	5.22	3.45	3.45	6.13	5.71	6.00	5.93	
Dirty	4.34	5.31	3.87	5.60	4.40	5.93	4.67	3.73	4.24	6.11	6.09	5.82	Clean
	4.54	6.04	4.01	6.33	5.01	6.28	4.72	3.61	5.38	6.54	6.59	6.36	
Dangerous	3.11	5.45	2.33	5.45	5.31	5.75	3.33	2.16	5.29	6.13	5.18	5.98	Safe
	3.74	6.13	2.32	6.27	5.55	6.01	3.65	1.90	5.72	6.49	6.67	6.46	
Tense	2.04	4.65	2.05	4.31	5.00	5.02	2.18	2.25	4.89	4.67	4.36	4.73	Relaxed
	2.23	5.45	1.99	5.26	5.07	5.17	2.30	1.77	5.00	5.10	4.96	5.35	
Worthless	4.25	5.54	3.53	5.51	5.33	6.27	4.27	3.64	6.16	5.69	6.29	6.18	Valuable
	3.94	5.93	3.06	6.00	5.46	6.19	3.91	1.90	6.39	5.71	6.61	6.30	
Sick	2.38	4.87	1.84	4.87	3.85	5.42	2.24	1.82	5.42	5.71	5.05	4.89	Healthy
	2.55	5.83	1.81	5.51	4.06	5.74	2.62	1.64	5.81	5.71	5.45	5.74	
Bad	4.00	3.88	5.53	5.45	5.73	4.20	3.80	5.53	5.73	5.62	6.13	4.89	Good
	4.19	5.90	3.78	6.07	5.65	5.96	4.16	3.25	5.94	6.00	6.57	6.39	

* The means are calibrated on the seven-point scale which was described in the footnote to Table 4.1. The high-education group consists of 55 persons who had at least some college training. The low-education group consists of persons who did not complete high school. The two groups were equated for the demographic variables of age and sex. To illustrate how the table is read, look at the foolish-wise scale for the concept *neurotic man*. On that scale the high-education group has a mean of 3.22 and the low-education group has a mean of 2.81. This indicates that the low-education group regards *neurotic man* as more foolish (less wise) than the high-education group does.

meanings of concepts encountered in everyday life such as father, me, and child. Some results reported in this chapter (see Tables 4.1 and 4.2) and in subsequent chapters show some interesting things about the meanings of everyday concepts. In order not to distract from the central theme of the book, no effort will be made to give a detailed account of the "incidental" findings. Two of the findings, however, are of particular interest.

The low-education group as compared to the high-education group gives more favorable ratings on most scales to the concept child, rating it, for example, as much more wise, intelligent, healthy, clean, and safe. Perhaps child-rearing is a problem only for the *middle class* in our society.

Another interesting finding is that the public at large expresses relatively unfavorable attitudes toward the concept old man. In comparison to concepts like me and average man, old man is rated as relatively unpredictable, cold, dirty, dangerous, worthless, and so on. Insofar as the results here are indicative of popular attitudes in general toward the aged, they exemplify a serious problem.

ALTERING PUBLIC ATTITUDES

Now that we know how the public *does* feel about the mentally ill, it is important to discuss the question, "How *should* the public feel?" What kinds of changes in public attitudes can realistically be expected?

In terms of the *evaluation* factor, it is probably unreasonable to expect that the public will ever react to the mentally ill as they do to "normal" people. Psychotics, neurotics, and emotionally disturbed people are often unpleasant to have around. They sometimes do dangerous things, they are often undependable or inefficient, and they often embarrass and provoke. The only realistic hope is that the public will come to devalue the mentally ill *less*. Both practical experience and our results indicate that the public's devaluation of the mentally ill (the stigma and the feeling of danger) is unreasonably extreme.

In terms of the *understandability* factor, the goals are quite clear. Hopefully the mentally ill will become as understandable and predictable as possible to the general public. Not only is this a laudable and reasonable goal in and of itself, but, as was hypothesized earlier in this chapter, the more understandable the mentally ill are to the general public, the more the public will react to them as sincere, clean, valuable, and safe.

SUMMARY

In Chapter 2 it was said that a careful distinction should be made between *information* held by the public and *attitudes* held by the public. A comparison of the results discussed in this chapter (relating to attitudes) with those in Chapter 2 (relating to information) shows why the distinction is crucial. Whereas the *information* held by the public is not really "bad" in the sense that the public is not grossly misinformed, the *attitudes* held by the public are as "bad" as is generally suspected. Whereas correctness of information correlates with demographic variables such as age and education, correlations between attitudes and such demographic variables are very small. Old people and young people, highly educated people and people with little formal schooling—all tend to regard the mentally ill as relatively dangerous, dirty, unpredictable, and worthless.

One of the most important findings is that there is a strong "negative halo" associated with the mentally ill; they are regarded as all things bad. Such unselectively negative attitudes may, in part, be due to a failure to observe and learn about mental-illness phenomena in daily life.

5

Public Attitudes toward

the Experts and Treatment

IF THE PUBLIC is to develop more constructive attitudes toward mental-health problems, it must have faith in the professionals who treat mental illness and in the treatment methods that are applied. The need to rely on professional advice and professional help is particularly crucial in the mental-health area. The preceding chapters have shown that people are afraid of mental-health problems and unsure what to do about them. Later it will be shown that even thinking about these problems causes anxiety (see Ch. 10). It is in situations of this kind that people most need professional help and should feel that the professionals are highly competent.

There are signs that public attitudes toward mental-health professionals (psychologists, psychiatrists, and kindred experts) are not all that they should be. These indications range from the fact that the psychiatrist joke is rapidly replacing the time-honored position of the traveling-salesman joke to the fact that people in trouble are sometimes reluctant to seek psychological and psychiatric aid. These signs are not easy to interpret, however, and more systematic evidence is needed before public attitudes toward mental-health professionals and treatment methods can be fully understood. With that aim in mind, this chapter will summarize several studies of public attitudes. The chapter will first treat attitudes toward mental-health professionals and then attitudes toward treatment methods and facilities.

ATTITUDES TOWARD MENTAL-HEALTH PROFESSIONALS

As in our studies of attitudes toward mental illness, we have studied attitudes toward professionals with a variety of instruments, concepts, and samples. In addition to studies which specifically examined public attitudes toward professionals, most of our experiments incidentally revealed attitudes toward professionals. (Related experiments will be discussed in later chapters.) This section reports in some detail the results of one of the major studies and draws on other studies for supplementary evidence.

In the first major study a special Semantic Differential form was administered to members of our opinion panel. Concepts were chosen to represent the principal professions that are directly or indirectly involved with mental-health problems. The following titles were selected for that purpose:

doctor	psychologist
physician	clinical psychologist
nurse	research psychologist
psychiatrist	mental-hospital attendant
psychoanalyst	social worker

In addition to the above, the concepts *me* and *mental patient* were used to provide further grounds for comparison.

Scales for the Semantic Differential form were selected to represent the four factors described in Chapter 4. In addition, a number of other scales, such as emotional-unemotional, masculine-feminine, and effective-ineffective, were chosen to get at particular aspects of public attitudes. The complete list of scales is given in Table 5.2.

TABLE 5.1. Demographic Characteristics of the Respondents (N = 207)

Characteristic	Percent	Characteristic	Percent
Age		*Years of education*	
15–24	14	under 8	2
25–34	16	8 (grammar-school	
35–44	26	graduate)	5
45–54	20	9–11	16
55–64	12	12 (high-school	
65 and over	12	graduate)	42
		13–15	21
Sex		16 and over (college	
Male	45	graduate)	14
Female	55		
		Annual income	
Marital status		under $1,000	9
Married	78	$1,000–1,999	6
Single	17	$2,000–2,999	9
Widowed/divorced	5	$3,000–3,999	13
		$4,000–4,999	14
Location		$5,000–5,999	16
Urban	62	$6,000–9,999	25
Farm	9	$10,000–14,999	6
Rural (nonfarm)	29	$15,000 and over	2

The Semantic Differential form was mailed to 239 panel members. None of the subjects had participated in related studies during the prior year. Of these, 207 forms, or 86.6 percent, were returned on time and were complete enough to be used in the analysis of the data. Table 5.1 shows some demographic characteristics of the respondents.

Three different analyses of the data were performed. Each involved computations of mean ratings for different groups of subjects on each scale applied to each concept (see Tables 5.2 and 5.3). Data are so arranged that a high score indicates a judgment toward the "favorable" end of a scale. The "unfavorable" pole of our seven-step scale is 1 and the "favorable" pole or adjective is 7. Some scales have no sharply defined "favorable" and "unfavorable" ends; in such cases (notably the masculine-feminine scale) one end is arbitrarily designated 7. The neutral or center point of 4 can be interpreted either as "don't know" or as a position of ambivalence.

To read the results in Tables 5.2 and 5.3 first locate any desired concept at the top of the table and then look down the column of numbers directly beneath the concept. Thus, *mental patient* is viewed by the total sample (see Table 5.2) as extremely unpredictable on the unpredictable-predictable scale and more or less at the neutral point on the boring-interesting scale, whereas *doctor* is viewed as both very predictable and interesting on the same scales. The tables of means provide many observations on the meanings of the individual concepts and also the concepts can be compared with one another.

The first analysis utilized the mean responses of the entire sample (see Table 5.2). Standard deviations were computed for each scale on each concept, and *t*-tests were run to assess the significance of particular differences between means of selected pairs of concepts on each scale.

A second analysis was undertaken to determine whether groups with different amounts of formal education showed marked differences in attitudes. The sample was divided into a low-education group, all 48 of whom had less than a full high-school education; a high-education group, whose 72 members all had at least some college training; and a third group (high-school graduates who did not go on to college) whose responses were not analyzed. Means and standard deviations were determined separately for the high- and low-education groups for each scale on each concept. Table 5.3 shows the results, reported as differences between the means of the two groups on each scale.

A third analysis was performed to see whether differences within and between the educational attainment groups would be more pronounced if factors rather than individual scales were used in the comparisons. For the *evaluation* factor, scores were averaged over the scales sincere-insincere, valuable-worthless, effective-ineffective, and dependable-undependable. For the *understandability* factor, scores were averaged over the scales predictable-unpredictable, straight-twisted, and simple-complicated.

TABLE 5.2. Mean Scale Positions for the Total Sample on Seven-step Semantic Differential Scales (N = 207)

Concept

Scale	Doctor	Physician	Nurse	Psychologist	Research psychologist	Clinical psychologist	Psychiatrist	Psychoanalyst	Social worker	Mental-hospital attendant	Me	Mental patient	
Insincere	6.46	6.42	6.43	6.09	6.26	6.13	6.07	6.00	6.22	5.71	6.22	3.86	Sincere
Unpredictable	5.88	5.87	5.85	5.01	4.99	5.22	4.81	4.81	5.51	5.38	5.24	1.69	Predictable
Weak	6.10	6.12	5.92	5.35	5.43	5.45	5.45	5.45	5.47	5.87	5.30	2.75	Strong
Slow	5.02	5.03	5.56	4.23	4.27	4.32	4.32	4.32	4.42	5.27	4.86	3.55	Fast
Delicate	5.23	5.34	4.98	4.49	4.70	4.55	4.60	4.44	4.67	5.75	4.84	3.46	Rugged
Cold	5.55	5.59	5.84	4.86	4.61	4.83	4.93	4.79	5.42	4.83	5.59	3.47	Warm
Dangerous	6.27	6.20	6.21	5.68	5.67	5.67	5.69	5.43	6.02	5.84	6.18	2.54	Safe
Tense	5.56	5.75	5.49	5.37	4.89	5.37	5.41	5.27	5.19	4.64	4.50	1.72	Relaxed
Worthless	6.65	6.67	6.55	5.98	6.13	5.96	6.06	5.84	6.09	6.22	5.44	3.78	Valuable
Ineffective	6.25	6.33	6.15	5.71	5.70	5.70	5.70	5.63	5.71	5.76	5.42	3.03	Effective
Complicated	3.46	3.53	4.16	3.31	3.04	3.31	3.18	3.16	4.22	4.39	4.43	2.74	Simple
Colorless	5.19	5.18	5.22	4.74	4.72	4.58	4.87	4.82	4.79	4.32	4.62	3.73	Colorful
Undependable	6.39	6.36	6.39	5.77	5.76	5.85	5.67	5.59	5.80	5.96	6.24	2.01	Dependable
Feminine	5.43	5.37	2.26	4.77	4.74	4.65	4.87	4.76	3.46	5.00	3.63	4.10	Masculine
Excitable	6.13	6.12	5.97	5.69	5.47	5.70	5.80	5.71	5.36	5.59	4.61	1.93	Calm
Boring	5.96	6.01	5.89	5.52	5.40	5.45	5.46	5.41	5.36	5.07	4.82	3.92	Interesting
Weak willed	5.97	5.95	5.81	5.51	5.44	5.42	5.72	5.41	5.35	5.72	5.45	3.44	Strong willed
Emotional	4.38	4.42	4.04	4.08	4.28	4.37	4.26	4.21	3.87	4.49	3.16	2.28	Unemotional
Twisted	5.94	6.01	5.87	5.47	5.46	5.37	5.41	5.30	5.46	5.52	5.92	2.24	Straight

TABLE 5.3. Mean Differences between High- and Low-Education Groups
(Low-education, N = 48; High-education, N = 72) *

Concept

Scale	Doctor	Physician	Nurse	Psychologist	Research psychologist	Clinical psychologist	Psychiatrist	Psychoanalyst	Social worker	Mental-hospital attendant	Me	Mental patient	
Insincere	.44 †	.23	.51 †	.15	.47	.01	.41	.25	.18	1.01 †	.08	−.81	Sincere
Unpredictable	.56	.09	.76 †	.31	.55	−.02	.78	.98 †	.06	.48	.47	.24	Predictable
Weak	.60 †	.34	.50 †	.30	.73 †	.24	.63 †	.52	.38	.39	.51	−.32	Strong
Slow	.73	.84 †	.56	.78 †	.68	.58	.26	.33	.79 †	.60	−.14	−.29	Fast
Delicate	.05	.12	.22	.35	.23	.35	.49	.11	.40	.30	.23	−.17	Rugged
Cold	.35	.71 †	.60 †	.38	.89 †	.61	.45	1.19 †	.13	.97 †	−.18	−.64	Warm
Dangerous	.27	.10	.55 †	.39	.37	.12	.53	.50	.47	.72 †	.31	−.06	Safe
Tense	.58	.72 †	.55	.53	.30	−.14	.46	.39	.34	.71	1.32 †	−.09	Relaxed
Worthless	.31 †	.17	.21	.17	.24	.04	.30	.03	.15	.59 †	.08	−.63	Valuable
Ineffective	.11	.27	.07	.09	.27	−.03	−.07	.09	.04	.60	.16	.44	Effective
Complicated	.62	.83 †	.06	.62	.71	.22	.71	1.34 †	.75	.30	.38	.38	Simple
Colorless	−.05	.22	.19	.42	.68 †	.09	.32	.33	.51	.91 †	.42	−.71	Colorful
Undependable	.22	.25	.26	.65 †	.20	.12	.51	.33	.05	.75 †	.04	.14	Dependable
Feminine	−.19	−.27	.11	−.22	−.16	.00	.15	−.06	.07	−.48	.23	.15	Masculine
Excitable	.38	.21	.11	.13	−.08	.01	.20	.00	.25	.56	.73	.17	Calm
Boring	.43	.45	.32	.46	.70	−.01	.64	.50	−.07	.66	.04	−.46	Interesting
Weak willed	.55 †	.77 †	.30	.38	.58 †	.42	.59 †	.29	.39	.71 †	.22	−.30	Strong willed
Emotional	−.21	−.09	.06	−.16	−.11	−.24	−.19	.17	−.17	−.18	.29	1.06 †	Unemotional
Twisted	.08	.13	.11	.14	.09	−.14	.28	.24	.07	.52	.13	.17	Straight

* Minus sign indicates a higher mean score for the high-education group.
† Difference significant at or beyond the .01 level by t-test.

Means were obtained on each of the two factors for the two educational-attainment groups (see Tables 5.4 and 5.5).

Results

There are at least two ways to interpret the results of Semantic Differential studies. An interpretation can be made either of the absolute ratings of each concept or of the comparative differences in ratings for different concepts. The distinction is crucial in this study, because an interpretation of the absolute results alone or of the comparative results alone would lead to faulty conclusions. We will discuss first some absolute results and then the implications of some comparative results.

PROPOSITION 5.1: **The public holds moderately high positive attitudes toward mental-health professionals.**

All of the professions studied were held in high esteem by the public, the mental-health professions included. The "mental" professions are rated as sincere, effective, dependable, and so on (see Table 5.2). This trend is illustrated by the fact that the mental professions have an average score on the *evaluative* factor of about 6.00 (see Table 5.4). Because the mean could not be larger than 7.00 and measurement error should make it smaller, a mean of 6.00 is, in absolute terms, a high positive rating.

TABLE 5.4. Mean Scores on the *Evaluative* Factor

Low-education group (N = 48)		High-education group (N = 72)		Total (N = 207)	
Concept	*Mean score*	*Concept*	*Mean score*	*Concept*	*Mean score*
Doctor	6.61	Doctor	6.33	Physician	6.45
Nurse	6.58	Nurse	6.33	Doctor	6.44
Physician	6.56	Physician	6.33	Nurse	6.38
Mental-hospital at-tendant	6.31	Social worker	5.97	Research psychol-ogist	5.96
Research psychol-ogist	6.13	Clinical psycholo-gist	5.91	Social worker	5.95
Psychiatrist	6.08	Research psychol-ogist	5.84	Clinical psycholo-gist	5.91
Social worker	6.08	Me	5.80	Mental-hospital at-tendant	5.91
Psychologist	6.02	Psychiatrist	5.78	Psychologist	5.89
Clinical psycholo-gist	5.94	Psychologist	5.76	Psychiatrist	5.87
Psychoanalyst	5.89	Psychoanalyst	5.71	Me	5.83
Me	5.88	Mental-hospital at-tendant	5.57	Psychoanalyst	5.76
Mental patient	3.09	Mental patient	3.21	Mental patient	3.17

TABLE 5.5. Mean Scores on the *Understandability* Factor

Low-education group (N = 48)		High-education group (N = 72)		Total (N = 207)	
Concept	*Mean score*	*Concept*	*Mean score*	*Concept*	*Mean score*
Nurse	5.52	Nurse	5.20	Nurse	5.32
Physician	5.37	Me	5.03	Me	5.22
Me	5.35	Physician	5.01	Physician	5.14
Doctor	5.32	Social worker	5.01	Mental-hospital attendant	5.10
Mental-hospital attendant	5.32	Doctor	4.90	Doctor	5.09
Social worker	5.30	Mental-hospital attendant	4.88	Social worker	5.08
Psychoanalyst	5.00	Clinical psychologist	4.64	Clinical psychologist	4.66
Psychiatrist	4.84	Psychologist	4.51	Psychologist	4.60
Psychologist	4.84	Research psychologist	4.35	Research psychologist	4.52
Research psychologist	4.75	Psychiatrist	4.24	Psychiatrist	4.47
Clinical psychologist	4.67	Psychoanalyst	4.13	Psychoanalyst	4.43
Mental patient	2.40	Mental patient	2.14	Mental patient	2.22

The findings here seem to contradict the premise with which this chapter began—that all is not right with popular attitudes toward the mental-health professions. There are three points that must be considered in order to understand the findings here. First, some comparative results, which will be discussed shortly, indicate that in a relative sense public attitudes are higher toward some nonmental professions than toward the mental professions. Second, a distinction must be made between attitudes toward professionals and attitudes toward the tools and methods used by professionals. A possibility which is often overlooked is that the public may place high evaluations on the mental-health professions but low evaluations on the techniques that the professions use. For example, the psychiatrist may be held in high esteem as an individual, but the techniques that he uses—psychotherapy, shock treatment, hypnoanalysis, and others—may be viewed with suspicion. Third, the public probably holds all professional people in high esteem. We would probably have found high evaluations placed on engineers, physicists, ministers, and others if we had included them in the study. Although the public may differentiate among professionals, the variations in its ratings of professionals is probably less important than its tendency to hold all professionals in high esteem.

PROPOSITION 5.2: The public places higher evaluations on professionals who treat physical disorders than on professionals who treat mental disorders.

There are large and significant differences between the concept doctor or physician and the cluster of concepts whose titles start with the morpheme "psych-." In the case of the comparison between doctor and psychiatrist, for example, psychiatrist is rated less favorably on every scale, with an average absolute difference of .50 scale unit. On 14 of the 19 scales, this difference is significant beyond the .01 level by *t*-test. When psychologist is compared to doctor, the average absolute difference (showing the doctor as more generally favorable) is significant beyond the .01 level 16 out of 19 times. In general, nurse is rated more favorably than psychiatrist. On 14 scales the differences are significant at the .01 level of confidence by *t*-test.

PROPOSITION 5.3: The public does not make connotative distinctions among the subprofessions in the mental-health field.

No significant differences are found among public attitudes toward the various subprofessions in the mental-health field, perhaps because the public does not differentiate between words beginning with the common morpheme "psych-." This is in sharp contrast to the care which mental-health professionals take to make distinctions between clinical and experimental psychologists, between psychoanalysts and psychiatrists, and between psychiatrists and psychologists. Although we have no data bearing directly on the point, some professional groups probably would rate themselves as more or less valuable and as more or less understandable than other professional groups. If, as is supposed, attitudinal distinctions among mental-health professionals are important to the professionals themselves, this is in strong contrast to the apparent lack of these distinctions among the general public. This may be true of all intraprofessional distinctions.

The failure of the public to distinguish among the subprofessions in the mental-health field should be interpreted with respect to the measuring instrument used. The Semantic Differential is intended to measure some aspects of connotative meaning or, in other words, the metaphorical implications of concepts. Consequently, the findings here do not mean that the public makes no distinctions at all among the subprofessions but only that it makes no connotative distinctions.

Additional Findings

There is an apparent tendency for the low-education group to rate the "mental" professions more highly than does the high-education group (see Tables 5.3, 5.4, and 5.5). However, the low-education group tends to rate *all* of the concepts in the study slightly more highly (with the exception of mental patient). Consequently this finding may be merely an artifact (response-set tendency) of the rating method. More extensive investigation is needed to show whether the low-education group actually has more positive attitudes toward the "mental" professions. If so, it would pose an interesting dilemma: it is the high-education group which has the most contact with the mental professions and knows more about them from school courses, reading, and conversation.

The concept *mental-hospital attendant* is given very favorable ratings (see Tables 5.2, 5.4, and 5.5), being rated more favorably than psychiatrist on 13 out of 19 scales. The evaluation is much higher among the low-education group than the high-education group. In this case there are comparative results to show that the difference between educational-attainment groups is not due solely to rating artifacts (see Table 5.4). On the list of concepts, the high-education group ranks *mental-hospital attendant* next to last, above only *mental patient,* while the low-education group ranks *mental-hospital attendant* high, above all of the "mental" professions. The low-education group rates *mental-hospital attendant* above the concept *me,* where the high-education group rates it below *me.* Even in the high-education group, however, *mental-hospital attendant* is given a moderately high evaluation. These findings are interesting in the light of the low wage scale of attendants in many places and the difficulties of recruiting capable people for the work.

There are no significant differences between the ratings of *doctor* and *physician.* Whereas in a technical sense the word *doctor* covers holders of numerous academic degrees besides those in medicine, the public tends to equate *doctor* with *physician.*

The underpaid and overworked *nurse* has one consolation: she is rated as very valuable and understandable by both high- and low-education groups.

The mean ratings of *mental patient* in this study confirm some of the comments made in Chapter 4. *Mental patient* is rated low on the *evaluative factor* and low on the *understandability* factor by both the low- and high-education groups.

The results reported here might be erroneously interpreted to indicate that the public considers practitioners of "physical" medicine—as compared to psychiatrists and psychologists—more capable of dealing with psychological problems. This is not so. From two additional studies we tried to learn whom the public would contact in case of mental illness in the family and whose professional advice the public would most trust. Item 4 in the association test (see Appendix 9) concerned whom the public would seek for "advice on mental-illness problems." In another study a pair-comparisons technique was used to determine the public's preference among psychiatrists, psychologists, medical doctors, ministers, and others as sources for advice (see Table 5.6).

TABLE 5.6. Interval Scales * of Preference for
Sources of Mental-health Information †

Question 1		Question 2	
Whose advice would you most trust in an article entitled, "How to Prevent Mental Illness?"		Whom would you see for advice if a close relative of yours showed signs of mental illness?	
Psychiatrist	.82	Psychiatrist	1.03
Psychologist	.47	Psychologist	.54
Medical doctor	.23	Medical doctor	.48
Minister	−.07	Minister	.04
A person recovered	−.25	Older relative	−.42
Lawyer	−1.20	A person recovered	−.61
		Lawyer	−1.06

* Preferences were made via pair-comparisons. Scale values were obtained by Thurstone's "law of comparative judgment," Case V.
† Administered to a sample of residents of Lafayette, Indiana ($N = 169$).

The two sets of data indicate the public considers the psychiatrist the final expert on the treatment of mental illness. The psychologist comes next, followed by medical doctor and then minister. Another interesting implication of these two studies is that the more severe the disorder is made to sound, the greater the tendency to call on a psychiatrist instead of a medical doctor. If you speak of "mental-health problems," the family doctor is favored by the public as a source of advice. If you speak of "mental illness," then the psychiatrist is favored over other professions as a source of advice. Because of the limited scope of the two studies, however, these results need to be confirmed by more substantial investigations.

In no instance did we find a strong tendency for the public to seek out religious institutions and ministers for help with mental disorders, which supports the conclusion in Chapters 2 and 6 that the public does not strongly associate mental-health problems with religious phenomena, practices, and institutions.

The findings in this chapter about mental-health professionals agree with those in Table 4.1 regarding attitudes toward the concept *psychiatrist*. The study reported in Chapter 4 employed only some of the scales and concepts used here, and none of the respondents in the two studies were the same. A number of other experimental studies which used such concepts as psychologist, psychoanalyst, and psychiatrists also confirm the conclusions reached here.

ATTITUDES TOWARD TREATMENT METHODS AND INSTITUTIONS

Earlier in the chapter we hypothesized that the "problem" is not so much that the public holds unfavorable attitudes toward mental-health professionals but that it holds unfavorable attitudes toward the techniques and procedures which the professionals use. Some evidence will be given here to support this hypothesis.

A number of our experimental studies (described in later chapters) incidentally measured public attitudes toward mental-treatment methods such as psychotherapy, shock treatment, and brain operations. Generally we found the public fearful and distrustful of these procedures. A small study was performed to help tie down these observations.

A special Semantic Differential form was administered to 109 high-school students in Danville, Illinois. Concepts for the form were chosen to provide a comparison between treatment institutions and methods for "physical" disorders (concepts like hospital, doctor, methods for treating cancer) and treatment institutions and methods for "mental" disorders (concepts like mental hospital, psychiatrist, methods for treating mental illness). The full set of concepts and scales is shown in Table 5.7. Because of the nature and size of the sample, the data should not be analyzed finely and the results should not be interpreted broadly. The results are used only to illustrate several general principles, principles that were strongly confirmed by the data.

PROPOSITION 5.4: **Mental-treatment methods and institutions are held in relatively low esteem.**

Mean scores on all scales and concepts (see Table 5.7) show large and consistent differences between ratings for the "physical" and "mental" institutions. For example, *hospital* is rated as much more valuable, safe, predictable, and understandable than *mental hospital*. The results for treatment techniques are less clear cut, although they are similar to those obtained for institutions. *Methods for treating broken bones* was used in the study because we thought that the public would react to it as representing a "tried-and-true" method of treatment. *Methods for treating cancer* was used because we thought the public would react to it with fear and puzzlement. Probably no other physical-treatment method is currently surrounded with the same amount of fear, mystery, and distrust. In comparing methods for treating mental illness with methods for treating cancer, we put the mental methods to their severest test. Our sample regarded the mental treatment methods (*methods for treating mental illness* and *shock treatment for mental illness*) as much more like cancer treatment than the treatment of broken bones. In general, cancer-treatment and the mental-treatment methods are regarded as less safe and understandable.

Without going into more detail about the specific findings in the study, we may say that the public does not trust mental-treatment methods and institutions as much as physical-treatment methods and institutions. The mean differences between the attitudes toward the two types of institutions are much more pronounced than are the mean differences between the attitudes toward the mental- and physical-health professions.

TABLE 5.7. Mean Semantic Differential Ratings of Treatment Institutions and Methods by 109 High-school Students *

Concept

Scale	Methods for treating broken bones	Methods for treating cancer	Methods for treating mental illness	Psycho-therapy	Psycho-analysis	Shock treatment for mental illness	Psychi-atrist	Mental-hospital doctor	Doc-tor	Insane asylum	Mental hospital	State hospital	Hos-pital	
Insincere	5.63	5.92	5.80	5.37	5.48	5.30	5.92	6.01	6.48	4.96	5.48	5.69	6.21	Sincere
Unpredictable	5.15	3.62	3.88	3.84	3.70	3.46	4.32	5.00	5.36	3.36	4.06	4.96	5.44	Predictable
Weak	5.14	4.13	4.67	4.34	4.43	4.60	5.17	5.62	5.95	4.43	4.84	5.33	5.64	Strong
Slow	3.69	3.00	2.86	3.59	3.44	4.09	3.76	4.13	4.98	3.12	3.28	4.25	4.81	Fast
Delicate	3.55	3.30	3.49	3.58	3.68	3.95	3.67	3.85	3.70	4.43	3.93	4.04	3.35	Rugged
Cold	4.60	4.43	4.58	4.40	4.35	4.14	4.58	4.82	5.27	4.31	4.58	4.83	5.31	Warm
Dangerous	4.78	3.64	4.51	4.41	4.71	3.82	5.51	5.64	5.90	3.92	4.52	5.31	6.05	Safe
Tense	4.07	3.38	3.89	4.42	4.35	3.54	5.14	5.21	5.53	3.27	3.72	4.20	4.84	Relaxed
Worthless	6.14	6.06	5.97	5.45	5.37	5.64	5.71	6.09	6.36	5.58	5.86	6.01	6.48	Valuable
Complicated	3.81	2.41	2.93	2.87	3.28	3.26	3.05	3.31	3.62	3.18	3.13	3.64	3.62	Simple
Undependable	5.50	4.22	4.94	4.73	4.97	4.40	5.21	5.77	6.03	4.86	5.05	5.67	6.14	Dependable
Masculine	3.71	3.74	3.75	3.53	3.73	3.75	3.49	3.26	3.01	3.66	3.75	3.74	4.14	Feminine
Excitable	4.21	3.97	4.24	4.31	4.38	3.38	5.27	5.27	5.74	3.64	3.83	4.38	5.13	Calm
Mysterious	5.20	3.49	4.19	4.00	4.36	4.02	4.50	5.27	5.70	3.94	4.33	4.80	5.28	Understandable
Weak willed	4.99	5.04	4.84	4.88	5.00	4.51	5.18	5.57	5.90	4.48	4.78	5.00	5.42	Strong willed
Emotional	3.62	3.23	3.52	3.30	3.49	3.00	4.13	4.17	4.40	3.24	3.29	3.63	4.08	Unemotional
Strange	4.68	3.41	3.91	3.43	3.54	3.65	4.09	4.38	5.57	3.27	3.62	4.14	5.38	Familiar

* Means were obtained for ratings made on seven-step scales. Consequently, the highest possible mean is 7.00, and the lowest possible mean is 1.00. The nearer the mean to 7.00, the more the concept is judged to be like the adjective on the right; the nearer the mean to 1.00, the more the concept is judged to be like the adjective on the left.

These comparisons support the hypothesis that what is "wrong" with public attitudes is not so much a distrust of the mental-health professionals as it is a distrust of the methods and institutions with which they are associated. Although this may seem like a hair-splitting distinction, it is very important for public-information programs. For example, rather than trying to convince the public that psychiatrists are intelligent, friendly, sincere persons (which the public already believes), it would be more to the point to convince them that psychotherapy, drug treatments, and other methods are safe and effective (assuming that would be appropriate).

An additional finding in Table 5.7 is worth noting. *Insane asylum* is rated less favorably than *mental hospital,* which in turn is rated less favorably than *state hospital,* showing that it is important what you call it—a point that will be discussed in detail in the following chapters.

The differences in attitudes toward the "physical" professions and the "mental" professions shown by these high-school students are similar to those shown by the panel respondents earlier in the chapter. Not only does this substantiate evidence cited in the first part of the chapter but it allows us to generalize with some confidence from the responses of this group of high-school students.

SUMMARY

Our surveys have shown that, although the public holds moderately high, favorable attitudes toward psychologists, psychiatrists, and kindred "mental" specialists, it holds much more favorable attitudes toward "physical"-treatment specialists, such as physicians and nurses. While the public makes a clear distinction between *doctor* and *psychiatrist,* it does not make connotative distinctions among the subprofessions in the mental-health field—psychiatry, psychoanalysis, clinical psychology, experimental psychology, and the others. Evidently it attributes a common meaning to all professional titles prefixed by the morpheme "psych-," which also connotes some of the characteristics of the mentally ill.

Our results indicate that what is "wrong" with public attitudes is not so much a degrading of the mental professionals as a degrading and distrust of treatment methods and institutions. When this finding is coupled with the fact that treatment methods and institutions are presently not as effective as we would like, the inevitable conclusion is that public attitudes really are not "bad" and irrational.

6

What the Mass Media Present

THE MEDIA OF MASS COMMUNICATION are commonly thought to exert a powerful influence on what the general public feels and believes. Consequently, we studied presentations dealing with mental-health phenomena in the mass media and the impact of the media on public opinion. This chapter will describe a content analysis of the mass media and Chapter 7 will discuss how mental-health information is processed through the media.

CONTENT-ANALYSIS PROCEDURE

Content analysis is a counting operation. Examples of things that might be counted are the number of metaphors in Shakespearean plays, the number of friendly references to a political candidate in newspapers, and the number of times that a propaganda source refers to a particular issue. Our content analysis counted the number of times that particular points of view about mental health were portrayed in samples of mass-media presentations.[1]

Coding Categories

In a content analysis, the people who do the counting are referred to as *coders* and the things that they count are referred to as *coding categories*. Usually coding categories are determined a priori, or "rationally," rather than deduced from empirical observations. Our content analysis departed from the customary dependence on "rational" categories. One of the principles which guided our study of information held by our three sources (the public, the experts, and the media) was that comparable measures should be used for all three. Consequently, the ten information

[1] The content analysis was directed by Dr. Wilbur Schramm and Dr. Wilson Taylor. (See Taylor, 1957, for a more technical explanation of the content-analysis procedure.)

factors that were used to study the public and the experts were also used to study the content of the media.

How the information factors were used to analyze the content of media presentations can be illustrated with one of the television programs "caught" in our sample. The program was a 15-minute crime drama. As the scene opens, a thief is sneaking through a clock shop. The shop is filled with ticking clocks and swinging pendulums. The thief enters a barred enclave in the room where the "safe" is placed. The barred door accidentally closes and locks, and the unfortunate thief must spend the night looking at and listening to a room full of clocks. When the proprietors arrive in the morning, the thief is staring glassy-eyed and mumbling incoherently. In the final scene he is carted away to a mental hospital.

How the content of this television presentation was analyzed will illustrate our general procedures. It was first necessary to decide whether any relevant material occurred. (How relevance was determined will be discussed later.) Relevant material was then "coded" on the ten information factors. A judgment was made as to whether the material affirmed each factor, repudiated each factor, or portrayed a neutral viewpoint (a neutral presentation either said or portrayed nothing relating to the ten factors or was a balance of pro and con). Scores of "plus," "minus," and "zero" were given for the results.

The television drama described above is relevant to our problem because the thief was referred to several times as being "out of his mind" and because he was placed in a mental hospital. The presentation was particularly relevant to two of our factors, "look and act different" (Factor I) and "immediate external environment versus personality dynamics" (Factor VII). The thief assumed a very bizarre appearance, which, if characteristic of the mentally ill at all, would be found only in the most severely ill. Consequently, the program was scored "plus" on Factor I. In the drama, the thief was "driven mad" by the ticking clocks. He entered the shop an apparently normal person (except for an unfortunate occupation) and left with a severe mental illness. The lesson that people might learn from this (fortunately people know better) is that one harrowing experience will bring on mental illness. Consequently, the program was scored "plus" on Factor VII. The details of the program supplied information enough to score some of the other information factors as either "plus" or "minus," and zeros were given to the remaining information factors because no related ideas were presented.

In addition to the ten factors, five supplementary content categories were employed. Counts were made of the number of portrayals of *supernatural* causes and cures associated with mental-health problems. Although supernatural explanations were generally rejected by the public, it was thought that some of the media presentations might deal with evil omens, visions, magic spells, and the like. The second supplementary category concerned the *approval of mental-health professions and facilities*. A "plus" was recorded if the portrayal suggested, for example, that psychiatrists usually do an effective job. An example of a "minus" situation is one in which the psychiatrist was in league with crooks and used his position to confine hapless victims in a mental hospital. Similarly, codings were made of portrayals relating to psychotherapy, mental hospitals, and specific forms of treatment. The third supplementary category concerned the *incidence* of mental-health problems: whether or not the presentation suggested that mental-health problems occur frequently in our society. For the fourth supplementary category, *methods of prevention and treatment*, coders simply listed all the suggested methods encountered in the media presentations. For the fifth supplementary category, *whom to approach for help* when mental problems occur, coders listed the kinds of persons suggested in the media presentations, such as ministers, psychiatrists, and lawyers.

In addition to the content categories, coders applied a number of space and time categories. For the printed media, the coders determined the amount of space taken up by each relevant message. For radio and television, coders noted the amount of time consumed by each relevant presentation—an hour, a half-hour, or only five minutes. The space and time categories were broken down in terms of the places in which relevant material appeared. For example, in the analysis of newspapers, each relevant item was classified into one of the following "location" categories: (1) news stories, features, and pictures, (2) paid advertising, (3) entertainment such as fiction, comics, and puzzles, (4) personal-advice columns on health and psychology and for the "lovelorn," (5) editorials, including political cartoons and "letters to the editor," and (6) all factual "how to" items, such as recipes, financial guides, and home-repair columns.

The ten factors and the supplementary categories were intended to measure the information stated and implied by mass-media presentations. In addition to these information-type measures, part of the content analysis was concerned with the attitudes suggested by the media presentations. For this, coders were asked to make judgments about the portrayals of the mentally ill and the persons who treated the mentally ill. Each character appearing in the media was rated on a series of seven-step attitude scales. The scales were bounded by polar adjectives such as safe-dangerous, strong-weak, and valuable-worthless. (This type of attitude-measuring instrument was used widely in our studies. It was described in more detail in Ch. 4.) The coders were not asked to rate their personal reactions to the characters portrayed but to try to make impartial judgments about the nature of the portrayals themselves.

Coder Selection and Training

The main job of the coders was to analyze media content on the basis of the ten information factors. Consequently, the coders had to be familiar with psychological concepts. Six undergraduate majors in psychology were employed as coders, and a psychology graduate student supervised their work. The coders were given six hours of training. The meanings of the information factors were explained in detail, and the coders practiced using the factors. One form of practice was to make a "blind" sorting of the 180 information items (the ones used in the original factor analysis) into their proper factors. Thus, given a statement like "The eyes of the insane are glassy," the coders had to guess the corresponding factor (in this case the correct answer was Factor I, "look and act different"). On the average the coders assigned 75-percent of the items correctly, giving us some confidence in their understanding and use of the factors. As another form of practice, the coders made content analyses of excerpts from newspaper articles and of contrived written messages. The results were compared with the codings made by psychologists on the research staff, which resulted in more exact specification of the procedures of analysis and continued training for coders.

Media Samples

A truly representative sampling of the content of the mass media would be an enormous research undertaking. Not only are there numerous arms of the media (films, books, newspapers, radio, television, and others), but there are numerous classifications of each. Even a representative sample of one arm alone, such as magazines, would require a diverse and extensive collection. In comparison to a truly representative sampling of media content, our sample was relatively weak.

TELEVISION. Television coverage was the most restricted of our media samples, because of the difficulties and expenses of content-analyzing television programs as compared to newspapers, magazines, and other media. The television sample was restricted to the total output—about 111 hours of transmission time—of a single VHF station, WCIA in Champaign, Illinois, for one full week, January 31 through February 6, 1955. In addition to local productions, this station offered more than 100 CBS, nearly 20 NBC, and several DuMont programs.

As was true in all of the content analyses, every minute of the telecasting was considered for material relevant to mental health. Thus our coders watched such apparently unrelated presentations as basketball games, stock-market quotations, and commercials, but we did not want to judge in advance where relevant presentations would be found.

Coders worked in shifts to analyze television programs, with one shift of three coders watching at all times. A room equipped with clocks, two television sets (in case one fell into disrepair), and partitions separating the coders from one another was specially prepared for the analysis. Supervisors were available to distribute and collect coding sheets and to answer coders' questions about technical procedures.

RADIO. The radio sample consisted of one week's total broadcasting by four stations, affiliated with four different networks, in four widely separated geographic areas of the United States. The broadcasts had been recorded in November and December 1953 for another project.[2] It proved much less tedious to analyze the radio recordings than it was to analyze "live" television. The coders were also able to play back portions of the program recordings to help them form judgments about the content categories.

MAGAZINES. In this sample were 91 different magazines, one issue of each, which were displayed on newsstands at about the same time in March 1955. These included comic books, news, pictorial, digest, "quality," health, women's, men's, teen-age, sports, farm, romance and confession, detective, film, and other magazines. We tried to gather as diverse a collection as possible, excluding only such highly specialized magazines as photography and "how to" publications. About 351,000 column inches of space were included.

NEWSPAPERS. Our newspaper sample was both the most extensive and the most representative for the country as a whole. The sample consisted of one week's "home" editions of 49 daily newspapers. The newspapers were proportionately representative of the geographic regions in the United States and proportionately representative of circulation size. The issues were spread over the month of October 1954. Involved were 317 separate issues with a total of 12,419 pages, containing approximately 2,086,423 inches—and every inch was searched for material relating to mental health.

CONFESSION MAGAZINES. In gathering the magazine sample discussed above, we found that "confession" magazines are saturated with material relating to mental illness, neurosis, and emotional disturbance. Consequently, a separate study was made of the mental-health content of confession magazines (see Appendix 11).[3] Different methods of content analysis were used on the confession magazines and the results were not combined directly with those from our four other media samples.

Some Technical Details

The general logic for sampling the media and analyzing the content was relatively clear. As is usually the case, however, we had to solve some knotty practical problems in the actual research. Some of these technical details will be discussed in this section.

[2] The recordings were made available by Dr. Dallas Smythe.
[3] The study was conducted by Dr. Wilbur Schramm.

THE SCORING UNIT. Before applying the content measures (the information factors, the supplementary categories, and the attitude ratings), we had to designate what the item, or the unit, for scoring would be. As a practical solution we defined units as separable programs in radio and television and separable "columns" in newspapers and magazines. Thus in radio or television, a half-hour comedy program, including commercials and other announcements, was scored as a whole and constituted a single item or unit. In magazines, a complete story or feature was considered a single item, including the continuation of the feature or story from page to page. If the story continued to another issue or if the feature reappeared regularly, the material in one issue was considered a single item, and the material occurring in subsequent issues was considered a new item. As for magazines, the entire content of each separable newspaper story and feature was considered as one unit. Some of the items or units in particular issues were an editorial column about the cold war, a syndicated short story, a Joe Palooka comic strip, an advertisement for television sets, and a front-page story about an airplane accident.

RELEVANCE OF CONTENT. The analysis consisted of a twofold set of decisions: first whether a particular excerpt from the media (a television program or a magazine story) contained material related to mental health, and, if so, how the material conformed to our coding categories (the information factors, the supplementary information categories, and the attitude ratings).

Relevance was determined on the basis of the definition of our project area: information and attitudes about mental disorder—the psychoses, the neuroses, and lesser disturbances. In choosing topics to study and in selecting relevant material from the media, we preferred to err toward overinclusion rather than toward underinclusion. Consequently, our studies include some findings relating to child-rearing practices, alcoholism, juvenile delinquency, and other phenomena that are usually considered parts of mental health. We considered such matters as relevant, however, only if they were specifically linked with a central theme of mental disorder and only if they were presented as relating to a disorder.

Thus material was considered relevant and analyzed if it presented anything directly or indirectly related to mental illness. For example, material would be considered relevant if one of the characters in a drama were spoken of as "insane," if someone were being treated by a psychiatrist, if a person's behavior was called "emotionally disturbed," or if someone exhibited any of the classical neurotic symptoms. Whereas in a sense relevant material was defined rather narrowly (concerning mental disorders), the indicants of these disorders in media presentations were construed rather broadly. In some instances, it was very easy to determine the relevance of a presentation for the content analysis, for example, a newspaper story about "an escaped mental patient." In other cases, the decision of relevancy was debatable. In all cases, material was considered relevant and analyzed only if two out of three coders, working independently, rated the media excerpt as relevant. Because, as we found later, the occurrence of relevant material is much the exception rather than the rule, the odds that two out of three coders would rate an item relevant "by chance" were relatively low.

PRELIMINARY SCREENING FOR RELEVANCY. Our first analysis was directed at television. There, relevance of material had to be judged immediately before the content-analysis procedures were applied. If the coder decided that the material was relevant, he marked it appropriately for content categories while the program was in progress. With radio programs, magazines, and newspapers, relevancy could be judged at any time before the content analysis was applied.

When we found that relevant material occurs relatively infrequently in television, we assumed that it would occur relatively infrequently in the other media as well. After inspection, much of the material could be discarded as clearly irrelevant (such as financial reports of civic organizations, most advertisements, articles about club meetings, weather maps, and musical programs). Thus, to reduce the work load, the original plan of having three coders judge the relevance of *every* media presentation was discarded in favor of a plan whereby only one coder would judge content relevancy in a preliminary screening. Material that was in no wise related could be thrown out in that screening. Then three coders would work over the reduced collection of material, and the final judgment of relevancy would be based, as before, on majority decision.

CONTENT-ANALYSIS RESULTS

How seriously can the results of the content analysis be taken? We have pointed out some of the frailties of the procedures that were used. Much of the data is judgmental and is no better or no worse than the subjective processes of the coders. Also, the content samples were, at best, only moderately representative of the media as a whole. In spite of the limitations of the content analysis and the modest proportions of our media samples, however, the results are so lopsided that we can reach some strong conclusions about the mental-health content of the mass media.

Time and Space

Seeking material directly related to mental-health problems (as we defined them) in the mass media is like looking for a needle in a haystack. If you search every inch of space in three different daily newspapers, the odds are that you will find only one item which is relevant. To find one relevant item it would be necessary to read, on the average, the entire content of two magazines. If you listened to one entire day of broadcasting of a radio station, you would, on the average, find about 2.3 programs with information or portrayals relevant to mental-health problems. An almost identical number of relevant programs would be expected in the entire daily telecasting of one station—2.4 programs which in some way relate to mental health problems. Thus we can conclude that:

PROPOSITION 6.1: Information concerning mental illness appears relatively infrequently in mass-media presentations.

The findings here contradict our original estimates of the prevalence of mental-health presentations in the mass media. We had guessed that relevant material was presented more frequently than it is. Before doing the study we tried to recall the number of presentations relating to mental-health issues that we had seen recently in newspapers, television, and the other media, but in so doing we did not fully consider the many programs that were irrelevant. Consequently, we overestimated, percentagewise, the occurrence of related material.

In all of the media samples combined, we found a total of 202 relevant items (items being defined as separate whole programs in radio and television and as columns, stories, and features in the printed media). Of the total, we found 120 items in newspapers, 49 in magazines, 16 in radio, and 17 in television. There were not enough items for us to compare their content similarities and differences or to demonstrate differences among subclassifications of the media. For example, it would have been interesting to determine whether the mental-health content of newspapers is generally different from that of television programs or whether the mental-health content of television news programs is different from that of evening drama programs. Because there were not enough relevant items to analyze separately, all of the relevant material was lumped together, providing an average profile of the information presented in the mass media.

Although we did not study the issue directly, it seemed to us that information relating to "physical" disorders—cancer, heart trouble, physical injury, and so forth—appeared more frequently than information relating to mental health. Perhaps the apparent relative scarcity of information relevant to mental-health problems is related to the findings (see Ch. 2) that public information is unstructured and uncrystallized. Problems of mental health may not be discussed sufficiently in the media, in schools, and in private conversation to permit the individual to develop a firm system of beliefs. More research is needed, however, to determine the amount of mental-health information in the media and, if, as our data indicate, such information is relatively scarce, to test the effect of this scarcity on public beliefs.

The Information Factors

To review: Two out of three coders had to be in agreement before material was classed as relevant and before content was coded on the information factors. Although basing the analysis on majority decisions reduced the total amount of data, it probably produced a more valid set of results.

While the data on the information held by the public and the experts was in seven-step-scale form and could be compared directly, the data from this content analysis had to be converted to the seven-step scale for comparison purposes. The data consisted of ratings by coders of the number of times that one pole of a factor was portrayed as compared with the other pole. For example, 80 instances were found in which the "immediate external environment" (Factor VII) was portrayed as being at the root of particular mental disorders. The opposite pole of the factor, "personality dynamics," was portrayed only 29 times. Thus Factor VII was attributed to be the cause in 73 percent of the classified presentations. Percentages of this kind were then converted to a seven-point scale (see Nunnally, 1957, for a description of the scaling procedure used). From these converted results we were able to compare the results from the mass media with the opinions held by the public and the experts (see Fig. 6.1).

The scaled factor scores for the media, represented by circles, are shown in Figure 6.1. Three factors (will power, sex distinction, and age function) occurred less than ten times in the media presentations and consequently offered insufficient grounds for making comparisons. The factor scores for the media are compared with the average responses given by experts and by members of the general public (shown in Ch. 2 without the content-analysis results). The results are quite clear. Not only are the views that the media present generally incorrect according to expert opinion but they are also far less accurate than the beliefs of the average man.

PROPOSITION 6.2.: **The media of mass communication generally present a distorted picture of mental-health problems.**

Although some mass-media presentations, especially those specifically designed to convey information about mental health, provide a valid picture of mental illness, the number of such programs is very small in comparison to those which incidentally portray mental illness in a misleading light. An individual is more likely to see some aspect of neurotic behavior portrayed on television in an evening drama program than in a public-information program.

In general, the causes, symptoms, methods of treatment, prognoses,

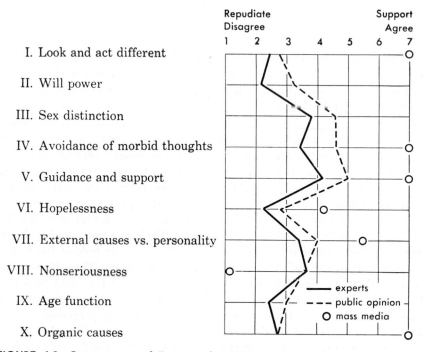

FIGURE 6.1. Comparisons of Experts, the Public, and the Mass Media on the Ten Information Factors

and social effects of mental illness portrayed by the media are far re-moved from what the experts advocate. (These findings from the infor-mation factors are supported by an independent study of confession magazines presented in Appendix 11.) In particular, media presentations emphasize the bizarre symptoms of the mentally ill. For example, infor-mation relating to Factor I was recorded 89 times. Of these, 88 affirmed the factor, that is, indicated or suggested that people with mental-health problems "look and act different"; only one item denied Factor I. In television dramas, for example, the afflicted person often enters the scene staring glassy-eyed, with his mouth widely agape, mumbling incoherent phrases or laughing uncontrollably. Even in what would be considered the milder disorders, neurotic phobias and obsessions, the afflicted person is presented as having bizarre facial expressions and actions.

The occurrence of mental disorder is explained in the media most often by pressures in the immediate external environment (Factor VII). The soap-opera heroine develops a neurosis because her husband dies in a plane crash, her little daughter is afflicted with an incurable disease, and all the family savings are lost in a fire. The "neurosis" goes away with a brighter turn of events. If the pressures of the immediate external environment are not brought in as causal explanations, organic factors are cited. A magazine fiction story might explain neurotic or psychotic behavior in terms of an old battlefield injury, a head wound in childhood, or physical privation such as thirst or hunger.

In the media, the person with a mental disorder most often receives help from some strong person in the environment who lends guidance and support. The strong individual may be a person who is professionally trained—a psychiatrist, "doctor," or nurse; equally often the guiding hand is that of a homespun philosopher who manages to say the right thing at the right time. Such cogencies as "The world is what you make of it" and "The past cannot hurt you" are portrayed as profoundly influencing the course of a disorder.

Supplementary Categories

Because only a few examples of the items in the media contained material which was related to the supplementary categories, there is little to report. For example, in the category "whom to seek for advice," we found that only eight psychiatrists, two "doctors," one psychologist, and one nurse were mentioned. These categories did provide one interesting bit of negative evidence: Although we had thought that the media might portray religion as being related to mental-health issues, it was seldom mentioned as an important variable. The same results held in a separate study of confession magazines (see Appendix 11). In this case, the media are in line with public opinion: our studies show that very few people associate mental-health phenomena with religion (see Chs. 2 and 5).

Attitude Ratings

The media samples portrayed 41 persons who could be classified as mentally ill. Of these, 21 displayed typical neurotic symptoms and 20 displayed typical psychotic symptoms. Three coders made attitude ratings of the 41 portrayals, and the median rating of the three coders on each Semantic Differential scale was used in the analysis. The resulting profile of the mentally ill in the mass media closely resembles the public's attitudes toward the mentally ill (see Ch. 4). Both psychotics and neurotics are portrayed as relatively ignorant, dangerous, dirty, unkind, and unpredictable. Neurotics were pictured as less dangerous, dirty, and unkind than psychotics, the latter being pictured as stronger and more active.

For what they are worth, the coders also made attitude ratings of the portrayals of the 12 "therapists" mentioned above. The resulting average profile is much the same as the attitude profile of the general public toward psychologists and psychiatrists (see Ch. 5). The media portrayals depict the therapist as being intelligent, kind, and valuable.

SUMMARY

Our results point to a seeming paradox: the ideas about mental health portrayed in the mass media are less "correct" in comparison to expert opinion than are the beliefs of the public at large. Where then did the public get its present body of information? Certainly not from an uncritical acceptance of media presentations. Perhaps, as has been suggested, the public is able to discriminate between "valid" information and unrealistic portrayals. If this is so, then the public probably does learn something from the "better" media presentations, although the number of such programs is relatively small.

The media are, of course, commercial ventures whose policies and presentations are determined in part by their internal needs. Presentations related to mental health are shaped by numerous hands—writers, editors, directors, media executives, commercial sponsors, and others. Perhaps it is necessary to emphasize bizarre symptoms in order to make the presentations more exciting and to enlarge their audience appeal. Perhaps the relatively restricted time period or space available is responsible for much of the oversimplified treatment of mental disorders. If the media took the time to illustrate the complexities of the learning processes that experts deem to be the important components in personality disorders, they might produce some very dull programs.

The communications media have adopted a stylized picture of mental-health problems which distorts reality, but is a useful device in drama, comedy, and other programs for the public. It would be a great waste, however, if the communications media did not eventually help to promote a healthy set of public attitudes and improve public understanding of mental-health phenomena. It is also to be hoped that more accurate information can be incorporated into effective forms of entertainment. Our content analysis was performed in 1954 and 1955. Presentations in the mass media may have begun to incorporate more adequate viewpoints about mental health since then. Chapter 7 will go more deeply into how the media select and shape presentations relating to mental health.

7

The Internal Processes

of the Mass Media

THE CONTENT-ANALYSIS RESULTS reported in the previous chapter show that, on the whole, the mass media of communications are not helping the public to learn about mental-health problems and are not promoting favorable attitudes toward the ill and toward treatment methods. (Those conclusions are also supported by some data to be reported in this chapter.) This is made doubly unfortunate when we consider that, because of the vast audiences which they attract, the mass media could serve a highly important function in purveying information and in softening the harsh attitudes held by the public.

Because of the potential importance of the mass media in our problem area, and because of the disturbing results obtained from our content analysis (Chapter 6), we decided to extend our studies of the mass media.[1] A subproject was organized and extensive studies were made over a period of two years. The primary purposes of the studies were (1) to determine why mental-health issues are treated as they are in the mass media, and (2) to gather some suggestions as to how the mass media can more effectively participate in future programs of mental-health education. Because of the scope of the studies and the bulk of the results, the detailed findings will be reported elsewhere.[2] This chapter will give only a summary of the major findings and conclusions.

METHODS OF INVESTIGATION

Three principal means were employed to study the mass-media processes: (1) trend analyses of the amounts and kinds of presentations

[1] With only minor changes, this chapter was adapted from material written by Dr. C. E. Osgood. The author wishes to reiterate his thanks to Dr. Osgood for this and his many other contributions to the research and to this book.

[2] The research reported in this chapter was undertaken primarily by Dr. G. Gerbner and Dr. P. H. Tannenbaum. Dr. Gerbner is presently preparing a detailed account of the research for publication.

relevant to mental illness appearing in the mass media over the years, (2) intensive interviews with key personnel in the media—writers, directors, producers, actors, managerial staff, and others, and (3) "case-history" studies of highly relevant portrayals (such as a documentary movie on mental illness), including as much as possible of the interplay surrounding their genesis and production.

TRENDS

The Reader's Guide to Periodical Literature was used as the basis for estimating trends in popular magazines, the period from 1900 to the present being covered. *The New York Times Index* was used for estimating trends in newspapers, the period from 1913 to the present being covered. The Production Code Administration of The Motion Picture Association of America reviews and classifies about 95 percent of the feature films exhibited in the United States; its classifications were used to estimate trends in the movies, for a period from 1944 to 1959. Our estimates of trends in television were based on the files of a network censor, which contained records of clearance of all old movies and filmed television shows telecast by that network—the period here is only from 1951 through 1958. In all cases, trends were analyzed both for sheer density of relevant material and also for the context (that is, type of movie, kind of magazine) in which the relevant material appears. This analysis was obviously "indirect" in the sense that we necessarily had to depend upon the categorizing criteria of the original coders in each medium.

Despite these limitations, certain rather significant trends appear. In the first place, for those periods where all of the trend analyses overlap, it is evident that the density of popular productions dealing with mental health and illness tends to covary in the various media. This suggests that there are basic cultural forces operating, affecting all of the media, which influence the probability of this particular topic being portrayed. Comparing just *The New York Times Index* and *The Reader's Guide*, for which a longer time period was available, it also appears that there is a consistent *lag* of a year or two for the "entertainment" (magazine) media behind the "news" (newspaper) media; for the shorter period in which movie and television trends are available, they also seem to lag behind the density changes found in *The New York Times Index*. This probably reflects a very general relation between "news" and "entertainment" media that might hold in any content area and should be studied. The "entertainment" media pick up matters of current popular interest and concern from the "news" and then move into the production of related portrayals—this production taking time. The relation between "information" and "entertainment" is further illustrated by the nature of the boom in television programs involving mental illness that occurred

TABLE 7.1. Number of Television Programs Dealing
with Mental Illness, 1951–1958

	1951– 1953	1954	1955	1956	1957	1958
Documentary programs	4	15	2	2	1	1
Other (features and films)	1	12	37	122	169	72

in the middle fifties. This is shown in Table 7.1, which compares "documentary" with "other" television programs.

It can be seen that the documentary-type presentation, presumably closest to public-service "information," appears first on the scene, has a brief increase, and then fades; the "fad" created is taken up in more "entertainment"-oriented productions, which have their burst and then, by 1958, begin to fade.

As to the over-all trends, it is, of course, difficult to relate density changes to any particular events in time; relevant material increased during the middle twenties, decreased during the depths of the Depression, picked up again during the middle thirties, decreased again during the years of World War II, increased tremendously during the late forties and early fifties, and is now, in all media apparently, on the decrease again. If we were to hazard a wild guess as to the dynamics here, it might be this—that concern with mental health and illness is essentially a "luxury item" as far as both the public and the media are concerned; it is easily pushed out when in competition with "serious" matters, like wars and depressions, and it flourishes relatively in times of peace and plenty.

Regardless of the accuracy of our guesses as to why the density of presentations relevant to mental illness increases and decreases over time, the fluctuating density is easy to see. Evidently, faddism determines the number of relevant presentations found in particular years; and just as other themes are popular for awhile, decline, and rise again later, the emphasis on mental-illness themes in the media is cyclic.

What is the context in which material relevant to mental health and illness typically appears? Here the trend data substantiate our content analysis. For feature films released during the period from 1950 through 1958, materials relevant to mental health and illness were relatively dense in crime, science-fiction and horror, and general drama movies and relatively scarce in western, adventure, and musical movies. Mental illness was frequently a significant element (noted in synopsis by coders) in drama and in mystery television productions, but seldom a significant element in comedy, western, or documentary television productions. Since *The Reader's Guide* does not index the "pulp" magazines, in which we had previously found the largest share of relevant material, no direct trend comparisons can be made. On the other hand, a second content analysis of all magazines found on the stands in a single month substantiates the earlier findings—detectives and confessions contain the most material, with personal advice, slicks, and quality periodicals contributing a share. It is again abundantly clear that the public is most likely to encounter material relevant to mental health and illness in the context of dramatic fiction—in close contact with the emotional states engendered by crime, horror, mystery, and deviant romance and confession. Given such a repetitive affective context, it is not surprising that public *attitudes* correspond closely with mass-media portrayals; the *information* implications are presumably sufficiently ambiguous, inconsistent, or in outright conflict with other sources of information that the public is not particularly influenced in this area.

DECISION-MAKING

Approximately 150 key people in the mass-media industries were interviewed in the course of our studies; they included executives, producers and directors, editors, writers, censors, public-relations men, officers of trade and professional organizations, and "mental" professionals (psychiatrists and others) who serve as consultants to the media. We feel that this is a reasonably large and representative sample of the people who make the crucial decisions as to what will be presented and how. Because this material was gleaned from comments made during informal interviews, we feel that it gains in richness what it may lose in rigor.

Decision-makers in the media do not speak with one voice—each has his own particular pattern of pressures and problems depending on his medium and his role within it—but they seem to share a common posture of trying to look many ways at once, and that rather anxiously. In deciding each particular *what, when, where* and *how,* they cast a very alert eye toward the "box office" or the "circulation figures," as the case may be; they take a good look at "what the public wants," or at least their own image of it; they simultaneously turn a wary eye toward the sources of censorship in their own medium as well as in the public at large—and they also glance at the public-service value of the potential product. Of course, the relative weight given to the public-service role of the product varies with the type and quality of the medium; it also varies, apparently, with the economic stress within any medium at any time. Movie producers in recent years, for example, have been especially leery of mental-illness themes and their box-office potential; a literary agent commented that magazine writers have been driven toward either the "shocker" or the "Pollyanna" extreme type of presentation in this area because of keen competition at the newsstands.

In general, the higher the quality of the medium the greater the stress on mental *health* (emphasis on positive living, being "upbeat") and the lower the quality of the medium the greater the stress on mental *illness* (emphasis on "shockers," appeal to public curiosity, and so forth). But this, too, reflects a complex of motives, not simply public service versus profit. Producers of quality television programs and magazines feel that there is a sordid, negative halo surrounding many mental-illness topics, retardation, and deviancy that is liable to "rub off" on the source, the star, the sponsor, and so on. As the story editor of one television drama program which had dealt with a number of these problems put it:

> Many viewers felt that Miss ———— [the star] should not do these stories; somehow it disturbs their image of her. We feel that they were good and important shows. We are not contemplating any more at the present time, however.

Several advertising-agency men admitted that sponsors generally forbid "downbeat" themes like mental illness; if it is presented at all, it should be positive in tone, with an uplifting moral. On the other hand, it was generally agreed that the portrayal of mental illness, particularly the more bizarre types of insanity, makes for dramatic audience appeal, and media people in the lower quality end of the continuum are not above using "mad-dog" material.

There are purely dramatic and production considerations, quite apart from either service or profit motives, which influence the portrayal of mental health and illness materials. A young production executive in a movie studio clearly expressed this conflict: "Neurotics are dull. Insanity has dramatic appeal. But it is evil to exploit this appeal. That is why it is a difficult subject to treat seriously." A television writer complained about the treatment of two of his mental-illness themes, saying,

> They butchered it because of the requirements of the star. You see, the star must be on-stage most of the time, and will share only one scene with the second lead. . . . The other was changed, too. The producer told me . . . he wanted danger in the script. . . . It should have been played quietly.

Many stressed the purely logistic requirements of magazine stories and television productions:

> Okay, so you have twenty-three minutes to establish your exposition . . . to delineate your characters, to work to your climax with as much action as possible. . . . You use as many short cuts as possible. . . . Often you fall back on the stereotype of mental illness of some sort which presumably your audience will understand without full pathological explanation.

Another writer pointed out that, while deviant behavior lends itself quite readily to drama and suspense, long and laborious therapy certainly does not—and therefore we find "cures" telescoped into a single traumatic incident, a "revelation" or the like.

Even in those media and among those media personnel where public-service motives are strongest, there is a serious question of how good a factual job they can do. The decision-makers in the mass media are part of the public too—albeit in the better educated, more sophisticated (and sometimes more cynical) segment. Many of them pointed to the ambiguities in this field, to the lack of agreement among experts, and to the chameleonlike changes in viewpoints. You could find some "expert" to support almost anything you might write, it was said. Another said it was very difficult, within the limitations of the production conditions of either the printed or electronic media, to present anything like a faithful picture of the devious intricacies of psychotherapy. This is one reason for the relative "play" given to physical developments, brain surgery, wonder drugs, and the like. The same lack of *understandability* of "mental" phenomena that we found in the general public also influences the decisions of media people, both in their expressed difficulty in filling a service role and in their exploitation of fear of the unknown.

This lack of security with the material, its significance, and its impact is probably one of the reasons why the media are so prone to "fads" in this sphere. Our interviewers were repeatedly told such things as "Mental illness is dead now—I wouldn't touch it. But let someone come out with another *Snakepit* and start another cycle, and I'll jump on the bandwagon." Of course, "faddism" is entirely general to the industry— we see it in the westerns, in the quiz shows, and even in cartoon ads— and it reflects insecurities in a highly competitive field. Attempts are often made by media decision-makers somehow to resolve or compromise service and profit motives. One editor in the "crime and detective" magazine field explained his avoidance of insane criminals on the ground that "readers tend to sympathize with mentally ill criminals, and that defeats the objective of showing that crime does not pay." A men's "adventure" magazine justified a "jazzed-up" horror story of the inside of a mental institution by claiming that it was "exposing conditions." The fact that mental illness is presented in fiction form (stories, television dramas, and the like) was often used as a justification for the mode of treatment. One fiction editor said she considered fiction the best medium for presenting such material, because "readers do not feel as directly involved in fiction as in a nonfiction article. They will often accept in fiction what might repel them in nonfiction."

The oft-heard justification for media decisions—that "they are merely giving the public what it wants"—seems to be more for outside consumption than a matter of inside belief. One television executive said he believed Gilbert Seldes was right when he stated that "TV is the only business in which the supply creates the demand." Our data make us think that this situation is rather characteristic of the popular-culture industries generally, not just limited to television. The pressures from advertisers to reach as wide an audience as possible, coupled with the requirement that media institutions make a profit, lead to a kind of conservatism and "faddism" that often inhibits creative innovation. The public is not given sufficient opportunity to sample; it is meaningless to talk about "what the public wants" when not enough alternatives are given. Many media people expressed their awareness of this fact, their concern with it, but also their inability to do anything about it. A few indicated their pleasure at the results of innovation:

> So we ran a study to determine how far we can go in giving our readers something different. The results, to my mind, exploded an old myth about medical journalism readership. They showed that people *will* read well-written, straightforward accounts without any sensational slant.

Our interview results *in toto* suggest that the media and the public are playing an elaborate, but largely unconscious, game with each other. The game might be called "peek-a-boo," and it deals in the main with the *images* that each has of the other. The media personnel have an image of what the public wants, which is based more on the interplay of forces within their own economic enterprise than upon any study of the public itself. The public has an image of media personnel, which is based more upon a single motive—"they are just making a living, doing what most *other* people want"—than upon any understanding of the complex pattern of motives under which they actually operate. Perhaps all communication media, e.g., Japanese drama, American newspaper formalism, tend to become more and more stylized and remote from valid images of the sources and receivers. Some media people were clearly aware of this: many of them referred to the great changes in public attitudes in the areas of human behavior that have occurred in the past two decades—the greater openness with which behavioral problems, even sex and mental illness, can be discussed—yet at the same time accepted a code for their own productions that takes scant cognizance of these changes.

GATEKEEPING

Regulation is inherent in mass production, and the products of the communication industries are no exception. Here, too, we find "quality control," and the people who exercise these controls are often referred to as the "gatekeepers." The formal procedures, institutions, and organization of censorship vary greatly with the medium of communication. One of the main factors determining this variation is the size and monopolistic character of the medium. Another is the size and character of the audience. Thus newspapers, with relatively diffuse ownership and audiences that are both restricted in size and mainly adult in make-up, also have decentralized "gatekeeping" activities—mainly vested in individual editors. A similar situation holds for magazines, whose audiences, with the exception of a few weekly "slicks," are even more specialized in age, sex, education, and other demographic variables.

In contrast with newspapers and magazines, in the movie industry and in the broadcast media of radio and television, with their more monopolistic concentrations and their relatively unrestricted audiences, we find more formalized, industry-wide censorship functions. The Production Code Administration of the movie industry screens about three to four hundred films a year and about twice as many scripts; it is a centralized "gatekeeping" authority. Beyond this, each major studio maintains a censorship staff which mediates between the PCA and that studio, providing more immediate, on-the-spot controls. The broadcast media have a somewhat different censorship organization, again in keeping with their structure. The National Association of Broadcasters maintains a small, industry-wide control which is mainly restricted to advertising content. Each major network maintains its own "continuity-acceptance" department, in which the major censorship of program content occurs. There is some degree of interaction among the "gatekeepers" in different networks. Between the movies and the broadcast media (particularly television), again because of differences in the make-up, setting, and control over audiences, we find certain differences in censorship—the fact that television is characteristically an intimate, family communication situation definitely influences the kinds of censorship functions.

Despite these differences in the formal organization of censorship functions in the different media, the actual policies and practices prove to be pretty much the same. This is because the patterns of forces shaping censorship policies and practices are generally similar. The self-regulation which characterizes the media, with its "codes of fair practice" and the like, developed mainly out of fear of regulation by others, specifically government censorship. The Hollywood Code and the individual network codes appeared within a few years of each other, the movie code in the early thirties and the broadcasting codes in the middle thirties, and both in response to moralistic pressures from religious organizations and the like which were having their reverberations in Washington.

The Production Code of the movie industry directly reflects this moralistic pressure, being chiefly concerned with matters of sex, crime, childbirth, religion, cruelty to animals, liquor, and respect to flags, institutions, and peoples of all nations, races, and professions. The network codes are somewhat less moralistic and more concerned with children's programs, public issues, and "the advancement of education and culture." Newspaper and magazine self-regulation is relatively more concerned with matters of slander and libel, since they deal more often with factual material relating to particular individuals. All of the media censorship operations are concerned with offending peoples' sensibilities and with "good taste," and particularly with avoiding offense to groups—particularly organized groups (religious, civic, racial, veterans, patriotic, and so on *ad infinitum*).

The handling of professional groups is particularly interesting in this connection. The "fair-treatment" clause of the Production Code says that nothing should be presented implying that all, or even a majority, of the members of any profession are unethical, immoral, given to criminal activities, or the like; furthermore, where a given member of a profession must be shown as a "heavy" or unsympathetic character, this should be offset by showing an upright member of the same profession who condemns the conduct of the unsympathetic character. That this "fair-treatment" clause does not necessarily result in fair treatment is indicated by some facts: In our study of all identifiable mentally ill male characters playing significant roles in movies since 1950, only 56 percent were shown as having any profession at all; of the one third of these who were members of recognized "professions," half were either scientists or psychiatrists. Comparing "physical" with "mental" doctors, physicians are twice as likely to be favorably portrayed and six times as likely to play "romantic" leads as psychiatrists and the like; on the other hand, the "mentals" were three times more likely than the "physicals" to be portrayed as mentally ill themselves.

However, this concern over fair treatment of professional and other groups does reflect the main theme running through all media-censorship operations, and this is *self-protection.* Unlike the government censor and many other private and institutional censors external to the communication media, the "gatekeepers" within the popular-culture industries owe their primary responsibility to the industry itself and its continued economic well-being. As one network censor put it, "Some producers are out for newspaper headlines, not just television programs. But controversy and sensational publicity hurt the network; we're here to protect it." Or another, "We're the conscience of the industry; conscience in our case means a nose for trouble." The "gate" that the media censors "keep" swings both ways: on the one hand, the censors monitor and control the communications product; on the other, they are the "radar" of the industry, receiving "feedback" which in turn influences subsequent production. The public is generally unaware of the sensitivity of the media to feedback. The products of these cultural industries go out into a great public void; box-office receipts, circulations lists, Hooper Ratings, and sales volumes give only the over-all picture, not the details of the impacts of product details—yet it is the details of the impacts with which the "gatekeepers" are mainly concerned. Our interview data show that a single sincere letter from an individual aroused by unfair treatment of some group (e.g., retarded children ridiculed) can set the entire censorship staff of a network aquiver.

The broad themes of media codes, *in practice*, tend to degenerate into the dismembered, superficial trivia of concrete "Do's and Don'ts" about words and phrases. In the mental-health area, lower echelon censors follow categorical rules to delete terms like "crazy," "looney," "idiot," "nuts"; yet the most bizarre total characterization may pass unchecked. "We can invent the most fantastic things," one studio censor said, "and no one complains. But the slightest error in the wearing of a uniform and we are flooded with letters." In one case, the PCA objected to the "repellent" nature of a movie treatment of a mental institution; a minor twist, "crusading for reform," was added, and the whole was passed. Suicide is sinful, according to the PCA code, but it is permissible with the mentally ill because they are not trying to evade justice. The words used by comedians, such as "You're *nuts!*" or "He was a *crazy*, mixed-up kid," are carefully screened for their possible implications of ridicule; yet, for "production" reasons, admittedly false "cures" of mental illness may be propagated without a qualm. The concern is with symbols, not with substance.

Why does the sublime in media codes tend to become the picayune in media practice? It seems to come down again to the major underlying theme behind media self-regulation—self-protection. It is difficult for the general public to perceive discriminatively and react explicitly to the complexities of characterization, to the building of stereotypes, or to the implications of dramatic devices which may create undesirable images and affects. On the other hand, the public can react definitely and often vigorously to *symbols*, even those whose significance it would be hard put to explicate. Thus misplaced military insignia, a wrongly made hospital bed, the use of the word "nigger" or the word "idiot" can serve to focus irritation while, for example, the consistent portrayal of Negroes in servile roles or of the mentally ill in homicidal contexts fails to have sufficient focus. The same thing applies to staffs of censorship departments who do the day-to-day red-pencilling: it is easy to follow a rule that says "strike the word *crazy* whenever you see it" but very difficult to follow one which says "reject instances of portraying the mentally ill as submen, displaying bizarre, stereotyped behavior." The "gatekeepers" of the industry are primarily concerned with avoiding negative feedback, not with raising the general cultural level of the public.

To say that the media "gatekeepers" are primarily concerned with self-protection is not to say that they are entirely unconcerned with public service. Our interview data are replete with comments of an earnest, and not pious, nature about the importance and difficulty of presenting a socially valid and useful image of mental illness. One censor speaks of staying up all night helping a studio writer recast his story along lines that put the mentally ill and the institutions for their care in a fairer light; the file of another contains a letter sent to all television writers and producers exhorting them to come up with something effective but valid for Mental Health Week; another includes in his training files articles from better sources on mental health and illness. It is also important to point out that it is the "gatekeepers" who are closest to, and most susceptible to, the pressures toward public service—they are the industry representatives who are responsible for interpreting feedback, from expert consultants as well as from the public at large, and transforming it into production policy.

The problem is not so much that of an unwillingness to perform a public service, for the media personnel are as, or more, civic-minded than the representatives of most business enterprizes, but a problem of *how*. The *how* of it involves (1) how to determine or be advised as to what constitutes "better portrayals" (and because of the many missing pieces in the storehouse of "mental" facts and the differences in opinions among experts, this is no easy matter), (2) how to shape such "better" portrayals to the mechanical and production requirements of the media, and (3) how to make such "better" portrayals sufficiently interesting to attract a wide audience.

EXPERTS

Since 1955 there have been at least three national and many regional conferences bringing together representatives of the mass media and the mental-health professions. The calling of these conferences reflected the increasing need felt on both sides for mutual understanding and assistance. Their occurrence has brought about a striking improvement in relations, but some of the old antagonisms still remain. To understand the antagonisms, as well as the accommodations, it is necessary to appreciate the motives and the anxieties of both sides. The "approach and avoidance" patterns in each case are complex, but it is only through gaining mutual understanding that the experts and the media personnel will be able to "use" each other effectively. And, incidentally, "use" of experts involves much more than consulting—it includes personal appearances, endorsements, programming suggestions, and sometimes even active collaboration in production of articles and programs.

Let us first take the point of view of the media man. The same underlying theme of self-protection we found elsewhere in media operations also appears in the use of experts. One old-timer in the movie industry put it quite bluntly—"We usually seek expert medical advice for protection. This is solely to the end that we would not make foolish or harmful technical blunders." The frequent and often strenuous search for endorsement of articles or programs by mental-health professionals reflects the same need for protection against negative feedback. Media people are also motivated toward service of the public and presentation of truth, particularly in areas like mental health, but the requirements of economic survival and of dramatic vitality, at least as they are interpreted, usually interact with the service motives:

> This was a documentary, and I felt barred windows were a natural part of the environment. The APA [American Psychiatric Association] did not like this. . . . It also gave us an opening high-angle shot, looking out from inside, from the patients' point of view.

The same needs for getting audience support often lead to selection of topics for portrayal and discussion—hypnotism, sleepwalking, dream symbolism, sex crime, and the like—that are more sensational than sound from professional points of view.

The media people also have their sources of anxiety when dealing with experts. One of these is fear of loss of independence in controlling their own products. Experts often "insist" where they are asked to "advise," and the newspaper man or television producer feels that, since he has the final responsibility, he must also exercise the final say. There is also a matter of professional pride at stake here—the reporter rebels at the expert's insistence that he be allowed to "check" the story before publication; not only does this imply inadequacy but it is usually interpreted as an infringement on his freedom. Media people also feel, and often correctly, that they know how to "reach" the public better than the expert in his ivory tower. They are afraid that if the expert has his way, all the life (and salability) of the product will be lost. On the other hand, there are often conflicts within the media industries themselves, usually between the "gatekeepers" and the production "decision-makers." Unfortunately, each can usually find his own "expert," and this does little to encourage reliance upon expert opinion in the mental-health field. Driven by his own complex set of motives, the media man is likely to select an expert who has the happy combination of professional prestige and sympathy with media-production needs.

What about the experts? The prime motive of the expert in mental health is certainly public enlightenment, but even here the situation is by no means simple. Experts closely identified with professional societies are likely to be concerned with "what is good for the profession"; those relatively remote from professional association, and hence with less professional status at stake, are sometimes motivated more strongly for personal publicity. Many men in private practice are frankly loathe to take time away from their patients—for monetary as well as ethical reasons—to serve as consultants to the communications industries. The expert is also motivated toward the portrayal of truth in his field, but where the media man's "other" motives lead toward more sensational treatment, the expert's "other" motives often lead toward softening the hard realities (for example, the APA didn't like showing barred windows in mental institutions, but they are certainly there in many).

Experts in the mental-health and other fields have often learned to beware of publicity the hard way. At one of the joint conferences between experts and media people, Dr. Finley Gayle told of how a reporter asked him to observe a lady wonder horse; he observed, said it was a smart horse but certainly no mind reader, and read in the newspaper that afternoon: "Dr. Finley Gayle Psychoanalyzes a Horse." Experts often find themselves in embarrassing positions when appearing in prestige roles in broadcast programs, for example, suddenly being asked to give on-the-spot psychiatric advice to members of the audience or to pick which girl will make the best wife for a quiz-show prize winner. Often they are expected to make public pronouncements on topics on which their professional knowledge forces them to be reticent—and this reticence is often interpreted by both media personnel and the public as professional incompetence. Experts are also loathe to give endorsement to articles and programs—unless they have control over the final product, which is seldom the case. The reason for experts' anxiety here is quite obvious: with their endorsement they are also staking their professional reputation, and they are not willing to endorse an "idea," no matter how sound, when the actual treatment of it may be entirely incompatible with their standards.

WHAT CAN BE DONE?

Today moves are being made from both sides to solve this problem. The mental-health professionals have become acutely aware of the role that the communications media must play in informing the public. Media professionals have become increasingly aware of the need for really expert advice if they are to play their public-service role effectively. Both the American Psychiatric Association and the American Psychological Association have recently set up staff positions and committees to work on public relations and communications problems—unfortunately, much of the advice to their members is still of the "beware-of-being-trapped" variety rather than information on how the media operate and hence how to be effective in the process. One network censor expressed the hope that, rather than the present "chaos" among professional consultants to the network, a central clearing house for professional advice could be set up. There have been several examples of excellent programs and program series in the mental-health field that have been written, produced, and cleared with complete collaboration at all stages between expert consultants and media personnel—so it can be done.

8

Opinions and Attitudes

of General Practitioners

IN EARLIER CHAPTERS we discussed information and attitudes about mental health held by three sources—the general public, the experts, and the media of mass communication. An equally important source is the general practitioner in medicine.[1] He stands in a key position as an advisor and referral agent. Moreover, because of his time-honored position as an advisor and confidant to the family, his attitudes toward the mentally ill and toward treatment methods may have an impact on the attitudes held by the general public. Much of the traffic to mental-health professionals is routed through the offices of general practitioners. The general practitioner is often consulted first about mental-illness problems, and he makes the decision as to whether or not a "mental" specialist should be consulted, and, if so, who should be consulted.

Survey results show that the public considers the general practitioner to be the first person to contact for advice about mental-health problems. For example, in one of our studies [2] the public was asked, "If I myself, or someone close to me, needed advice on mental-health problems, I would consult a. . . ." The question was followed by alternatives such as minister, psychologist, family doctor, and psychiatrist. The family doctor was favored by 47 percent of the respondents. The next most popular choice was the psychiatrist, with 28 percent of the responses.

Further evidence comes from a study of 508 persons in Phoenix, Arizona, conducted by the Institute of Social Research at the University of Michigan (Survey Research Center, 1950). They conclude, "The most frequent avenue for help of a professional nature [for nervous conditions], as seen by respondents, was general medical practitioners." Thus the

---

[1] The main study reported in this chapter was conducted by Dr. Edward Ware.

[2] This sample consisted of 101 persons from the vicinity of Lafayette, Indiana. See Appendix 9 for the questionnaire and Chapters 4 and 5 for other results.

general practitioner stands as the gatekeeper in the communication chain between the general public and the mental-health professionals. Also, as the research evidence will show, the general practitioner actually treats many cases of mental illness himself instead of referring them to specialists.

MEASURES

A three-part questionnaire was used to study the information and attitudes held by general practitioners. The first section (see Table 8.2) contained some of the information items used in the studies of the public (see Ch. 2) and in the studies of mental-health professionals (see Ch. 3). The second section contained specific questions about the availability of psychiatric consultants, referral practices, and the effectiveness of various methods of "mental" treatments (see Tables 8.3 through 8.6). The third section was a Semantic Differential form, of the type illustrated in preceding chapters, concerning concepts such as psychiatrist, mental hospital, and neurotic person (see Tables 8.7 through 8.9).

SAMPLE

To obtain a representative sample of general practitioners, the questionnaires were sent to 1,000 of the approximately 25,000 members of the American Academy of General Practice.[3] This sample was randomly selected (every twenty-fifth member listed in the Academy directory) and covered 49 states. In all, 431 completed booklets were returned, 323 in response to the first mailing and 108 in response to a follow-up letter. Because we were sampling from a rather active and busy group, a return of 43 percent was considered adequate.

Eleven items were selected from the first section of the questionnaire to test the differences between responses to the first and second mailing. The purpose of these tests was to see if those who responded only after a follow-up letter differed in their responses to the questionnaire from those who responded to the first mailing. A *chi*-square test was performed on each of these pairs of items. None of the differences on these 11 tests approached statistical significance. In other words, the late returns were not significantly different from the early returns. To the extent that it is valid to project the responses of the late returns to the hypothetical responses of physicians who did not return their questionnaires, the statistics suggest that the sample results were not grossly affected by nonresponse bias. This finding lends some confidence to the generalization of results beyond our particular sample of general practitioners.

[3] We would like to thank the American Academy of General Practice for their cooperation and assistance with this survey. Particular thanks are due to Mr. M. G. Hermetet for his advice and assistance.

TABLE 8.1. Age and Residence of the General-practitioner Sample

Population of residence	Percent	Age	Percent
rural	2	25–34	17
under 1,000	3	35–44	34
1,000–5,000	10	45–54	32
5,000–25,000	24	55–64	13
25,000–75,000	19	65–74	3
75,000–250,000	15	75–84	1
250,000–500,000	6		
500,000–1,000,000	6		
over 1,000,000	7		

RESULTS AND CONCLUSIONS

The physicians in our sample practice in areas of widely varying population and represent a wide age range (see Table 8.1 for some demographic characteristics).

Table 8.2 lists the mean responses of general practitioners to a set of information statements. Responses of mental-health experts (psychiatrists and psychologists) and members of the general public are also available for six statements. The responses of general practitioners lie between the extremes posed by the mental-health experts and the public and are generally much closer to the former. Insofar as the information items are useful as a test of correctness of information, the results indicate that the information of the general practitioners is "good."

Referral Practices

Almost all general practitioners (91 percent) state that psychiatrists are available for case referral (see Table 8.3). We had guessed that psychiatrists would be less available, particularly for the many general practitioners who reside in small towns (Table 8.1 shows that 23 percent of our sample lives in towns with a population under 5,000). Perhaps the reason for the preponderance of "yes" answers to the question is due to the phrasing "in or near" the community of the physician. Modern transportation, which makes cities 50 and 100 miles away accessible, may have reduced the feeling that psychiatrists are scarce.

Referral to a psychiatrist is most often made in two circumstances: (1) when the patient himself requests referral and (2) when, in his own judgment, the physician thinks it is advisable (see Table 8.3). The opin-

TABLE 8.2. Mean Responses to a Set of Information Statements *

Item	General practitioners	Experts	General public
The best way to mental health is by avoiding morbid thoughts.	3.57		
There is not much that can be done for a person who develops a mental disorder.	1.49	1.29 †	1.96 †
Mental disorder is one of the most damaging illnesses that a person can have.	4.50		
Children sometimes have mental breakdowns as severe as those of adults.	5.98		
Nervous breakdowns seldom have a physical origin.	3.84		
Most of the people in mental hospitals speak in words that can be understood.	5.62	5.85	5.49
Mental health is largely a matter of trying hard to control the emotions.	3.14	2.36 †	4.31 †
If a person concentrates on happy memories, he will not be bothered by unpleasant things in the present.	2.71	2.69	4.24 †
The mentally ill have not received enough guidance from the important people in their lives.	4.35		
Women are as emotionally healthy as men.	4.89		
The seriousness of the mental-health problem in this country has been exaggerated.	2.04		
Helping the mentally ill person with his financial and social problems often improves his condition.	5.48		
Mental patients usually make a good adjustment to society when they are released.	4.44		
The good psychiatrist acts like a father to his patients.	3.79	3.69	5.11 †
Early adulthood is more of a danger period for mental illness than later years.	4.22		
Almost any disease that attacks the nervous system is likely to bring on insanity.	1.72	2.21 †	3.37 †
You can tell a person who is mentally ill from his appearance.	1.83		
People who become mentally ill have little will power.	2.24		
Women are more likely to develop mental disorders than men.	3.39		
Most mental disturbances in adults can be traced to emotional experiences in childhood.	4.86		

* These means were derived from a seven-point scale with 1 representing extreme disagreement and 7 representing extreme agreement.

† These ratings were significantly different at the .01 level by *t*-test from the ratings of general practitioners on the same items.

TABLE 8.3. Answers to Questions about Referral Practices

Question	Answer				
1. Are psychiatrists available in or near your community to whom referrals can be made?	*Yes* 91% *No* 9%				
2. In which of the following circumstances do you refer patients to psychiatrists?	Almost always	Usually	Some-times	Almost never	No answer
a. When the patient himself asks to be.	76%	16%	6%	1%	1%
b. When the patient's family asks that he be.	33%	34%	25%	7%	1%
c. When my own cognizance dictates.	70%	22%	6%	1%	1%
d. When it will help the patient's home, family, and personal adjustment.	42%	34%	19%	4%	1%
e. When a psychiatrist can do it quicker.	12%	28%	35%	23%	2%
3. Of the patients you have referred to a psychiatrist and have subsequent knowledge about, a. What percent have been helped *considerably?*	54% (average)				
b. What percent have been helped *very little* or *not at all?*	30% (average)				

ions of the patient's family seem to have considerably less influence in determining psychiatric referral.

Of the cases that he refers to psychiatrists, the "average" general practitioner thinks that 54 percent are helped considerably and 30 percent are helped very little or not at all (Table 8.3). This tends to show that, on the average, general practitioners regard the results of psychiatric treatment as only moderately good, or poor.

General practitioners recognize that psychological problems play a very important part in bringing business to their doors. A sizable percentage (31) of the difficulties presented to general practitioners are judged to be largely "mental" in origin (Table 8.4). The question was stated in an extreme form—"brought on by." Evidently 31 percent of the cases are judged to be almost entirely the result of "mental" causes. If the question had been phrased "contributed to by mental problems" or "aggravated by mental problems," the percentage would probably have been even higher.

When patients require treatment for mental illness, the general practitioner often provides that treatment himself. Most general practitioners (77 percent) say that they treat patients with some kinds of mental illness rather than refer them to a psychiatrist or other specialists. This question was also worded in an extreme way in order to prevent ambiguity: it

TABLE 8.4. Answers to Questions about Mental Problems and Treatment

Question	Answer
1. In your opinion, what percent of your patients who complain of physical symptoms have their disorders brought on by "mental" problems?	31% (average)
2. Do you treat any kinds of mental illness yourself rather than refer the patient to a psychiatrist or other mental specialist?	*Yes* 77% *No* 23%
3. If yes (to question above), roughly what percent of patients with mental problems do you treat yourself?	47% (average)

employed the term "mental illness" rather than terms which might imply either less severe or more widespread difficulties. Considering the specification of mental illness, the result is something of a surprise. More surprising, the average physician among those who do treat mental cases (the 77 percent who answered "yes" to the second question) states that he treats 47 percent of the mental cases that he encounters. These findings have several important implications. First, many "mental" patients are treated by general practitioners. Second, the fact that general practitioners treat many patients cannot be due to the nonavailability of psychiatrists and other specialists, for 91 percent of the general practitioners stated that psychiatrists were available for referral. Evidently, the majority of general practitioners feel that they are properly trained and equipped and that they should treat many of the "mental" problems which they encounter. As gatekeepers to the mental specialists, general practitioners keep the gates partially closed, and they probably exert a selective influence on the clientele of mental specialists.

General practitioners do not often refer patients with mental problems to specialists other than psychiatrists (see Table 8.5). If another resource is used, it is most often a "clergyman," an interesting result in light of the findings from the study of public information. This study revealed that the public places little credence in religious explanations and treatment for mental disorder. In another study (see Table 5.6) "minister" was ranked far down on a list of persons to seek for advice about mental problems. In practice, however, ministers do a considerable amount of counseling for adjustment problems, and pastoral counseling is increasing. Probably much of this "business" comes through referrals from those general practitioners who do not want to, or feel competent to, treat mental problems themselves or who do not choose to refer cases to psychiatrists.

TABLE 8.5. Referral of Patients with Mental Problems to Professionals
Other Than Psychiatrists

Patients referred to:	Often	Sometimes	Never	No answer
Psychologist	3%	34%	55%	8%
Lay analyst	0%	5%	82%	13%
Social worker	5%	39%	47%	9%
Clergyman	17%	66%	14%	3%
Lawyer	2%	35%	52%	11%
Other	3%	6%	27%	64%

Treatment Methods

Of the various methods for treating mental illness listed in the questionnaire, general practitioners placed considerably more faith in shock treatment (see Table 8.6). Because of their respect for surgery in general, we had supposed that general practitioners would place considerable emphasis on brain surgery for mental illness. The average rating of the effectiveness of brain surgery, however, is relatively low (mean of 3.18). General practitioners show a moderate, but not high, respect for "psychological" methods such as psychoanalysis and occupational therapy. Although these are regarded as somewhat effective, both are regarded as considerably less effective than shock treatment.

TABLE 8.6. General Practitioners' Ratings of the Effectiveness
of Some Procedures Available to Psychiatrists

Psychiatric procedures	Mean *
Shock (electric or insulin)	5.41
Psychoanalysis	4.66
Occupational therapy	4.47
Tranquilizing drugs	4.36
Group therapy	4.30
Hypnoanalysis	3.67
Brain surgery	3.18
Psychodrama	2.97

* Ratings were made on a seven-point scale: 7 would mean "highly effective," 1 would mean "highly ineffective," and 4 would mean "average."

Attitudes toward Mental Health

The Semantic Differential results are presented in Tables 8.7, 8.8, and 8.9. Let us first look at the results as summarized in Table 8.7, which

TABLE 8.7. Mean Scores on the *Evaluative* and *Understandability* Factors

Concept	Evaluation *	Understandability †
General practitioner	6.41	4.86
Psychiatrist	6.08	4.14
General hospital	6.11	4.33
Mental hospital	6.02	4.04
Psychotherapy	5.85	3.53
Tranquilizing drugs	5.40	3.99
Psychotic person	3.20	2.03
Neurotic person	4.44	3.06
A person who has ulcers	5.60	4.05
A person who has epilepsy	4.95	3.88

* A score of 7 represents extremely high *evaluation,* and 1 represents extremely low *evaluation.* This factor contains the scales worthless-valuable, insincere-sincere, and ineffective-effective.

† A score of 7 represents complete *understandability,* and 1 represents incomprehensibility. This factor contains the scales unpredictable-predictable, twisted-straight, and complicated-simple.

shows the mean scores for all concepts on the *evaluative* and *understandability* factors. The most obvious trend is that the general practitioner views himself as slightly more "good" and "understandable" than the psychiatrist. The difference in *evaluation* is relatively small and may only indicate the natural pride which any individual has in his own professional speciality. The difference in *understandability* is more marked, showing that general practitioners regard "mental" treatment as relatively mysterious and difficult to understand. (The public reacts in the same manner.) This is also borne out by the difference in *understandability* attributed to *general hospital* and *mental hospital.*

General practitioners have a fairly high respect for psychotherapy (mean *evaluation* of 5.85), more so, for example, than for tranquilizing drugs (mean *evaluation* of 5.40). This is interesting because general practitioners are well acquainted with the use of various drugs but few of them are well trained to perform psychotherapy.

Evidently, general practitioners have much the same feelings toward neurotics and psychotics as do members of the general public. (Compare the results in Tables 8.7 and 8.8 with those shown in Table 4.1 for the general public.) General practitioners rate the mentally ill as low on *evaluation* and *understandability,* rating psychotics much lower than neurotics on both of these characteristics. These negative attitudes are shown more specifically in Table 8.8. Neurotics and, to a greater extent, psychotics are viewed as weak, foolish, twisted, complicated, and ineffective. Psychotics in particular are viewed as dirty, highly unpredictable, and highly dangerous.

TABLE 8.8. Mean Semantic Differential Ratings for 413 General Practitioners *

Scale	General practitioners	Psychiatrists	General hospital	Mental hospital	Psychotherapy	Tranquilizing drugs	Psychotic person	Neurotic person	A person who has ulcers	A person who has epilepsy	
Unpredictable	5.55	4.82	5.20	4.64	3.59	3.91	1.65	3.53	5.06	3.74	Predictable
Tense	4.01	4.38	3.77	3.84	4.36	5.23	2.05	1.71	1.51	3.13	Relaxed
Worthless	6.59	6.30	6.52	6.43	6.05	5.89	3.21	4.96	5.93	5.15	Valuable
Dangerous	5.94	5.72	5.97	5.63	5.38	4.59	2.17	4.73	5.54	4.27	Safe
Weak	5.78	5.35	5.37	5.09	4.66	4.68	3.70	3.35	4.79	4.25	Strong
Dirty	5.88	5.65	5.67	4.90	5.02	4.90	3.51	4.79	5.40	4.43	Clean
Foolish	5.93	5.94	5.25	5.34	5.71	4.96	3.27	3.84	4.91	4.33	Wise
Twisted	5.73	5.10	5.20	4.80	4.81	4.56	2.26	3.23	4.55	4.25	Straight
Insincere	6.43	6.16	5.77	5.82	5.91	4.78	3.77	4.75	5.51	5.08	Sincere
Complicated	3.31	2.50	3.60	2.67	2.19	3.49	2.17	2.41	2.53	3.64	Simple
Ineffective †	6.22	5.78	6.03	5.72	5.61	4.44	2.63	3.62	5.36	4.61	Effective

Concept

* These means were derived from a seven-point scale with 1 representing close association with the terms on the left of the table, and 7 representing close association with the terms on the right. The data are so arranged that the higher scores generally indicate the "favorable" end of the scale.

† A different "effective-ineffective" scale was employed for the responses shown in Table 8.6. Consequently, the results there and in the table above differ by small amounts.

Such negative attitudes certainly raise problems since 77 percent of the general practitioners in our sample say that they treat some kinds of mental illness themselves—and that they treat roughly 50 percent of the patients with mental problems they see (see Table 8.4). If in fact the average general practitioner considers the patient with a mental disturbance to be low on *understandability* (unpredictable, twisted, and complicated), one must wonder how effectively he can treat such a patient—particularly when he places such a low *evaluation* on him (seeing him as foolish, dirty, and highly dangerous).

To provide a basis of comparison for attitudes toward the mentally ill, the Semantic Differential form contained the concepts *a person who has epilepsy* and *a person who has ulcers*. As we hypothesized, people with both of these illnesses are rated as considerably more valuable and understandable than are people with the two mental illnesses mentioned (psychotics and neurotics). The only surprising finding is that the ulcer patient is rated as considerably more valuable than the epilepsy patient (mean *evaluation* ratings of 5.60 and 4.95 respectively). This may reflect the more "mental" and "abnormal" implications of epilepsy as compared with ulcer conditions. Or it may be that the typical ulcer patient is, or is perceived to be, hard working and achieving, and thus, in the eyes of general practitioners, valuable.

For some of the concepts on some of the scales used in the Semantic

TABLE 8.9. Mean Semantic Differential Ratings for a Sample of 109 High-school Students Compared with Those for the Sample of General Practitioners *

	Concept								
Scale	Psycho-therapy		Doctor †		Mental hospital		Psychiatrist		
	GP	HS	GP	HS	GP	HS	GP	HS	
Unpredictable	3.59	3.84	5.55	5.36	4.64	4.06 **	4.82	4.32	Predictable
Tense	4.36	4.42	4.01	5.53 **	3.84	3.72	4.38	5.14 **	Relaxed
Worthless	6.05	5.45 **	6.59	6.36	6.43	5.86 **	6.30	5.71 **	Valuable
Dangerous	5.38	4.41 **	5.94	5.90	5.63	4.52 **	5.72	5.51	Safe
Weak	4.66	4.34	5.78	5.95	5.09	4.84 **	5.35	5.17	Strong
Insincere	5.91	5.37 **	6.43	6.48	5.82	5.48	6.16	5.92	Sincere
Complicated	2.19	2.87 **	3.31	3.62	2.67	3.13	2.50	3.05 **	Simple
Ineffective	5.61	5.11 **	—	—	5.72	5.30	5.78	5.43	Effective

* Ratings for general practitioners are taken from Table 8.8; those for high-school students are taken from Table 5.7 and from other studies described in Chapter 5.

† General practitioners rated the concept *general practitioner;* high-school students rated the concept *doctor.*

** These ratings were significantly different from the ratings of general practitioners at the .01 level by *t*-test.

Differential form for general practitioners, comparable ratings are available for a sample of high-school students (see Ch. 5). Those comparable results are shown in Table 8.9. Because the attitudes expressed by high-school students toward mental-health concepts are not grossly different from those expressed by the general population, any large differences in Table 8.9 are worth noting.

Statistically significant differences in attitudes between general practitioners and high-school students are marked by two asterisks. Most of the significant differences show that, in comparison to high-school students, general practitioners have "better" attitudes toward professionals, psychotherapy, and mental hospitals. Two exceptions are on the scale tense-relaxed: general practitioners rate themselves and their brothers in psychiatry as more tense than the public does. Evidently, general practitioners are more aware than the public that physicians work in an atmosphere of stress.

Differences among Doctors

So far we have been reporting the average, over-all data for the sample of general practitioners. There is reason to expect, however, that medical men will differ among themselves. We might anticipate differences in attitudes and beliefs to appear as functions of such things as their age, their location, the proportion of patients with mental illness they treat themselves, and so on. Since we have a large sample (431 respondents), we are able to investigate sets of interrelationships within the population of general practitioners, using correlational techniques. A number of pivotal fact and opinion items were correlated with each other and with certain attitude items. The major results are summarized in Table 8.10.

Although all of the relationships presented in Table 8.10 are based upon correlations significant at the .01 level, the actual magnitude of these correlations is small. With an N of 431, a correlation of .123 is significant at the .01 level. The correlations range between .123 and .328. Therefore we must look upon them as indicating significant trends but not as definite predictors (for example, just because a general practitioner is a young man does not definitely mean that he treats more of his own patients with mental problems, although it is *more likely* that he does).

The trends revealed here are very consistent and interesting. It is clear that the *younger doctors* are more sensitized to symptoms of mental illness in their patients, are more likely to treat such patients themselves, see these problems in terms of personality development rather than as matters of will power, and put less faith in tranquilizing drugs. In other words, in perfectly parallel fashion to our findings about the lay population, younger men in the medical profession appear to be more sophisticated about problems of mental health and illness. Whether this merely reflects changes in the general culture over several generations or changes in the training of general practitioners in medical schools cannot be determined from our data.

Doctors from smaller communities are more likely to think that the patients they refer to psychiatric services for treatment are helped by this treatment and that mental patients make good adjustments when released from treatment. By way of internal consistency, we find that those general practitioners who think more people referred to psychiatric services are helped are also the ones who see both *psychotherapy* and *psychiatrist* as more valuable, predictable, strong, wise, sincere, and effective. Encouraging is the fact that the general practitioners who tend to treat their own mental patients are usually younger, more perceptive of symptoms of mental illness, more concerned with the childhood origins of these difficulties, and more likely to see neurotic people as understandable.

It is interesting to compare the patterns of correlations for those doctors who believe in shock-treatment therapy with the patterns of correlations for those doctors who believe in psychoanalysis. The more a doctor has faith in shock therapy, the more patients he sees as being helped by psychiatric referral, the more he thinks patients will make good adjustments when released, the more effective he judges psychotherapy to be, and the more clean and sincere he judges the psychiatrist to be. On the other hand, the more a doctor has faith in psychoanalysis, the more he believes mental problems to have their origins in childhood, the more predictable, strong, wise, and valuable (as well as effective) he judges psychotherapy to be, and the more effective (as contrasted with clean and sincere) he judges the psychiatrist to be. In other words, belief in "physical" (shock) treatment is associated with belief in the effectiveness of psychotherapy and the cleanness and sincerity of the psychiatrist, whereas belief in "mental" (psychoanalytic) treatment is associated with belief in the wisdom and predictableness of psychotherapy and the effectiveness of the psychiatrist. To put this contrast even more crudely, for those who believe more in shock treatment, it is the treatment that is effective and the psychiatrist who is well intentioned, while for those who believe more in psychoanalysis, it is the psychiatrist who is effective and his treatment wise, strong, valuable, predictable, and so forth.

Finally, we find among general practitioners the same cluster of beliefs about the nature and treatment of mental problems as was discovered in the population as a whole: those who recommend avoiding morbid thoughts as a key to mental health also stress the importance of controlling the emotions, also see the psychiatrist as playing the role of a father with his patients and giving them the authoritative guidance they missed earlier in life, and also consider the problems of both neurotic people and patients with epilepsy to be *simple*. And the doctors with this cluster of beliefs tend to be the *older* men in the profession.

TABLE 8.10. Correlations (Significant at the .01 Level) among Fact, Opinion, and Attitude Items Across 431 General Practitioners

1. *The older the general practitioner is:*
   a. the more populous is the area in which he practices;
   b. the smaller the percentage of patients with physical symptoms he judges to have mental problems;
   c. the smaller the percentage of patients with mental problems he treats himself;
   d. the more mental problems are considered matters of controlling the emotions;
   e. the more a psychiatrist is assumed to act like a father to his patients;
   f. the less mental disturbance is assumed to be traceable back to emotional experiences in childhood;
   g. the more safe, clean, and simple *psychotherapy* is judged to be;
   h. the more clean and sincere *tranquillizer drugs* are judged to be;
   i. the more unpredictable and tense *a person with epilepsy* is judged to be;
   j. the more clean and simple *psychiatrist* is judged to be.
2. *The greater the percentage of patients with physical symptoms judged to have mental problems:*
   a. the younger the general practitioner is;
   b. the greater the percentage of patients with mental problems the doctor treats himself;
   c. the more mental disturbance is believed to be due to lack of guidance;
   d. the more mental disturbance is assumed to be traceable back to emotional experiences in childhood.
3. *The greater the percentage of patients referred to psychiatrists that are judged to be helped:*
   a. the smaller the population area in which the doctor practices;
   b. the greater the judged effectiveness of shock treatment;
   c. the more mental patients are believed to make good adjustments when released;
   d. the more predictable, strong, wise, valuable, sincere, and effective *psychotherapy* is judged to be;
   e. the more predictable, relaxed, valuable, safe, strong, clean, wise, straight, sincere, and effective *psychiatrist* is judged to be.
4. *The greater the percentage of mental patients treated by a general practitioner himself:*
   a. the younger the doctor is;
   b. the greater the percentage of patients with physical symptoms he judges to have mental problems;
   c. the more mental problems he believes are traceable back to emotional experiences in childhood;
   d. the more predictable *a neurotic person* is judged to be;
   e. the less simple *a person with epilepsy* is judged to be.
5. *The more effective shock therapy is judged to be:*
   a. the greater percentage of patients referred to psychiatrists that is believed to be helped;
   b. the more effective psychoanalysis is judged to be;
   c. the more mental patients are believed to make good adjustments when released;
   d. the more effective *psychotherapy* is judged to be;
   e. the more clean and sincere *psychiatrist* is judged to be.
6. *The more effective psychoanalysis is judged to be:*
   a. the more effective shock treatment is judged to be;

  b. the more mental problems are believed to be traceable back to emotional experiences in childhood;
  c. the more predictable, strong, wise, valuable, and effective *psychotherapy* is judged to be;
  d. the more effective the *psychiatrist* is judged to be.
7. *The more "avoiding morbid thoughts" is believed to be the best way to maintain mental health:*
  a. the older the general practitioner is;
  b. the more controlling the emotions is believed to be necessary for mental health;
  c. the more psychiatrists are believed to act like fathers to their patients;
  d. the more it is believed that mental patients have not received enough guidance from important people in their lives;
  e. the more simple *a neurotic person* is judged to be;
  f. the more simple *a person with epilepsy* is judged to be.
8. *The more damaging mental illness is judged to be:*
  a. the more *seldom* mental illness is believed to have a physical origin;
  b. the more it is believed that the mentally ill have not received enough guidance from important people in their lives;
  c. the less strong and wise *a neurotic person* is judged to be;
  d. the more dangerous *psychotherapy* is judged to be;
  e. the more dangerous *a person with epilepsy* is judged to be.
9. *The more mental patients are thought to make good adjustments when released:*
  a. the greater the percentage referred is judged to have been helped;
  b. the more effective shock treatment is judged to be;
  c. the more a psychiatrist is believed to act like a father to his patients;
  d. the more valuable *a neurotic person* is judged to be;
  e. the more predictable, safe, and effective *psychotherapy* is judged to be;
  f. the more valuable, safe, wise, straight, sincere, and effective a *psychiatrist* is judged to be.
10. *The more mental problems are believed to be traceable back to emotional experiences in childhood:*
  a. the younger the doctor is;
  b. the greater the percentage of patients with physical symptoms judged to have mental problems;
  c. the greater is the percentage of patients treated by the general practitioner himself;
  d. the more effective psychoanalysis is judged to be;
  e. the more predictable, valuable, strong, wise, and effective *psychotherapy* is judged to be;
  f. the more predictable *psychiatrist* is judged to be.

FINDINGS

The substance of our study of a sample of general practitioners can be summarized and discussed in terms of a number of propositions:

PROPOSITION 8.1: **General practitioners in medicine are "gatekeepers" between the general public and psychiatry.**

The truth of this proposition could probably have been inferred without our research. The survey results, however, help to clarify the position of the general practitioner as the "gatekeeper." First, the public views the general practitioner as the first person to contact for advice and information about mental health problems (Appendix 9). Second, general practitioners state that a sizable percent of their patients are primarily troubled by "mental" problems. Third, nearly all general practitioners are aware of psychiatric referral sources, and many referrals are made. Fourth, and as important as the number of referrals, many "mental" cases are not referred, but are treated by general practitioners themselves. Therefore, as decision-makers they often influence the kinds of problems that reach psychiatrists.

PROPOSITION 8.2: **A sizable proportion of all mental patients are treated directly by general practitioners.**

The information obtained about this proposition is probably one of the most valuable results of the survey. Most general practitioners say that they treat some cases of mental illness. On the average, those who do so say that they treat about half of the mental cases which they encounter. Because general practitioners far outnumber psychiatrists and other "mental" specialists, the indication is that much of the out-patient treatment given for mental problems comes from general practitioners.

Our research suggests that some additional information should be obtained from general practitioners. It would be interesting to learn what kinds of mental problems are dealt with by general practitioners and what kinds are referred elsewhere. We suppose that general practitioners are more likely to treat the neuroses and lesser disturbances rather than the psychoses. It would also be interesting to learn what kinds of treatment general practitioners give to the mentally ill. Our results show that general practitioners have a high regard for shock treatment. Does this imply that general practitioners often employ shock treatment with their patients, or does this reflect their experience with patients who received shock treatment after referral to psychiatrists? Also, it would be important to determine the degree to which tranquilizers and other drugs are used to treat mental problems.

On the other hand, general practitioners do have moderately high respect for psychotherapy and psychoanalysis. Does this mean that they apply their own versions of various types of psychotherapy to their own patients? Or is the treatment mostly in the form of an everyday friendly discussion of the patients' problems? These are important questions for further study.

PROPOSITION 8.3: **General practitioners tend to have as negative attitudes toward the mentally ill as do members of the lay public.**

We were surprised to find in our data such strong negative attitudes toward concepts like *neurotic person* and *psychotic person* being expressed by general practitioners. The mentally ill (particularly psychotics) are regarded not only as twisted, dirty, ineffective, and dangerous but also as unpredictable and complicated. Considering the frequency with which general practitioners treat patients with mental difficulties themselves, we are forced to ask to what degree such attitudes influence the effectiveness of their treatment.

PROPOSITION 8.4: **General practitioners have moderately favorable attitudes toward mental-treatment specialists, methods, and institutions.**

Although the survey results show that general practitioners place slightly higher evaluations on themselves and their own institutions than they do on "mental" specialists and methods, the over-all attitude displayed toward "mental" facilities can be described as "not bad." They place moderately high evaluations on psychiatrists, mental hospitals, psychoanalysis, psychotherapy, and other related concepts.

The relatively favorable attitudes expressed by general practitioners may be largely abstract. They give particularly high ratings to psychiatrists, for example, on such scales as valuable-worthless and sincere-insincere. When general practitioners are asked more concretely what percentage of the cases referred to psychiatrists are actually helped, however, they rated psychiatric treatment as "helping considerably" in only about half of the cases and as helping "little or not at all" in about one third of the cases. Also, general practitioners do not give very high ratings to psychiatrists on "effectiveness" (see Table 8.8). In other words, general practitioners apparently have high respect for psychiatrists as persons and respect for what they are *trying* to do; however, they do not believe that the total "mental" treatment is, at present, highly successful.

As the proposition above states, the attitudes of general practitioners toward the *evaluation* of "mental" treatment are generally good, although they tend to regard mental specialists, institutions, and methods as not *understandable*. For example, they rate psychiatrists, relative to themselves, as considerably less predictable and straight and as more complicated. Part of the relatively low *understandability* may be realistically attributed to the complexity and the many unknowns in mental treatment. The low *understandability* ratings also probably indicate that it would be good if general practitioners had more opportunity to learn about psychiatric and psychological methods—particularly so if general practitioners continue to perform such a large volume of treatment of mental patients.

PROPOSITION 8.5: **General practitioners vary among themselves in terms of certain consistent patterns of beliefs, attitudes, and practices.**

The concern which could reasonably be felt about the over-all data described above—specifically, that general practitioners with intensely negative attitudes toward the mentally ill are involved in a considerable amount of treatment—is partially allayed by our correlational findings within the sample of general practitioners.

Younger doctors are more alert to mental disturbances and see these problems as developing out of personality dynamics, and are more likely to treat their own patients. These younger practitioners are more likely to see psychotherapy and psychiatrists as more complicated and difficult, but they also see neurotics as (potentially?) more understandable. Furthermore, those who view mental disorders as most serious and damaging tend to look to "mental" rather than to "physical" etiology and treatment. It is the older doctors who tend to view mental health as simply a matter of avoiding morbid thoughts, controlling the emotions, accepting wise advice from a fatherly figure, and so on.

SUMMARY

The results from our survey suggest that general practitioners hold reasonably correct *information* about mental-illness phenomena, but their *attitudes* toward the mentally ill are as "bad" as those expressed by the general public. Although their over-all attitudes toward the mentally ill can be characterized as "bad," they range from "very good" to "very bad." In particular, younger, better-informed physicians tend to have "better" attitudes; fortunately, it is these physicians who are more prone to treat "mental" problems rather than refer them to specialists.

Interestingly enough, many general practitioners treat certain kinds of mental problems themselves, in spite of the fact that psychiatric care is available in or near their communities. Their reluctance to refer patients to mental-health professionals may be explained, in part, by the fact that they regard psychiatric treatment as not highly effective, even though they express high regard for psychiatrists as persons.

Our survey has given us some facts, but it raises more questions—and they are serious questions. How can the family doctor—who is typically the first contact of the person under stress—be provided with the kind of information he needs to play his important gatekeeping role? What sorts of criteria does he use in determining the existence and extent of mental problems? What selective influence does the general practitioner have upon the kinds of problems ultimately referred to specialists? What kind of treatment does the general practitioner give in those frequent cases where he tries to handle the problem himself? What are the outcomes of treatment by the general practitioner as compared with the specialist?

PART

II

Studies of Information Transmission

and Attitude Change

9

Public Interest

in Mental-health Topics

IN ORDER TO DEVELOP more effective programs of public information, it is important to learn what kinds of communications the public is willing to receive: the necessary first step in establishing a communication program is to "capture" an audience.

In totalitarian societies, audiences can be "captured" by flooding the communications media with particular types of messages and by forcing people to receive selected messages in schools, industrial-training programs, and other state-organized activities. In less restrictive societies, such as ours, individuals have considerable latitude in choosing messages. They can select among available communications by moving radio dials, switching television channels, reading selectively in the printed media, participating in discussion groups of their choice, attending particular lectures, and merely changing the subject in informal discussions.

We need to know two things about public interests: (1) What kinds of mental-health topics presently interest the public? (2) How can the public interest in mental-health topics be increased? The first part of the chapter will describe a questionnaire study of current public interests, and the second part of the chapter will describe an experimental investigation of some factors which influence public interests.

A QUESTIONNAIRE STUDY OF PUBLIC INTERESTS

A questionnaire concerning the interest value of various mental-health topics was sent to 200 members of our opinion panel. The first of two parts of the questionnaire examined public interest in mental-health topics as compared to other topics, such as sports, news, and drama. The second part concerned relative public interest in different kinds of mental-health information, for example, whether the public is more interested in learning about psychotherapy than about rehabilitation. In both parts of the questionnaire the items consisted of groups of four titles, and the subjects ranked the titles in order of interest. The first part of the questionnaire contained 15 items (the complete questionnaire is presented in Appendix 5). The subjects were told that "the questionnaire concerns the things that you like to read about, listen to on the radio, and see in movies and television." They were instructed to rank the four titles in each item from 1, "most interest," to 4, "least interest." Here is a sample item from the first part:

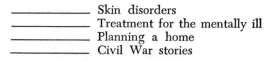

In the first part of the questionnaire, one of the four titles in each item concerned a mental-health topic, a second concerned physical health, a third concerned "entertainment," and a fourth concerned "information." (In some cases it was difficult to distinguish entertainment from information.) The 15 titles in each of the four sections were randomly assigned to the 15 items, and the four titles in each item were randomly ordered. Following are three examples from each of the four types of titles used in the first part of the questionnaire:

Mental Health

The beginning of a "nervous breakdown"
"Nerve" drugs
Psychological treatment

Physical Health

How to live with heart trouble
Do you have an allergy?
Preventing a cold

Information

The family car in 1970
World news
How to make you own furniture

Entertainment

How they climbed Mount Everest
Life in the Old West
Musical programs

The second part of the questionnaire concerned the relative interest in mental-health topics, with various subtopics being compared to one another. One of the items was as follows:

_____ What churches can do for the person who worries too much
_____ Knowing emotional disorders when you see them
_____ Help for an emotional disorder
_____ How a mental-hospital patient acts

The titles used in the second part were compounded in terms of a factorial design which considered (1) the severity of the mental disorder and (2) the aspect of the disorder which was discussed. (The design is presented in Table 9.1.) Severity was broken down into three levels: psychosis, neurosis, and neurotic trends. The aspects considered were causes, symptoms, treatment, rehabilitation, and social effects. Terms such as "mental-hospital patient," "mental illness," and "insanity" were used to refer to psychosis. Neuroses were denoted by "nervous breakdown," "neurotic," and "emotional sickness." Neurotic trends, disturbances without gross debilitation, were denoted by terms such as "a person who worries a great deal," "emotional problems," and "nervous disposition." The three kinds of disorders are not sharply differentiated; however, they probably represent a hierarchy of severity in popular thinking.

Statements about *causes* were such as: "What makes an individual . . . ," "How . . . comes about," and "What causes . . ." Statements about *symptoms* were denoted by such phrases as: "The signs of . . . ," "How to recognize . . . ," and "Knowing . . . when you see it." Statements about *treatment* used phrases such as: "What can be done for . . . ," "The treatment of . . . ," and "Helping the person who . . ." The *rehabilitation* category concerned the movement of the successfully treated individual back into society, using phrases like: "Recovering from . . . ," "How the . . . moves back into society," and "How people react to someone who has had . . ." The *social effects* were denoted by phrases such as: "The cost to the society of . . . ," ". . . in the armed forces," and "How the community can aid . . ."

There are 12 content combinations in the factorial design. Nine statements were composed for each combination; for example, the statement "The treatment of mental-hospital patients" is the combination "psychosis

TABLE 9.1. Mean Preference Ranks for Content Combinations *

Aspect	Severity Level			
	Psychotic	Neurotic	Neurotic trend	Row means
Cause	2.63	2.10	2.17	2.30
Symptoms	2.23	2.09	2.46	2.26
Treatment	2.41	2.56	2.38	2.45
Rehabilitation	2.43	2.64	2.61	2.56
Social effects	2.76	3.11	2.91	2.93
Column means	2.49	2.50	2.51	

* Each mean rank was obtained by averaging the ranks given by each individual to the nine titles in each content combination and averaging the results over 190 respondents. Consequently, each mean rank is based on 1,710 (9 times 190) separate preference decisions. Column and row means were obtained by averaging the table entries for each column and each row.

and treatment." The 108 titles obtained in this way were randomly clustered into 27 items, like the example shown above. (See Appendix 5 for the complete questionnaire.) Subjects were required to rank-order the topics in terms of what they would like to learn more about.

The questionnaire was mailed to 200 members of our opinion panel, and 190 were returned in time to be used in the analysis.

Analysis of Data

The first step in analyzing the data was to find the mean rank for each of the four titles in each question. The mean ranks are restricted to the range of 1.00 to 4.00. A mean rank of 1.00 would indicate that everyone chose the topic over the other three. A mean rank of 4.00 would indicate that no one chose the topic in preference to the other three. A mean rank of 2.50 indicates that the topic was chosen an "average" amount by the group. A typical set of mean ranks is as follows:

1.90	Advice on personal problems
2.60	Psychotherapy
3.02	Shock treatment
2.48	Advice on child-rearing

The respondents expressed most interest in "advice on personal problems," least interest in "shock treatment," and about average interest in the other two topics.

PROPOSITION 9.1: **Mental-health topics have moderately high-interest value.**

This proposition is based on the results from the first part of the questionnaire. The mean rank for the 15 mental-health topics is 2.46, very close to the average for all topics in the study. The important point is that mental health held its own with the physical-health, information, and entertainment topics which were compared to it. Mental-health topics will probably be received with about the same average "popularity" as competing topics. If we had compared mental-health topics with ones that are usually not popular enough to appear frequently in the media, such topics as "sheep shearing," "the sewer system in Dallas, Texas," and "recent trends in corporate finance," then mental-health topics would probably have appeared very popular.

The first part of the questionnaire was neither extensive nor finely gauged enough to produce precise conclusions about the exact amount of public interest in mental-health topics as a whole. The only point that should be made is that, when mental-health topics are compared in popularity to other topics, as a group they compete well.

One way to interpret the results from the first part of the questionnaire is to compare mental-health topics with physical-health topics. Although the average interest ratings for the two are not significantly different, there are some interesting differences when the severity of the physical disorder is considered. Topics concerning severe physical disorders—cancer, heart trouble, and polio—are more "popular" than mental-health topics, but topics concerning less severe physical disorders—such as diet, dental care, allergies, and others—are less popular. (The complete results are presented in Appendix 5.)

PROPOSITION 9.2: **Public interest is much higher for some mental-health topics than for others.**

From the second part of the questionnaire it was found that public interest varies considerably among different kinds of mental-health topics. Table 9.1 shows the mean rank for each content combination. Grand means for rows and columns are shown at the sides and bottom of the table. When the severity of mental disorders are compared, there are no significant differences in over-all preference for information. The grand means for columns are almost identical—2.49, 2.50, and 2.51. But there are substantial differences in the row grand means (significant beyond .001 level by analysis of variance) which show the order of preference for the five aspects of mental-health information: (1) symptoms, (2) causes, (3) treatment, (4) rehabilitation, and (5) social effects. Most marked is the lack of interest in "social effects," with statements such as the following receiving very low-interest scores in their respective questions. (The mean ranks of the items are also given.)

3.18	Emotional problems in government service
3.41	The cost to society for the treatment of neurosis
3.20	The effect of emotional disorder in industry
3.39	The cost to the community of mental illness

The over-all trend is for the public to want to learn about immediate personal aspects of mental health: What causes it? How can you recognize it? What can be done to handle the immediate problem? The more distant the topic from the individual's immediate personal concern—the obstacles for a person who is moving back into society after mental illness, the function of community agencies in helping the mentally ill, the long range effects of mental illness in society—the less interest is generated in the public (see Appendix 5).

Topics which concern the appearance of the mentally ill *after* the disorder is underway receive relatively low-interest scores. The mean ranks of several of these are as follows:

2.80	How a neurotic person acts
3.28	How a mental-hospital patient acts
2.66	The appearance of a person who worries a great deal

The public is interested in the *early* symptoms or warnings that a mental illness is likely to occur. For example, the topics "How to tell when a nervous breakdown is coming on" and "How to recognize mental illness" received high-interest scores, each with mean ranks of about 1.65. The public interest in symptoms is, then, to learn the "danger signals" in order to avoid the problem or seek help. Another observation (see Appendix 5) is that the public's interest in mental-health topics is motivated more by a search for "help" than by intellectual curiosity.

The findings from the questionnaire study suggest that mental-health information will be sought more often if the messages attempt to allay immediate fears and offer some information about the causes and early signs of mental disorder. (Some relevant experimental findings will be discussed in the next section.) Apparently it would be rather difficult to interest the public in information about the wide social problems connected with mental health and mental disorder. This is unfortunate because the immediate problems which the public fears need the attention of organized community, industrial, and governmental programs and institutions.

EXPERIMENTAL STUDIES OF PUBLIC INTERESTS

PROPOSITION 9.3: **Public interest in communications about mental illness is increased when the messages reduce anxiety and provide solutions to problems.**

One of the primary factors affecting public interest is the topic itself. To take an extreme case, regardless of how the topics were treated we would probably find more widespread public interest in "sexual freedom in Sweden" than in "the repair of typewriters." The purpose of the questionnaire study was to determine the inherent interest value of mental-health topics as a group and of subtopics in the area. We found that mental-health topics as a group tend to have moderately high interest value, and the interest value varies considerably for subtopics.

In addition to the subject of the topic itself, public willingness to receive messages relating to a topic probably is influenced by the ways in which the messages are composed. For example, if messages on atomic warfare are composed in such a way as to frighten rather than to dispel fear, the public might be loathe to receive them. This section will report some research evidence on the effect that three message variables have on the public's expressed preferences for particular topics.

The first variable under study is the relative amount of "message anxiety." A message is said to have relatively high "anxiety" if it pictures people in physical danger, pain, fear, and embarrassment and relatively low "anxiety" if it does *not* picture people in physical danger, pain, fear, and embarrassment. The term "anxiety" as used here refers only to what the message says, which does not insure that states of anxiety are actually generated in our subjects. However, differences in anxiety treatment, as in this experiment, actually produce differences in the anxiety reactions of subjects who read the messages (see Ch. 10).

The second variable considered is the degree to which messages give apparent solutions to a problem. A message is said to have "no solution" if it raises a number of questions and gives no answers; a message is said to have a "solution" if it answers the questions which it raises.

The third variable being studied concerns the relative personal or impersonal phrasing of the message. A message is said to be "personal" if it is phrased in the second person and invites "identification" by describing how events would affect the reader. A message is said to be "impersonal" if it is phrased in the third person and describes the effects of events on "other people."

The experiment described in this section grew out of an earlier experiment [1] which employed the same treatment variables. The primary results from the earlier experiment were that (1) messages which are low in anxiety generate more public interest than messages which are high in anxiety, (2) messages with solutions generate more public interest than messages without solutions, and (3) personal versus impersonal treatment has little, if any, effect on public interest.

Messages

In the second experiment each message, one page of written material, was read by individual respondents. All of the messages concerned methods for treating mental-hospital patients. Eight specific treatments were discussed: shock treatment, psychoanalysis, occupational therapy, hydrotherapy, drug treatment, group therapy, psychodrama, and hypnotherapy. Eight different versions were composed for each of the eight topics, embodying all possible combinations of the factorial design given in Table 9.2. For example, one of the possible combinations is 1a-2b-3a (or simply a-b-a), a message with relatively high anxiety, no solution, and phrased in personal terms. To illustrate how the messages looked in their final form, here is the above combination of effect levels applied to the shock-treatment topic:

[1] The study is not described in greater detail because the design was complex and the results were inconclusive. In the earlier study we were interested both in the combinations of message variables that promote public interest at one point in time and in the serial effects of the message variables over time. Messages were composed in terms of the combinations shown in Table 9.2, and different sets of messages were sent to 42 subjects on four different occasions. There were no significant serial effects. The over-all influence of message variable combinations was as described above. If we had made a rigorous statistical test of the findings, it would have been necessary to test subjects on more occasions. Instead, it was decided to perform a simpler study with a larger sample, the results of which are reported in this chapter.

One method of treating patients in mental hospitals is called "shock treatment." By imagining yourself going through the actual steps of treatment, you can visualize how this process works. A special electrical machine is used actually to send an electric current through your brain. First, you are brought into a room containing a bed and the electric shock machine. A doctor and several attendants prepare you for the treatment. The electrodes are attached to your temples, and at the proper moment the power is turned on. You would immediately slump into unconsciousness. The shock would affect your brain and nervous system in such a way as first to tense your body muscles and then to cause a series of violent jerking movements which would last for half a minute or more. You would remain unconscious for about an hour, awakening in a dazed state. In this period following the shock treatment, you would be somewhat less irrational than before and it would be possible to discuss your problems with you. The effect of the "shocks" plus the later discussion might help you, as it has helped many patients, to get gradually better. The patient usually receives a series of treatments over a period of several months.

There are many unsolved problems involving the use and effectiveness of shock treatments. It is not certain whether the treatments produce only temporary help or could actually effect any long range improvement in your condition. Even if shock treatments are permanently helpful, it is not known precisely how they act on the brain or what other effects they have on the individual.

The above message was changed from the combination a-b-a (high anxiety-no solution-personal) to a-a-a (high anxiety-solution-personal) by adding the following solution to the end of the message:

However, recent research has clarified some of these questions, and studies which are now underway should provide a clearer picture in the future. It is being learned what types of patients benefit most from shock treatments, how to identify these patients, and how to conduct the treatments to insure maximum success.

Relatively high-anxiety messages were differentiated from relatively low-anxiety messages according to the amount of danger, harm, and embarrassment portrayed. Messages were changed from personal to impersonal simply by discussing the treatment procedures as they are experienced by other individuals. A portion of the shock-treatment topic with relatively low-anxiety and an impersonal approach is as follows:

One method of treating patients in mental hospitals is the so-called "shock treatment." This treatment is actually misnamed in that the patient is not shocked in the same sense in which the word is used in everyday life. Instead, the patient undergoes a type of electrical treatment which is less painful than many routine medical treatments. The patient is brought into a room and placed in a restful position on a bed. The machine attachments are placed against the patient's temples, and the doctor adjusts the machine to send a weak electric current to the patient. This current immediately puts the patient to sleep. After going to sleep, the patient's body muscles become tense and then "jerky" for about half a minute. The patient remains asleep for about an hour, awakening in a dreamy state.

Eight versions were made of the psychoanalysis topic, the drug-treatment topic, and the other topics in a similar fashion, making a total of 64 different messages. The 64 messages were then sorted into eight groups of eight messages each. Treatment topics appeared only once with each combination of message variables.[2]

TABLE 9.2. Factorial Design for Interest Experiment

Effect	Levels	
1. Anxiety	a. High anxiety	b. Low anxiety
2. Solution	a. Solution present	b. Solution absent
3. Personal approach	a. Personal	b. Impersonal

Subjects

The subjects consisted of 288 members of our opinion panel. (To refresh the reader's memory, the panel represents an approximate minia-ture of the U.S. population in terms of education, age, sex, and other demographic characteristics.) For this study, people with less than eight years of formal education were excluded because the experiment required a considerable amount of reading and an understanding of a few technical terms.

Administration of Materials

Each subject was mailed a packet of eight messages and told that the purpose of the study was "to determine what you would like to learn more about." The subject was instructed to read all eight messages (which had been randomly ordered in the packet) and rank them from 1 to 8 in terms of interest. Number 1 was to be placed on the message which most inter-ested the subject, number 2 was to be placed on the message which was second in interest, and so on. An effort was made to create a realistic choice situation by telling the subject that, if more messages were sent, his choices in the first testing would determine the kinds of messages which he would receive later.

[2] The messages in each group were combined so that each subject received one, and only one, message on each topic; and each subject received one, and only one, message representing each of the eight possible treatment combinations. This insured, for example, that a subject would not receive two versions of the shock-treatment topic or two messages with the treatment combination of high anxiety-no solution-impersonal.

TABLE 9.3. Mean Interest Ranks and Preference Order

Topic	Message-variable combination							
	1 Anx.-sol.-per.		2 Anx.-sol.-imper.		3 Anx.-no sol.-per.		4 Anx.-no sol.-imper.	
	Mean rank *	Rank †	Mean rank	Rank	Mean rank	Rank	Mean rank	Rank
Hydrotherapy	4.63	4	4.56	3	4.09	1	4.86	7
Group therapy	4.56	6	4.61	7	4.97	8	4.49	4
Tranquillizers	4.55	5	3.57	1	4.80	7	4.77	6
Psychodrama	5.60	5	5.60	6	6.03	8	5.66	7
Shock treatment	4.82	5	4.56	3	5.26	8	4.77	4
Psychoanalysis	4.59	7	3.75	3	4.95	8	4.56	6
Occupational therapy	4.28	6	2.68	1	4.38	7	4.26	5
Hypnotism	4.67	4	5.11	7	5.00	6	5.15	8
Grand mean of preference ranks	4.71		4.31		4.93		4.81	
Rank total		42		31		53		47
Over-all preference order		5		4		8		7

* Each mean rank was determined by summing the ranks given to the particular interaction of topics and message-variable combination by 36 people and dividing by 36.

Analysis and Results

Mean ranks were determined for each interaction between topics and message-variable combinations. Mean ranks were restricted to the range of 1 to 8. A mean rank above 4.00 indicates relatively low public interest, and a mean rank below 4.00 indicates relatively high public interest. The means were then ranked over the eight combinations of message variables separately for each topic. These rankings over message variables were subjected to analysis of variance by ranks test (Walker & Lev, 1953, pp. 438–440). The analysis is summarized in Table 9.3. The analysis of variance by ranks test indicates the probability is less than one in 500 that the differences in mean ranks are due to sampling error only. Consequently, it is reasonable to infer that the public interest in a topic is affected by the combinations of message variables under investigation.

In particular, the combination of anxiety-no solution-personal engendered the least public interest, and, at the other extreme, the combination no anxiety-solution-impersonal created the most public interest. In those messages with anxiety, the public interest was raised by providing a solution. In raising the interest level of anxiety-provoking messages, of Message-variable Combinations on Each Topic

5 Nonanx.-sol.-per.		6 Nonanx.-sol.-imp.		7 Nonanx.-no sol.-per.		8 Nonanx.-no sol.-imper.	
Mean rank	Rank	Mean rank	Rank	Mean rank	Rank	Mean rank	Rank
4.95	8	4.28	2	4.74	5	4.82	6
4.38	2	4.49	3	3.90	1	4.54	5
3.91	2	4.10	3	4.26	4	4.92	8
4.62	3	4.20	1	4.84	2	5.47	4
4.97	6	4.38	1	4.57	2	5.13	7
2.97	1	3.63	2	3.82	4	3.97	5
2.70	2	2.85	3	4.20	4	4.49	8
4.05	1	4.54	3	4.74	5	4.37	2
4.07		4.06		4.38		4.71	
	25		18		27		45
	2		1		3		6

† The eight message-variable combinations are ranked separately for each topic. Rank 1 is given to the most preferred combination in each topic.

providing a solution was apparently more influential than using an impersonal style. These findings confirm the results of the earlier study.

Statistical comparisons were made between the two levels in each message variable. The first step in this analysis was to rank the means in Table 9.3 from 1 to 64. Separate tests were then made of the differences between levels in each of the three message variables, using the Mann-Whitney "sum of ranks" test (Walker & Lev, 1953, pp. 434–435). Messages without anxiety created more interest than messages with anxiety ($p = .01$), and messages with solutions created more interest than messages without solutions ($p = .02$). The over-all difference between personal and impersonal approaches is not significant.

It is possible that the results reported here are specific either to topics concerning the treatment of the mentally ill or to topics which bear some characteristics in common with the treatment of the mentally ill. Both intuition and our previous research findings indicate that mental illness is a topic which usually creates anxiety (see Ch. 10 for evidence relating to this point). Thus, the messages that we labeled "low anxiety" might be "high anxiety" in an absolute sense. If we had worked with a subject matter in which anxiety is generally low in an absolute sense, the combinations of message variables might have had different effects on public interest. For example, if the messages had discussed fishing, it might have been necessary to raise anxiety, use a personal approach, and provide no solution (by leaving some unanswered questions about the art of angling) in order to promote public interest. There is some evidence in Table 9.3 to support the contention that the results reported here are specific to "high-anxiety" subject matter. Whereas the combination anxiety-no solution-personal generally promoted the least public interest in most of our topics, it promoted the most public interest in the hydrotherapy messages. This inconsistency seems to indicate that the hydrotherapy messages were all low in anxiety regardless of the effort to make half of them relatively high in anxiety. It is rather difficult to build anxiety into a message concerned with a warm bath.

Whereas the results reported here may be applicable to other topics which tend to generate anxiety, such as cancer treatment and atomic warfare, they are most directly related to the communication of information about the treatment of the mentally ill. Possibly many of the efforts to communicate information about mental illness are not meeting with public acceptance because of the way in which topics are treated. For example, a film dealing with mental illness might raise anxiety by picturing the agonies of the sick. Further, the film might be made personal by inferring that "this can happen to you or to someone in your family." Finally, the film might, and probably would, have no solution in the sense that many of the questions raised in the film would not be answered. The results suggest that the public would be more attentive to communications concerning mental illness if anxiety were reduced and some relatively concrete answers were given. Until more straightforward answers (solutions) are available, the raising of anxiety will apparently reduce public willingness to receive communications about mental illness.

There are some interesting parallels between the results found here regarding willingness to receive communications and results reported by Hovland, Janis, and Kelley (1953, Ch. 3), regarding the effectiveness of communication. One study which used dental-hygiene messages found that messages with "minimal fear appeal" were more effective in influencing opinions than messages with "strong fear appeal." These results directly parallel our findings that "nonanxiety" messages (similar to those that Hovland et al. refer to as "minimal fear appeal" messages) generate more public interest than "anxiety" messages.

Hovland et al. (pp. 60–66) hypothesize that "threat" messages (similar to our anxiety-personal combination) will have more influence on opinions if they provide "reassuring recommendations" (solutions). This hypothesis parallels our finding that the combination anxiety-personal-solution promotes more public interest than the combination anxiety-personal-no solution. These parallels suggest that some of the factors which increase public willingness to receive communications about a topic may also increase persuasive effectiveness of communications. Chapter 10 will discuss some experimental results relating to the above hypothesis.

SUMMARY

Two studies of public interest in mental-health topics were reported here. The first, using a questionnaire designed to compare public interest in mental health with public interest in other topics and the appeal of various subtopics in the mental-health field, suggested that mental-health topics "compete" well with other fare in the mass media. More importantly it was found that the public is much more interested in certain kinds of mental-health topics than in others. In general, the public interest is centered on the immediate, personal aspects of mental-health problems and, in contrast, their interest in the broad social problems relating to mental health is rather low.

The second study measured the effects on public interest of three message variables in mental-health presentations. The three variables were (1) the degree to which the message raises anxiety, (2) the degree to which the message provides a solution to a problem, and (3) the degree to which the message is made "personal" rather than "impersonal." It was found that public interest is raised when messages tend to alleviate rather than increase anxiety and when messages provide solutions to problems. Much mental-health information currently being conveyed to the public probably is self-defeating because it decreases public interest by raising anxiety and providing few real solutions to the problems it discusses.

10

Anxiety in Mental-health

Communications

EARLIER CHAPTERS REPORTED that topics relating to mental illness tend to create anxiety, and anxiety has an important in-influence on public reactions to communications about mental illness. Chapter 9 discussed several studies which reported the effects of anxiety on the public's interest in mental-health topics. The results of the studies were clear: the higher the anxiety in mental-health messages the less willing the public is to receive the communications. But these studies raise another question: Does anxiety have a "bad" effect on public attitudes toward mental-health concepts? That is, regardless of their effect on the public's interests, do messages with relatively high anxiety promote unfavorable attitudes toward mental patients, psychiatrists, treatment methods, and related concepts? Two experiments were performed to answer this question. These studies also considered a number of other communication variables.

Preliminary Evidence

Before the two experiments on the effects of anxiety are reported, some evidence showing that communications relating to mental illness actually generate anxiety will be cited. The public views the mentally ill as frightening, rating them as unpredictable, dirty, and dangerous (see Ch. 4). Moreover, the public does not have complete confidence in the professionals who treat mental disorders and the treatment methods that are employed (see Ch. 5). Mental-health topics in general provoke anxiety and embarrassment. Several of our studies led us inevitably to this conclusion.

In one pilot study involving a group of college students, we applied a free-association word list using terms like emotion, psychiatrist, mental illness, and insane, and "filler" terms like chair, house, and school. We were surprised to find a considerable amount of blocking and overt embarrassment on associations to the terms relating to mental illness. This offered one more bit of circumstantial evidence to indicate that topics relating to mental illness usually generate embarrassment and anxiety.

More evidence for this hypothesis was found in our experimental studies of attitude change and information transmission, where we often required subjects to rate messages about mental illness as safe versus dangerous, tense versus relaxed, anxious versus calm, and so forth. In comparison to the control messages which were unrelated to mental illness, the messages about mental illness are usually rated as more dangerous, tense, anxious, and so on.

We performed two small studies in order to examine directly the extent to which the topic of mental illness is considered frightening. In the first of these, 44 subjects were asked to rank nine topics in order of decreasing anxiety, rating the most frightening topic with a 1, the next most frightening with a 2, and so on (see Table 10.1). Treatment methods relating to mental illness were not only rated as more anxious than coal mining, working in a lumber yard, and printing, but also as more frightening than methods, such as "operations," for treating physical diseases.

In a second small study, 39 subjects were asked to rate several stories in terms of anxiety. While the first study was concerned with the anxiety generated by mental-illness topics in general compared to a wide range of topics like coal mining and printing, this study was concerned with the anxiety created by topics about the treatment of mental illness compared to treatments for other kinds of sicknesses. This was a stringent

TABLE 10.1. Average Anxiety Rankings * of Topics

Topic	Average rank
A story about various ways of brainwashing prisoners of war.	2.58
A story about various ways of treating physical diseases, such as operations and x-ray treatments.	4.69
A story about various ways of treating mental patients, such as shock treatment and psychoanalysis.	4.06
A story about automobile accidents.	3.22
A story about some methods of coal mining, such as how the tunnels are constructed to get at the coal.	6.07
A story about working in a lumber yard.	8.18
A story about various ways of physically torturing prisoners of war to obtain information from them.	1.31
A story about some of the operations involved in printing, such as setting up the press run and stacking the printed material.	7.80
A story about the various duties of an engineer on a cross-country railroad train.	7.09

* The lower the average rank the higher the rating of anxiety.

TABLE 10.2. Mean Ratings of the Anxiety Present in Stories about Mental Illness and Other Topics *

Topic	Average rating
The life story of a man who is now in a mental hospital.	3.94
The life story of a man who is now in a tuberculosis sanitorium.	3.82
The story of what goes on during a visit to a psychiatrist.	4.59
The story of what goes on during a visit to a doctor.	4.56
The story of what goes on during a visit to a dentist.	4.29
The story of how a patient feels while he is being treated for insanity in a mental hospital.	3.19
The story of how a patient feels while he is being treated for a serious illness in a hospital.	3.54
The story of how a patient feels while he is being treated for cancer in a hospital.	3.01

* The means are restricted to the range of 1.00 to 5.00. The lower the mean, the more anxiety connected with the story.

comparison because topics relating to serious physical illness tend to create a relatively high level of anxiety. The subjects rated each of eight topics on a five-point scale (see Table 10.2).

There was surprisingly little difference between anxiety ratings for the life story of a man with tuberculosis and that of a man with a mental illness. Moreover, the story about a man being treated for a mental disorder was rated as more frightening than the story about a man being treated in a hospital for a serious illness. In this case the terms which labeled the illness as "insanity" and the hospital as "mental" were the only differences between the two stories. Evidently the words connected with mental illness are enough to make a topic more frightening.

As we had expected from our general research experience, in terms of anxiety ratings, mental-illness topics lie somewhere between topics about "ordinary" diseases and topics about severe illnesses such as cancer and heart disease. Even topics associated with the dreaded word "cancer" are only slightly more frightening than topics associated with the word "insanity."

On the basis of accumulated evidence, we offer the following proposition:

PROPOSITION 10.1: Communications relating to mental illness usually create a fairly high level of anxiety.

EXPERIMENT 1: ANXIETY AND SOLUTION VARIABLES

The first experiment to be discussed in this chapter was modeled after the experiment discussed in Chapter 9 which studied the effects on public interest of three communication variables: (1) high versus low anxiety, (2) solution versus no solution, and (3) personal versus impersonal style. The first experiment studies only two variables, relative anxiety and solution, because the third variable, personal versus impersonal style, had produced no significant results. The purpose of this experiment was to learn whether anxiety level and a solution influence public attitudes in the same way that they influence public interest.

Experimental Materials

Short written messages about two treatments for the mentally ill, psychoanalysis and shock treatment, were prepared. Two topics were chosen because it was felt that the particular topic might interact with the effects of the two variables. Eight different versions of each were composed, reflecting all possible two-way combinations of the two experimental variables, anxiety and solution. For example, one message had relatively high anxiety and a solution; another message had relatively low anxiety and no solution. The factorial design is outlined in Table 10.3.

Differences in structural properties, such as sentence length, sentence structure, and paragraph length, were minimized. All eight messages began with the same first paragraph, word for word. The high- and low-anxiety versions of the messages differed only with respect to slight changes in phrasing in the second paragraph. For example, the relatively high-anxiety message for the shock-treatment topic described a patient as being "carried into the room and strapped into position," whereas the low-anxiety message read, "brought into the room and placed in a restful position." Other than these slight differences, the same basic facts were presented in both versions.

The no-solution messages were changed to solution messages by the addition of a few sentences at the end which assured the reader that the problems were being solved. To illustrate how the messages looked in their final form, the following is the message on shock treatment with no solution and relatively low anxiety.

> Mental illness is a very important problem in the United States. There are about 700,000 mental patients in mental hospitals, and one half of all hospital beds are occupied by mental patients. Doctors estimate that

TABLE 10.3. Factorial Design for Experiment 1

Variable	Treatment	
Topic	psychoanalysis	shock treatment
Anxiety	relatively high	relatively low
Solution	present	absent

one out of every ten people born in the United States right now will have to spend some time during his life in a mental hospital. Doctors also estimate that one person out of every sixteen is suffering from serious mental problems.

A psychiatrist is a medical doctor who has had special training with mental illness and who often works in mental hospitals and supervises the treatment which the patients receive. One method of treating mental patients in mental hospitals is called "shock treatment." This treatment is actually misnamed in that the patient is not shocked in the sense in which the word is used in everyday life. The patient undergoes a type of electrical treatment which is actually less painful than many routine medical treatments. The patient is brought into a room and placed in a restful position on a bed. A psychiatrist and several attendants prepare him for the treatment. Then electrodes are attached to his temples and a special machine is used to send a weak electrical current through his brain. The patient slips into unconsciousness. The shock affects his brain and nervous system in such a way as to first mildly tense the body muscles and then cause a series of slight jerking movements which last for a half-minute. The patient remains asleep for about an hour, awakening in a dreamy state. In this period following the treatment, he is more rational than before and it is possible for the psychiatrist and other therapists to discuss his problems with him. The effect of the "shocks" plus the later discussions often help many patients to get gradually better.

There are many unsolved problems involving the use and effectiveness of "shock" treatments. It is not certain whether the treatments produce only temporary help or whether they actually cause long-range improvement in the patient's condition. Even if shock treatments are permanently helpful, it is not known precisely how they act on the brain, or what other effects they might have on the individual.

To illustrate how anxiety and solution were manipulated, the following is the high-anxiety and solution version of the message above.

Mental illness is a very important problem in the United States. There are about 700,000 mental patients in mental hopitals, and one half of all hospital beds are occupied by mental patients. Doctors estimate that one out of every ten people born in the United States right now will have to spend some time during his life in a mental hospital. Doctors also estimate that one person out of every sixteen is suffering from serious mental problems.

A psychiatrist is a medical doctor who has had special training with mental illness and who often works in mental hospitals and supervises the treatment which the patients receive. One method of treating mental patients in mental hospitals is called "shock treatment." This treatment is well named in that the patient is actually shocked in the sense in which the word is used in everyday life. The patient undergoes a painful type of electrical treatment which is more agonizing than other medical treatments. The patient is carried into a room and strapped into position on a bed. A psychiatrist and several attendants prepare him for the treatment. Then electrodes are attached to his temples and a special machine is used to actually send a powerful electric current through his brain. The patient immediately slumps into unconsciousness. The shock affects his brain and nervous system in such a way as to first tense the body muscles and then cause a series of violent muscle jerks which last for a half-minute. The patient remains unconscious for about an hour, awakening in a confused state. In this period following the shock treatment, he is usually less irrational than before and it is possible for the psychiatrist and other therapists to discuss his problems with him. The effect of the "shocks" plus the later discussions often help many patients to get gradually better.

There are many problems involving the use and effectiveness of shock treatments. It is not certain whether the painful treatments produce only temporary help or whether they actually cause any long-range improvement in the patient's condition. Even if shock treatments are permanently helpful, it is not known precisely how they act on the brain or exactly what other effects they have on the individual. However, recent research has clarified many of these questions, and studies now under way should provide an even clearer picture in the future. Recent evidence indicates that many of the questions associated with shock treatment will be answered in the next few years. It is being learned what types of patients benefit most from shock treatments, how to identify these patients, and how to conduct the treatments to insure maximum success.

To measure the effect of the experimental variables on attitudes toward mental-health concepts, a Semantic Differential form was used. Scales were included to measure the factors of *evaluation* and *understandability*. Analyses were also made of other scales and combinations of scales (see Table 10.4). Concepts such as *the message you have just read* and *mental patient* were used (the full list is given in Table 10.4).

In addition to the Semantic Differential, a comprehension test was constructed for each of the two topics to measure amount of "learning." Each test consisted of six multiple-choice items, with six alternative answers for each. The items dealt only with information that was worded identically in the four versions of each topic.

Subjects and Procedures

The subjects were 392 high-school students, diverse as to year in school and performance on an intelligence test. The subjects were tested during one school day in their regular study-hall meetings. They were simply told that they were "participating in a study of writing styles." The entire administration of the test materials was performed by the experimenters; the teacher of the study hall sat in the back of the room and did not participate. The messages and test materials were passed out in random order. Each subject read only one message. Questions about the instructions were answered, but no other information about the test materials was given. After the testing was completed, the experi-

TABLE 10.4. A List of the Measures Obtained for Experiment 1, with Summaries of Important Findings

Measure number	Semantic Differential scales and factors	Analysis of variance results
	Concept: *The article you just read*	
1	*Understandability* (unpredictable-predictable, mysterious-understandable, complicated-simple)	Low-anxiety group rates as more understandable. Significant beyond the .001 level.
2	*Evaluative* (bad-good, worthless-valuable, foolish-wise)	
3	Certainty (uncertain-certain, incorrect-correct, indefinite-definite)	
4	Convincing-unconvincing	
5	Interesting-dull	
6	Unsure-sure	
	Concept: *Ways of treating mental patients*	
7	*Understandability*	Low-anxiety group rates as more understandable. Significant beyond the .01 level.
8	*Evaluative*	
9	Successfulness (ineffective-effective, unsuccessful-successful)	
10	Moral-immoral	
11	Dangerous-safe	Low-anxiety group rates as safer. Significant beyond the .05 level.
12	Painful-pleasant	High-anxiety group rates as more painful. Significant beyond the .0001 level.
	Concept: *Shock treatment*	
13	*Understandability*	Low-anxiety group rates as more understandable. Significant beyond the .01 level.
14	*Evaluative*	
15	Successfulness	
16	Moral-immoral	
17	Dangerous-safe	Low-anxiety group rates as safer, beyond the .001 level.
18	Painful-pleasant	High-anxiety group rates as more painful, beyond the .0001 level.
	Concept: *Psychoanalysis*	
19	*Understandability*	Low-anxiety group rates as more understandable when tested against "within." Interaction of message versus anxiety level also significant. Both significant beyond the .05 level.

Measure number	Semantic Differential scales and factors	Analysis of variance results
	Concept: *Psychoanalysis*	
20	*Evaluative*	Low-anxiety group rates as more "good," beyond the .05 level.
21	Successfulness	Low-anxiety group rates as more successful, beyond the .05 level.
22	Moral-immoral	
23	Dangerous-safe	Low-anxiety group rates as more safe, beyond the .05 level.
24	Painful-pleasant	High-anxiety group rates as more painful (beyond .001 level) when tested against "within" mean square. Interaction of anxiety level versus message also significant, beyond the .05 level.
	Concept: *Mental patient*	
25	*Understandability*	Low-anxiety group rates as more understandable when tested against "within" mean square. Interaction of message versus anxiety also significant, beyond .05 level.
26	*Evaluative*	
27	Anxiety (helpless-secure, frightened-fearless, worried-carefree)	
28	Excitability (emotional-unemotional, tense-relaxed, excitable-calm)	
29	Moral-immoral	
30	Safe-dangerous	High-anxiety group rates as more dangerous, beyond the .05 level.
	Concept: *Psychiatrist*	
31	*Understandability*	Low-anxiety group rates as more understandable, at the .05 level.
32	*Evaluative*	
33	Anxiety	
34	Excitability	
35	Moral-immoral	
36	Safe-dangerous	
	Concept: *Yourself*	
37	*Understandability*	Low-anxiety group rates as more understandable, beyond the .05 level.
38	*Evaluative*	
39	Anxiety	
40	Excitability	
41	Moral-immoral	High-anxiety group rates as more immoral, beyond the .05 level.
42	Safe-dangerous	

TABLE 10.4. A List of the Measures Obtained for Experiment 1,
with Summaries of Important Findings (*continued*)

Measure number	Analysis of variance results
	Comprehension test score
43	No-solution group obtains higher score, beyond .05 level.

menters explained the nature of the study and frankly answered any questions the students had.

Results

For the purposes of analysis, the 392 subjects were divided into eight groups (49 subjects in each), each reading one of the message-treatment combinations (two topics, two anxiety levels, and solution absent or present). On each of the eight groups 43 measures were made. Means and standard deviations were obtained for each of the measures for each of the groups. In addition, a two (shock treatment versus psychoanalysis) by two (high versus low anxiety) by two (solution versus no solution) analysis of variance was performed on each of the 43 measures. A summary of the major results is presented in Table 10.4.

Before discussing the main results of the study, a preliminary result should be mentioned. While we assumed that the amount of anxiety was manipulated by the different message versions, it was important to learn whether subjects actually reacted differently to the "high" and "low" versions. To test this, subjects were asked to rate the concept *ways of treating mental patients* on the scales safe-dangerous and pleasant-painful. Students who read the high-anxiety versions rated them as significantly more dangerous and painful (see Table 10.4). Thus we can maintain with some confidence that differences in ratings in the experiment were actually due to differences in the subject's anxiety reactions to the messages.

The Effects of Anxiety

The ratings of subjects who received the relatively low-anxiety messages were different from those who received the high-anxiety messages to a statistically significant degree on a number of variables. In every case, the low-anxiety message was associated with "better" attitudes than was the high-anxiety message (see Table 10.4).

Although definite differences between the high-anxiety and low-anxiety groups are found on most of the scales, the most striking differences are found on the *understandability* factor. The low-anxiety groups rated all seven concepts as more understandable (see Table 10.4). As we typically find in our communication experiments, even the self-concept follows the trend. The difference on the *understandability* factor is evidently a difference in the *feeling* that mental-health concepts are more understandable. The message versions differed little or not at all in factual content. The results of the *comprehension test* offer more direct evidence: the difference between average scores obtained from the high-anxiety and low-anxiety groups is not statistically significant.

The effects of the anxiety variable on the *evaluation* factor also indicate the relative advantages of low-anxiety messages over the high-anxiety messages. The groups which received the relatively low-anxiety versions rated all of the seven concepts as more "good" than did the groups which received the relatively high-anxiety messages. Although the difference for individual concepts was statistically significant in only one case (psychoanalysis), when the results for the seven concepts are combined and a *t*-test applied to the combined results, the relatively low-anxiety groups are found to have given a higher *evaluation* to the concepts at the .01 level of confidence. Here again we find that an increase in the amount of anxiety in mental-health messages tends to decrease the "favorableness" of readers' attitudes. This effect seems to generalize not only to the message itself and to related concepts but also to the self-concept. The results show that anxiety has an over-all "bad" effect. For example, treatment methods were consistently rated as more "successful" by the low-anxiety group than by the high-anxiety group. In addition, the high-anxiety group consistently rated treatment methods and themselves as being less "moral" than did the low-anxiety groups.

Solution versus No Solution

The results left little doubt that anxiety has an over-all bad effect on attitudes. The next question is whether or not the solution variable plays a part. When all messages with solutions are compared with all messages without solutions, the answer is very clear: no discernible (and certainly no significant) differences are found. In none of the 42 Semantic Differential results does the solution variable produce statistically significant differences (see Table 10.4).

In spite of what was said above, the solution variable does produce substantial results. There is a strong interaction between relative solution and relative anxiety. Whereas the presence of a solution, as opposed to no solution, tends to promote favorable attitudes *when anxiety level is high*, it works the other way when anxiety is low.

The effect of solution was analyzed by comparing mean ratings given

TABLE 10.5. Grand Means Obtained Over "Favorable" Directions for All Scales and All Mental-health Concepts *

Anxiety

		High	Low	Row means
Solution	Present	4.67	4.83	4.75
	Absent	4.56	4.92	4.74
	Column means	4.62	4.88	

* Ratings were made on seven-step scales. A rating of 7 would be the most favorable rating possible. Each of the four means in the box is significantly different from each of the others (beyond the .01 level by *t*-test).

on all mental-health concepts by the various groups. For each Semantic Differential scale, the "favorable" end was designated 7 and the "unfavorable" end was designated 1. Each scale has a definite favorable-sounding end, for example, "understandable," "moral," "safe," and so on. Favorableness ratings were then averaged for the first six concepts listed in Table 10.4. Combined favorableness ratings were averaged separately for each of the four treatment conditions of both topics (shock treatment and psychoanalysis). The results are shown in Table 10.5.

Although the differences between mean favorableness ratings shown in Table 10.5 are small in an absolute sense, it should be recognized that the comparison was a very stringent test. There is little reason to believe that the treatment of the topic should affect some of the attitude ratings. For example, there is no obvious reason why any topic version should affect the moral-immoral ratings of *psychiatrist*. An over-all comparison tends to "dilute" the larger differences. This effect is illustrated in Table 10.5 which shows that the over-all difference between the high- and low-anxiety messages is small, in spite of the fact that some of the differences for "anxiety" on individual scales and concepts are large (see Table 10.4). The advantage of an over-all comparison, such as the one used here, is that it indicates whether or not one message treatment is generally "better" than another.

In spite of the apparent smallness of the differences between message-treatment conditions, the four means are all statistically different from one another beyond the .01 level by *t*-test. The interaction between the

TABLE 10.6. Grand Means for *Understandability* Ratings on All Mental-health Concepts °

Anxiety

		High	Low	Row means
	Present	4.07	4.22	4.14
Solution				
	Absent	3.85	4.35	4.10
	Column means	3.96	4.28	

° Means were obtained for the first six concepts listed in Table 10.4. The *understandability* factor was measured by the scales understandable-mysterious, predictable-unpredictable, and simple-complicated. A score of 7 means "completely understandable"; a score of 1 means "completely not-understandable"; and a score of 4 means "neutral."

effects of anxiety and solution is most prominently represented on the *understandability* factor. Grand means were obtained for the mental-health concepts on the *understandability* factor for each of the four treatment conditions. The results are shown in Table 10.6.

The differences in Table 10.6 are more sharply emphasized than those shown in Table 10.5. Again it is seen that under both "solution" conditions high anxiety is "bad" in that it leads to lower reactions of *understandability*. This is shown by the column means: high-anxiety messages have a grand mean of 3.96 and low-anxiety messages have a grand mean of 4.28.

Like Table 10.5, Table 10.6 shows that the presence or absence of a solution has no over-all effect—row means are 4.14 and 4.10 respectively. The interaction effect, however, is apparent. When anxiety is high, solution messages lead to higher *understandability* ratings than do no-solution messages. The difference is significant beyond the .01 level by *t*-test (using each of the individual concept means for *understandability* as a score). The difference is in the other direction for low-anxiety messages: the messages and related concepts are rated as more understandable when no solutions are given! The difference is small, but it is statistically significant beyond the .05 level by *t*-test.

Regarding high-anxiety messages, one point is clear: the absence of a solution has a "bad" effect in that *understandability* is diminished and other unfavorable attitudes are engendered. Because messages about mental illness generally raise anxiety, more favorable attitudes should result generally if solutions are present.

Although the effect of solution on high-anxiety messages is clear, how do we explain the effect of solution on low-anxiety messages? Although the difference is small in an absolute sense, it is consistent and statistically significant: in low-anxiety messages, the presence of a solution is "worse" than no solution. We are not sure what the explanation is, but we think it relates to something that was said in Chapter 9 regarding the variables that influence public interest in mental-illness topics. There it was found that the absence of a solution is generally "bad" in that it lowers public interest. However, it was hypothesized that in messages where the anxiety is low, solution would work the other way: the absence of a solution would promote interest.

The seemingly paradoxical finding about the effect of solution in low-anxiety messages probably relates to a point which will be made more explicit in Chapter 17, that the "average" man is very gullible about mental-health issues and will believe almost anything that he is told. This gullibility is due, in part, to the anxiety usually raised by topics relating to mental illness. We were surprised to find that college students, high-school students, and "average" adults believed some of the oversimplifications and false information in our experimental messages, but they did. It may be that when people are less anxious, they are more critical. If that is so, subjects who were not made anxious by receiving one of our high-anxiety messages may have reacted "negatively" to our oversimplified solutions. As is found in many of our communication experiments, over-all "negative" reactions sometimes generalize to concepts relating to the communications. These assumptions, however, hang on the thin threads of several guesses about the psychological processes involved. The time-honored dictum should be invoked: more research is needed.

EXPERIMENT 2: GENERAL ANXIETY REACTION

The second study was intended to replicate part of the findings from the first study and to answer other questions as well. Before describing this experiment, it is important to distinguish between two uses of the word "anxiety." The term *message anxiety* will be used in describing Experiment 2 to refer to the relative amount of danger, violence, and embarrassment reported in the message. This use of the word *anxiety* refers to the way in which the message is prepared and does not necessarily concern the way people react when they receive the message. The term *anxiety reaction* will be used to refer to an emotional response. In a number of studies we have found that mental-illness topics tend to induce an anxiety reaction regardless of how the topics are treated. A question which naturally arises from these results is whether the anxiety reaction for different topics interacts with the manner in which the topics are treated.

In the experiment to be described, we studied the interaction of the general anxiety reaction to three different topics with two levels of message anxiety. We took three topics (coal mining, printing, and treatments for mental illness) and treated each of them two ways. One message version contained a lot of message anxiety: it discussed a considerable amount of physical danger and embarrassment. The other version avoided discussing physical danger and embarrassment as much as possible. We then studied the interaction of the three topics and the two treatments as they affected attitudes and imparted information.

Experimental Materials

Three topics, methods for treating mental patients, coal mining, and printing, were selected. A small pretest with 30 subjects was sufficient to indicate that these topics produced different anxiety reactions. Subjects were asked to rank the topics in terms of how frightening they were, and the three topics were found to be significantly different from one another. The order from most to least frightening is, as might be expected: treating mental patients, coal mining, and printing.

A short message was prepared on each topic. The messages were matched in terms of length and sentence structure. Then two variants of the standard messages for each topic were constructed, one with a relatively large amount of danger, violence, and embarrassment and one with a relatively small amount of each. The two versions for each topic differed only in the use of 20 words and phrases. Other than these relatively slight differences, the same basic facts were presented in both versions.

The mental-illness topic used in this study was a combination of the two mental-illness topics used in the first study. The amount of anxiety was manipulated in ways illustrated in the discussion of Experiment 1.

The Semantic Differential was used to measure attitudes. Each subject rated the concepts: *the article you have just read, coal mining, printing, methods for treating mental patients, mental hospital, mental patient, a coal miner, a pressman,* and *me.* The *evaluation* and *understandability* factors were applied to each concept. In addition, an *excitement* factor (dull-interesting, calm-emotional, and colorless-colorful), a *danger* factor (dangerous-safe, risky-secure, and tense-relaxed), an *anxiety* factor (carefree-worried, fearless-frightened, and calm-jittery), and a *potency* factor (delicate-rugged and weak-strong) were measured when they were appropriate to a concept. The subjects were also asked to rate how interesting they found the material and how much they would like to read material written in the same way on the same topic. Lastly, they took a comprehension test on the messages they had read.

Procedure

The subjects, 288 high-school students, were tested during one school day in their regular study-hall meetings. The entire administration of the test materials was performed by the experimenters; the teacher in charge of the study hall sat in the back of the room and did not participate. The materials were passed out in a random order. Each subject read only one message. Questions about the instructions were answered, but no other information about the test materials was given. After the testing was completed, the experimenters explained the nature of the study and frankly answered any questions the students had.

Results

For the purposes of analysis, subjects were divided into six groups corresponding to the six message treatments—three topics and two levels of anxiety for each. Separate analyses of variance were performed for each Semantic Differential scale, or factor.

The results are clearly negative; no identifiable trends appeared. The only exception is that consistent, and statistically significant, differences were found for the "topic" classification. This only proves what we have found in many other studies: people who receive communications about mental illness subsequently express different attitudes than people who receive messages not relating to mental illness.

Regarding the interactions that we expected to find between topics and anxiety levels, no consistent trend developed. Several of the inter-action variances were statistically significant, but the patterns of inter-action were inconsistent.

Even more disappointing than not finding the expected interactions, the main effect of "anxiety" failed to produce significant differences. The same result is obtained when statistical comparisons are made separately for the topic relating to mental illness. This fails to support the numerous, highly significant differences found between high- and low-anxiety messages in the first study.

We do not know why the second study turned out as it did. Like most experimenters we often find that a seemingly good idea does not pay off and that negative results obtain. It is surprising, nevertheless, to find strong positive results in one study and completely negative results in a replication of it. It is doubtful that the negative results were due to the limited number of subjects: 288 students participated. Nor were the results due to computational errors; the data had been re-analyzed from scratch. It is also difficult to explain the negative results in terms of the mental-illness topic. The topic was a combination of the two topics used in the first study, both of which were successful in differentiating high- and low-anxiety conditions. Until the influence of anxiety is substantiated in another study, the following proposition will remain tentative:

PROPOSITION 10.2: **Relatively low-anxiety treatments of mental-health communications are related to more favorable attitude changes than are relatively high-anxiety treatments.**

Relative solution was not a variable in the second study; consequently nothing was found to mar the results obtained from the first study. In the first study, the results regarding "solution" were not strong, but they were consistent and the trends were statistically significant. Thus, we offer the following proposition.

PROPOSITION 10.3: **When a message is anxiety-provoking, more favorable attitude changes develop if a solution is presented than if a solution is not presented.**

SUMMARY

In previous chapters it was hypothesized that communications about mental illness tend to make people "anxious" and that the anxiety which is aroused has a detrimental effect on public attitudes toward mental-health concepts. Some research evidence for these hypotheses was presented in this chapter.

To support the hypothesis that communications about mental illness make people anxious, we cited a variety of circumstantial evidence and the results of two small studies. In these studies, subjects were asked to rate the amount of anxiety associated with mental-illness topics and with topics not related to mental illness. In comparison to the others, topics related to mental illness received fairly high ratings of anxiety.

We conducted two experiments to determine the influence of anxiety induced by written messages on attitude changes. In the first study the messages dealt with two treatments for the mentally ill, psychoanalysis and shock treatment. To test the effect of two communications variables, anxiety and solution, four versions of each topic were composed, a high and low version for each variable, resulting in eight different messages. A group of subjects read the messages and then made attitude ratings of concepts relating to the mentally ill and the treatment of the mentally ill. Regarding anxiety, the results were clear: high-anxiety messages had a "bad" effect in that they promoted relatively unfavorable attitudes toward mental-illness concepts. Regarding "solution," the results were more complicated: whereas the presence of a solution did not promote favorable attitudes when anxiety was low, it did promote favorable attitudes when anxiety was high. In other words, the presence or absence of a solution apparently matters only when messages are relatively high in anxiety, and, in that case, more favorable attitude change results if a solution is present. Because messages relating to mental illness usually raise anxiety, it would probably be a good general policy to provide "solutions" (if they are available).

The second experiment, a partial replication of the first, also attempted to test the effect of anxiety and, in addition, to determine the interaction of anxiety with different topics. The results from the study revealed no identifiable trends, casting some suspicion on the findings from the first study on the effects of anxiety. Nevertheless, because the results from the first study were so definite, we can tentatively conclude that anxiety-provoking messages about mental illness generally create "bad" attitudes.

11

The Language Problem

IN THE COURSE of studying the development and change of popular conceptions of mental-health phenomena, we became gradually aware of the importance of the language problem. Language is not simply a passive tool which can be used equally well to convey different points of view. Language, in part, predetermines the hypotheses, beliefs, and attitudes that people hold about natural and social phenomena. Words are the building blocks in persuasive communication efforts, and unless the public's vocabulary has certain optimum properties, either a new terminology must be introduced or communication efforts will not have the desired effect.

This chapter will touch on a few of the important characteristics of the popular language used to discuss mental-health phenomena. We were forced to consider language problems because of the obvious importance they have for studies of persuasive communications. Although we performed several studies specifically designed to uncover some of the characteristics of popular language, much of the material in this chapter is based on evidence from the studies discussed in previous and subsequent chapters.

THE NATURE OF THE PROBLEM

PROPOSITION 11.1: **There is a shortage of terms.**

Our over-all experience has led us to conclude that the public's vocabulary for discussing mental-health phenomena is quite limited. In searching for terms to use in questionnaire studies (see Ch. 2), we were able to find only a small number that people commonly used. Some of these are "insane," "mentally ill," "neurotic," and "nervous breakdown." There is an extensive slang vocabulary, populated with terms like "nuts," "bats," and "head-shrinker," but these terms are neither universally used nor suitable for use in public-information programs.

Most members of the public probably have no standard counterparts for terms such as Oedipus complex, positive transference, anal compulsive-ness, regression, and catharsis. This does not necessarily mean that the public is ignorant of the phenomena or that the average person is in-capable of discussing such matters. It does mean, however, that the public possesses no standard vocabulary. Consequently, when the mental-health professional tries to communicate to the public, he must often re-sort to homey analogies and round-about examples.

The public must understand a wide range of concepts if it is to be able to distinguish among phenomena. The ability to use only a narrow range of concepts makes for stereotypical reactions. The value of a stand-ard terminology is illustrated by the way in which the public has learned about recent advances in rocketry. Quick public acceptance of such pre-cise terms as "orbit," "re-entry," and "countdown" has made rocketry a familiar field. Our studies suggest that the public understands too few mental-health concepts to be able to broaden its understanding of the field.

PROPOSITION 11.2: **The language suggests misleading explanations.**

Language influences not only how people talk but much of what they think as well. Particular terms suggest explanations, and it is hard for the individual to avoid certain logical consequences. For example, it seems that the term "mental," when used to modify a disorder such as in "mental illness," suggests that the disorder is without cause. The public tends to think of a mental disorder as being "uncaused." If a cause can be stated, then the disorder is no longer mental, as the reasoning goes.[1] Therefore, if you ask the individual, "What causes mental disorder?", he is faced with a seeming paradox. In the same way, the term "neurosis" indicates tenseness and anxiety (see Ch. 4), and members of the public probably find it difficult to consider neuroses in which the symptoms are torpidity and shallowness of feeling. Another example is that "intelligence" has come to imply moral and useful behavior, and to the public it is para-doxical to think of the person with low intelligence as being useful and prudent. Many other terms suggest incorrect causes, symptoms, and social effects of mental disorder. Consequently, more valid systems of under-standing cannot be built up until a less biased set of terms has been adopted.

PROPOSITION 11.3: **The language is not well anchored semantically.**

The public probably does not have concrete referents for many of the terms which they use. For example, even though most persons use the term "neurotic," it is doubtful that they often label the real-life actions of other people as "neurotic" or that they would recognize neurotic be-havior in their families or among friends. Although people can talk in the

[1] These results were reported by Dr. Shirley Star at the meeting of the American Association of Public Opinion Research, Washington, D. C., in 1957.

abstract about neurotic behavior, they tend to interpret real neurotic behavior as stupidity, meanness, fakery, or some other foible of human behavior.

If, as we suppose, the terms are not well anchored semantically, at least two implications follow. First, in the long run, popular terms (currently used and new terms) must become attached to more concrete events and behaviors. If semantic referents are lacking, the public will not be able to use effectively new information about mental-health phenomena. If we were to teach a person how to control a particular insect, that knowledge would go largely to waste if he could not recognize the insect when he saw it. The same need for semantically anchored concepts occurs in purveying mental-health information.

Secondly, the information that the public has about mental-health phenomena exists largely as an abstract system, and the system is not anchored well enough in everyday experience. People can verbalize "correct" methods for solving problems, but, because of their inability to translate their own verbalizations into concrete events and actions, they cannot solve the problems when they arise.

There is one encouraging facet in this situation. From the standpoint of teaching the public new terms, the present lack of semantic anchoring is good. It is far easier to teach new labels than to revise old ones.

PROPOSITION 11.4: **The terms bear strong negative connotations.**

Our studies of public attitudes (see Chs. 4 and 5) show quite clearly that the terms used in the mental-health field carry connotations of low esteem, distrust, and fear. Consequently, any public-information program using these terms would probably fail. One of our studies demonstrates this point clearly. The study concerned the effect of "mixing" concepts on public attitudes. A form of the Semantic Differential was administered to a diverse collection of 160 persons in Lafayette, Indiana. In the first part of the form, the subjects rated concepts like *mother, father, insane woman,* and *neurotic man.* In the second part of the form, subjects rated mixtures of concepts given in the first part, like *insane mother, neurotic father,* and so forth. The purpose of the study was to determine how the concepts would "mix," which would provide some clues about ways of changing popular attitudes. We found that concepts did not "mix."

For example, we knew from previous studies that *mother* would receive high positive evaluations and that *insane woman* would receive negative evaluations. How would the public rate *insane mother?* A more positive evaluation for the mixed concept than for *insane woman* would have indicated one way in which attitude change might be effected. Conceivably, a radio program or magazine article could indicate that many of the women in mental hospitals are mothers. However, the concepts did not mix in the expected manner. The mixed concept *insane mother* was rated *more* negatively than *insane woman,* indicating that, if anything, an insane mother is more reprehensible than an insane woman without the accompanying symbol of motherhood.

The results for some of our experimental studies of attitude change show that public attitudes toward some terms and concepts are fixed and nearly immovable. For example, we found very little attitude change toward the concept *insane man*. When we translated *insane man* into concepts like *mental-hospital patient* and *mentally ill person*, however, attitude changes occurred.

The "mixtures" study and the attitude-change studies illustrate how difficult it is to promote more favorable, or even neutral, attitudes toward existing public concepts, such as "insane" and "neurotic." The far easier course is to adopt new symbols, ones that are at least neutral in the public mind.

THE IMPORTANCE OF LABELS

It might be argued that the importance of terms applies only to the terms themselves and not to the phenomena which they denote. For example, even though people manifest more negative attitudes toward the concept *insane man* than they do toward the concept *mental patient,* does the use of one label rather than the other make any difference in their attitudes toward a person who is mentally ill? An experiment will be described here which shows that "what you call it" is important.[2]

In the experiment each subject read one of two paragraph descriptions of persons suffering from mental disorders.[3] The two paragraphs, a description of a paranoid case and a description of a chronic anxiety case, are presented below:

> This is about a man. He is very suspicious; he doesn't trust anybody, and he's sure that everybody is against him. Sometimes he thinks people he sees on the street are talking about him or following him around. A couple of times, now, he has beaten up men who didn't even know him, because he thought that they were plotting against him. The other night, he began to curse his wife terribly; then he hit her and threatened to kill her, because, he said, she was working against him, too, just like everyone else.

> ---

> This is about a man. He has a good job and is doing pretty well at it. Most of the time he gets along all right with people, but he is always very touchy and he always loses his temper quickly if things aren't going his way, or if people find fault with him. He worries a lot about little things, and he seems to be moody and unhappy all the time. Everything is going

[2] The experiment discussed in this section was designed and executed by Dr. T. R. Husek.

[3] The stories were obtained from an interview schedule developed by the National Opinion Research Center for a study of popular orientations toward mental illness. The study was directed by Dr. Shirley Star.

along all right for him, but he can't sleep nights, brooding about the past and worrying about things that *might* go wrong.

Four versions of each story were used in the experiment. The first version of each story was exactly as given above. In the remaining three versions the first sentence was modified. In one version the stories were introduced with "This is about a mentally ill man." In another version the stories were introduced with "This is about an emotionally disturbed man." In the fourth version, the two stories were introduced with "This is about an insane man." This provided a total of eight paragraph descriptions, four for each of the two cases. The first version of each case was not labeled; the other three versions were labeled with three different terms denoting mental disorder.

After reading one version of one of the two cases, each subject was asked to make attitude ratings of the case. To estimate the extent to which the labels influenced attitudes toward the case described, the ratings of subjects who had read one of the labeled versions were compared with the ratings of subjects who had read the unlabeled version. The different effects on attitudes induced by the three different labels were also examined.

Test Materials

Each test booklet contained one version of one of the stories, followed by a Semantic Differential form. On the first page of the Semantic Differential the label that was applied to the particular version of the story appeared as the concept to be rated. The group which read the unlabeled description was asked to rate "the man in the story." The group which read the story introduced by the sentence "This is about a mentally ill man" was asked to rate "the mentally ill man in the story," and so on for the other two versions. On succeeding pages of the Semantic Differential form subjects were asked to rate the labels generally. That is, the subjects who read the unlabeled case and rated "the man in the story" on the first page of the form subsequently rated "mentally ill man," "emotionally disturbed man," and "insane man." In this way each subject rated all of the labels, either as applied to the case he read or as abstract terms. This provided us with a three-way comparison: the effects of the cases without labels, the effects of the cases combined with labels, and the effects of the labels by themselves.

Subjects and Procedures

The subjects were 440 high-school students, who were randomly assigned in groups of 55 to each of the eight treatment conditions (two cases and four versions of each). The students were tested in study-hall sections. They were told that they were "participating in a study of writing style." As was our usual procedure, the students were told that the results of the experiment would have nothing to do with their school grades and that their individual responses would be kept confidential. Except for these short introductory comments, all experimental materials and measures were self-explanatory.

Analysis and Results

Mean Semantic Differential ratings were obtained for each treatment group on each of seven factors and scales. The results are shown in Table 11.1. The results for the paranoid case are shown in the first two columns; the results for the anxiety case are shown in the last two columns. Semantic Differential results for the *evaluative* factor are shown in the first section of the table; results for *understandability* are shown in the second section; and so on to the bottom section of the table which shows the results for "emotionality" (a cluster of scales including emotional-unemotional, tense-relaxed, and excited-calm).

Several examples of the results in Table 11.1 may make the table more understandable. In the first row of the first column of the table the entry is 3.27. This shows that, for the paranoid case, the group which received the version introduced by "This is about an insane man" gave an average rating of 3.27 (slightly "bad" in meaning) on the *evaluative* factor to the concept "insane man in the story." The second entry in the first column (3.73) shows that the paranoid case was rated as "better" (higher on *evaluation*) when the case description was introduced with "This is about a mentally ill man." The third entry in the first column (3.85) shows the effect on *evaluation* when the paranoid case is introduced with "This is about an emotionally disturbed man." In the fourth row of the table, lying between the first and second columns, the mean of 3.15 is the rating given to the paranoid case when none of the three labels above is used in introductory sentences, in which instance the concept was "the man in the story."

The second column of Table 11.1 shows the average ratings given to the labels alone. Thus the first row of the second column shows that the average rating of "insane man" is 3.34 by subjects who did *not* read a version of the paranoid case introduced by "This is about an insane man."

The mean ratings for the labels alone are shown in the second column and also in the fourth column of Table 11.1. The means in the second column were obtained from subjects who read some version of the paranoid case. The means in the fourth column were obtained from subjects who read some version of the anxiety case. Because the corresponding entries in columns two and four are so much alike, the differences are probably due to sampling error.

From previous studies we knew that different ratings would be given to the labels when presented alone. This is amply evidenced in Table 11.1.

TABLE 11.1. Mean Semantic Differential Ratings of Labels,
of Cases, and of Labels Applied to Cases [*]

Rating	Label	Paranoid case		Anxiety case	
		Label with story	Label alone	Label with story	Label alone
Evaluative	Insane man	3.27	3.34	4.68	3.45
	Mentally ill man	3.73	3.97	4.88	4.04
	Emotionally disturbed man	3.85	4.13	4.70	4.32
	None (man in the story)	3.15		4.68	
Understand-ability	Insane man	2.84	2.09	3.00	2.13
	Mentally ill man	2.68	2.67	2.81	2.70
	Emotionally disturbed man	2.15	2.68	2.56	2.64
	None (man in the story)	2.24		2.84	
Sickness †	Insane man	6.27	6.11	5.25	5.90
	Mentally ill man	5.95	5.76	5.13	5.41
	Emotionally disturbed man	5.82	5.23	4.62	4.98
	None (man in the story)	5.55		4.59	
Immoral **	Insane man	4.99	5.05	4.08	5.08
	Mentally ill man	4.24	4.23	3.64	4.28
	Emotionally disturbed man	4.59	4.25	3.99	4.04
	None (man in the story)	5.19		3.77	
Dangerous ††	Insane man	6.41	6.22	4.26	5.90
	Mentally ill man	6.10	5.28	4.00	4.93
	Emotionally disturbed man	6.15	4.79	3.99	4.51
	None (man in the story)	6.08		3.69	
Anxiety	Insane man	6.13	5.74	5.63	5.48
	Mentally ill man	5.93	5.53	5.46	5.39
	Emotionally disturbed man	6.19	5.47	5.58	5.50
	None (man in the story)	6.32		5.55	
Emotionality	Insane man	6.36	5.89	6.17	5.81
	Mentally ill man	6.01	5.60	6.31	5.73
	Emotionally disturbed man	6.23	5.98	6.22	6.14
	None (man in the story)	6.63		6.04	

* Each mean is based on the scores of 55 students. The higher the mean, the more the meaning is like the factor name. For each of the two cases, the means in each row of the tables are based on different groups of subjects, and the means in each column are based on different groups of subjects.
   † Healthy-sick scale; high mean indicates "sick."
   ** Moral-immoral scale; high mean indicates "immoral."
   †† Safe-dangerous scale; high mean indicates "dangerous."

For example, in the second column of the table "emotionally disturbed man" is considerably higher on *evaluation* (mean of 4.13) than "insane man" (mean of 3.34). As another example, "insane man" is rated as much more "dangerous" than "mentally ill man."

Do the three labels receive different ratings when they are applied to case descriptions? Table 11.1 shows that the answer is definitely "yes." For example, when the paranoid case is introduced with "This is about an insane man," the case is given an *evaluative* rating of 3.27; when the same case is introduced by "This is about an emotionally disturbed man," the *evaluative* rating goes up to 3.85. Analysis of variance tests were made of the between-labels differences for each of the seven factors and the scales shown in Table 11.1. Three of these are significant beyond the .01 level. These are for *evaluation, understandability,* and the scale healthy-sick. The results indicate that when labels are applied to cases, the label which is used makes a difference.

Another question is related to the one discussed above. Do the cases receive different attitude ratings when they are not labeled than when they are labeled? One way to think about the question is to consider the entries in columns one and three as "mixtures" of two elements: the case itself when no label is applied and one of the three labels when rated alone. Ratings for the cases alone are shown between columns one and two and between columns three and four opposite "None (man in the story)"; the means for the labels alone are shown in columns two and four. The entries in columns one and three then show "mixtures" of cases with labels; for example, the first entry in the first column (3.27) can be thought of as the results of "mixing" the label "insane man" (mean rating alone of 3.34) with the "paranoid case" (mean rating of 3.15 when presented without one of the three labels).

How do the labels and cases "mix"? In most instances the rating of the mixture lies somewhere between the mean rating of the case alone and the mean rating of the label alone. On some scales the label tends to "draw" the mixture near to itself, and on other scales the case exerts more "pull" than does the label. One way to estimate the over-all importance of labels is to obtain the average distance of labels from the respective mixtures and to compare this with the average distance of the case itself from the respective "mixtures." For the paranoid case, the mean absolute difference in ratings for the labels alone and labels applied to cases is .39, and for the case alone and the labels applied to cases, .38—an almost identical average distance. Different results are found for the anxiety case. There labels have a mean absolute difference from mixtures of .52, and cases have a mean absolute difference of .22.

The attitudes expressed toward labels applied to cases are determined in about equal "amounts" by the labels alone and by the case alone for the paranoid case. For the anxiety case, the case alone is over two times as "important" as the labels in determining the attitudes expressed toward labels applied to cases. Such average effects, however, should not be taken too seriously. The relative influence of labels and cases in determining the meaning of cases with labels differs markedly in terms of the case and the Semantic Differential scales being inspected. In some instances the label appears to be much more important than the case description and in other instances the reverse is true.

In order to specify more definitely the relative effects of case descriptions and of labels, a range of cases broader than only two would have to be studied. Results from this study, however, support our contention that labels are important determiners of attitudes toward the mentally ill.

Some results from the study suggest two hypotheses for future investigations. (1) Labels are more influential determiners of attitudes when they are applied to relatively unfamiliar phenomena. This is suggested by the finding from the study (see Table 11.1) that labels appear to be more important determiners of attitudes for the paranoid case than for the anxiety case, probably because the average person is less familiar with paranoid behavior than with anxious behavior.

(2) Labels are more influential determiners of attitudes when they are perceived as being realistically related to the phenomena described. Although we have no direct evidence to support this view, most people would probably consider the labels "insane man" and "mentally ill man" as more appropriate for the paranoid case than for the anxiety case and the label "emotionally disturbed man" as more appropriate for the anxiety case than for the paranoid case. These expectations are borne out by the results in Table 11.1, where, in general, the labels of "insane" and "mentally ill" are more influential (exert more "pull") on the paranoid case than is the less appropriate label "emotionally disturbed." Conversely, "emotionally disturbed" generally exerts more "pull" on the anxiety case than do the two less appropriate labels.

A NEW TERMINOLOGY

What we mean by introducing a new terminology is not necessarily inventing new words and teaching them to the public, but rather translating mental-health phenomena into terms that the public already understands. We might, for example, translate neurotic behavior into terms like "emotional instability," "shyness," "tension," and "moodiness." The problem is to translate behavior into terms that clearly define the phenomena, yet are connotatively unbiased.

In one of our studies we investigated the translation of terms. Members of our opinion panel made Semantic Differential ratings of popular terms like "insane" and "neurotic" and of possible translation terms like "extremely withdrawn," "oversuspicious," and "emotionally immature." (The results are presented in Appendix 5.) We found, for example, that the label "extremely withdrawn" has a much less negative connotation than the labels "insane" and "mentally ill."

We also found that, among terms which can be used to describe the same behavior, such as an "emotionally unbalanced person" and an "emotionally sick person," the inclusion of words connotive of physical illness seems to have a favorable influence. For example, an "emotionally sick person" is rated as less negative than an "emotionally unbalanced person."

Another finding is that the adjective "aggressive," when used to modify a mental disorder, produces favorable or at least neutral public attitudes. This is a clear instance in which the experts and the public use a term differently. Whereas highly aggressive behavior often signifies a behavioral disorder to experts, "aggressive" means something "good" to the general public. In this and many other instances, ineffectual communication efforts result because the experts and the public use terms differently and because information sources, in writing pamphlets for example, incorrectly interpret the popular usage of terms.

SUMMARY

Our research experience leads us to believe that much of the problem of engendering more adequate information and more helpful attitudes is a language problem, and that one of the first orders of business in organizing effective information programs is to improve the terms and concepts which are used. Basically, we have found four things that are "wrong" with the available terminology: (1) there is a shortage of terms available for communicating about mental-health phenomena; (2) the terms often suggest misleading explanations; (3) the terms are not well anchored semantically; and (4) the terms bear strong negative connotations.

We do not mean to imply that *only* a language problem is at issue. People would be no less afraid of a lion if we hung a sign around his neck saying "pussycat." Some changes in terminology, however, are a *prerequisite* to the effective communication of information about mental health.

The language problem is far wider than our project, and it is the responsibility of professionals in the mental-health field and the sources of public information to devise a suitable language with which to communicate. Our purpose has been to show some of the criteria for developing an adequate terminology and to suggest some ways in which the effectiveness of terms can be studied.

12

Message Certainty and

the "Destruction" of Information

IF PUBLIC-INFORMATION PROGRAMS on mental health are to succeed, we must know how to structure the communications. What does the public really *want* to know? What *should* the public be told?

Clearly the public lacks information about mental illness (it is more *uninformed* than *misinformed*), but it is hungry for factual information about ways of handling or avoiding mental illness. Yet mental-illness topics tend to create anxiety, although that anxiety can be partially relieved when messages contain "solutions." Unfortunately, providing solutions is not an easy task. Not only do the professionals have a relatively meager storehouse of facts about mental health which can be easily communicated to the public but also some of what they believe to be correct today may prove to be incorrect tomorrow. Professionals are unsure about much of what they "know" in the mental-health field.

Because of the uncertain state of popular thought about mental illness, the variable of *message certainty* emerges as a potentially important factor. Message certainty is the degree to which a communication presents its "facts" as proven certainties. As a point of communication strategy, should mental-health communications be worded to sound certain of their information or should they mirror the uncertainty that is often felt by professionals in the field? If it would be dishonest to discuss all mental-health topics with certainty, would it be better to communicate only that information for which there are good grounds for speaking with sureness?

The problems involved in message certainty are more complicated than appear at first thought. For example, suppose that the public is told with certainty that a particular drug relieves a particular mental illness. What will be the effect if later the public must be told that the first message was wrong, that the drug does not work as anticipated? Will this build-up and letdown process do more harm to public attitudes than if no information had been given originally or than if the information had been given tentatively?

Message certainty can be thought of as a continuum ranging from "certainly true" to "tentatively true" through neutral to "tentatively false" and, finally, to "certainly false." Looking at the problem in that way, how does the negative side of the continuum affect public attitudes? In many of the communications about mental health and illness, the negative side of the continuum is used almost exclusively. For example, the public is told what does not cause mental disorder and what does not cure mental disorder. If the beliefs controverted in the message are actually held by some members of the public, negative messages serve to *destroy* existing information. (It should be reiterated that the term "information" is being used to encompass all verifiable statements, regardless of whether they are actually correct or incorrect.) Then, as another consideration, it is important to study the effect of information destruction on public attitudes.

This chapter will report the results of three studies concerning the effects of various aspects of message certainty on public attitudes. Also, results from studies reported in previous chapters and in succeeding chapters will be used to round out the picture of "certainty" as an important variable in communication.

STUDY 1: MESSAGE CERTAINTY

The first study [1] was concerned with both message certainty and the destruction of information. On one testing occasion, subjects were given messages which varied in certainty. Immediately afterwards, attitudes toward mental-health concepts were measured on a Semantic Differential form. Another group of subjects received control messages unrelated to mental health. These subjects also rated the same concepts on the Semantic Differential used with the experimental group.

Two weeks later, the subjects received messages which stated that the material they had previously read was incorrect. The control subjects also read the negation messages. All subjects were then measured on the same Semantic Differential concepts used for the first testing.

An experimental design was used which allowed us to determine (1) whether or not the differences in certainty produced differences in attitudes toward the mental-health concepts on the first testing; (2) whether or not the experimental messages (the messages about mental health) produced different attitudes from the control messages; (3) whether or not the control groups' attitudes became less favorable after reading the negation message; (4) whether or not the experimental groups reacted differently to the negation message than the control groups; (5) whether or not the high- and low-certainty experimental groups reacted differently to the negation messages.

[1] The study was designed and conducted by Dr. T. R. Husek.

Experimental Materials

Six different one-page messages were used in the first testing. Two messages described a possible physiogenic cure for schizophrenia; two discussed the use of tranquilizing drugs in curing mental disorders; and two were standard control messages, one on the Great Barrier Reef in Australia and the other on Starved Rock State Park in Illinois.

The experimental messages were variants of ones that had produced "favorable" attitude changes toward mental-illness concepts in previous studies. To insure that the only variable being manipulated was the certainty expressed, the high-certainty messages were matched with the low-certainty messages in terms of their structural properties. That is, both the high and the low message for schizophrenia had approximately the same number of words and sentences and had similar sentence structure. They were written so that the only difference between the messages was the degree of certainty. For example, one sentence in the high-certainty message read, "The years of research by scientists are beginning to pay off in valid conclusions." The comparable sentence for the low-certainty message was, "The years of research by scientists are beginning to pay off but only in tentative conclusions." Similarly, the two messages on tranquilizing drugs were varied in terms of certainty. The control messages were approximately the same length as the experimental messages.

The full body of the high-certainty schizophrenia experimental message is as follows:

> The problem of mental illness is becoming increasingly important in the world today. Research is gradually bringing the more immediate physical diseases under control, and more and more attention is being paid to mental disorders.
>
> The results of the work on mental disorders can be summarized briefly. The years of research by scientists are beginning to pay off in valid conclusions. Millions of dollars have been spent trying to understand mental illness, and our knowledge of mental disease is quite impressive from a scientific point of view. The research findings regarding schizophrenia, a form of insanity, are a good example. Schizophrenia is by far the most important and dangerous mental disorder in the world today. Scientists working with schizophrenia have discovered a copperish substance in the blood which is related to the disorder. This copperish substance is present in the blood of schizophrenics and is not present in the blood of the large number of normal people who have already been tested. Scientists believe that this substance is definitely the basic cause of schizophrenia. Some scientists have performed experiments in which some schizophrenic patients have been cured after taking medicines which reduced the amount of this copperish substance in the blood stream. Evidence is being gathered all the time concerning the importance of this substance with respect to mental illness.

It is certain that within a few years scientists will fully understand schizophrenia and will have perfected methods for eliminating it from the earth.

The full body of the low-certainty schizophrenia experimental message is as follows:

The problem of mental illness is becoming increasingly important in the world today. Research is gradually bringing the more immediate physical diseases under control, and more and more attention is being paid to mental disorders.

The results of the work on mental disorders can be summarized briefly. The years of research by scientists are beginning to pay off but only in tentative conclusions. Millions of dollars have been spent trying to understand mental illness, but our knowledge of mental disease is quite scanty from a scientific point of view. The research findings regarding schizophrenia, a form of insanity, are a good example. Schizophrenia is by far the most important and dangerous mental disorder in the world today. Scientists working with schizophrenia believe there is a copperish substance in the blood which might be related to the disorder. This copperish substance seems to be present in the blood of schizophrenics and has not been found thus far in the blood of those normal people who have already been tested. Scientists believe that this substance is possibly one of the causes of schizophrenia. Some scientists have performed experiments which seem to suggest that a schizophrenic patient may have been cured after taking medicines which reduce the amount of this copperish substance in the blood stream. Evidence is being gathered all the time concerning the possible importance of this substance with respect to mental illness.

It is possible that within a few decades scientists will better understand schizophrenia and improve methods for eliminating it from the earth.

The full body of the "negation" message on schizophrenia is as follows:

The problem of mental illness is becoming increasingly important in the world today. Research is gradually bringing the more immediate physical diseases under control, and more and more attention is being paid to mental disorders.

The results of some of this work on mental disorders can, unfortunately, be summarized very briefly. The findings regarding schizophrenia are a good example. Schizophrenia is by far the most prevalent and dangerous mental illness. Some recent research has indicated that scientists do not understand how schizophrenia is caused. Scientists know very little about mental illness, and although some scientists thought they had found a copperish substance which caused schizophrenia, it now turns out that their hopes were not well founded. They do not understand schizophrenia. Patients have been cured after taking a substance which reduced the amount of this copperish substance in the blood stream of schizophrenics, but now it is felt that these cures were the result of the added attention and treatment these patients received along with the substance. The cures were not related to the copperish substance. The reduction of the amount of copperish substance did not produce the cures. However, research in other areas of mental illness may turn up something which will be of value in treating mental disorders.

It is certainly possible that some day scientists will understand schizophrenia and they may even find an easy cure for it.

The Semantic Differential was used to measure attitudes. The factors of *understandability, evaluation,* and *potency* were used, along with the scales safe-dangerous and effective-ineffective. The concepts used were: psychiatrist, mental patient, a person who has schizophrenia, tranquilizing drugs, mental illness, ways of treating mental patients, and me. Nine-point scales were used. The subjects were also asked to evaluate the success of the treatment which was described in the message, and they indicated what they felt the chances were that one of their best friends would become mentally ill sometime in his life. On the first testing, subjects were asked to rate the "certainty" and "understandability" of their respective messages.

Subjects

The subjects were 144 high-school juniors and seniors, none of whom were taking courses in psychology or mental hygiene. They were selected to range widely in terms of their school grades and performance on the school intelligence tests.

Procedure

The subjects were tested during regular class meetings. Five classes were used. The entire administration of the test materials was performed by the experimenter; the teacher of the class sat in the back of the room and did not participate. The subjects were told that they were "participating in a study of writing styles." They were asked to read the messages and then to respond to the Semantic Differential material. Questions about the instructions were answered, but no other information about the test materials was given. The subjects were not told that the experimenter would return later for additional testing.

After two weeks, the tester returned to the high school. He administered the forms with the statement that the instructions would be self-explanatory. The instructions reiterated that the study was an investigation of writing styles. On this testing, all subjects received negation messages (of the form illustrated previously for schizophrenia). The two groups that had received the high- and low-certainty messages on schizophrenia respectively were given the negation message on schizophrenia. The two groups that had received the high- and low-certainty messages on tranquilizing drugs respectively were given the negation message on tranquilizing drugs. Of the two groups that had received control messages (one on the Great Barrier Reef and the other on an Illinois state park), one received the negation message on schizophrenia and the other received the negation message on tranquilizing drugs.

On the day following the last testing, the experimenter returned to the school and visited all of the classes that had been tested. He explained the nature of the experiment, and answered frankly questions from the students about the plan and purpose of the experiment.

Results

The total pool of subjects was divided into six groups for purposes of analysis. The six groups are described in Table 12.1. Each of the six groups responded to 39 variables on the first testing and 37 on the second (the first testing also included ratings of *certainty* and *understandability* for the messages themselves). Means and standard deviations for each group for both testings for all of the variables were computed. This resulted in 420 means and 420 standard deviations, too much material to present here. Consequently, to summarize the results, grand means were computed over all the scales representative of various factors (such as *evaluation* and *understandability*) and over the six concepts relating to mental health (*psychiatrist, mental patient,* and so forth). These are presented in Table 12.2.

Since we prepared messages that we assumed differed in certainty, a primary question is whether the subjects perceived the relative degrees of certainty. The subjects were asked to rate the messages they had read in terms of whether the message was "certain" or "uncertain" on a nine-step scale. The high-certainty messages were actually rated as being more

TABLE 12.1. The Messages Received by the Six Treatment Groups for Study 1

		First Session	Second Session
Group 1		High-certainty message on schizophrenia	Negation message on schizophrenia
Group 2		Low-certainty message on schizophrenia	Negation message on schizophrenia
Group 3		Control message	Negation message on schizophrenia
Group 4		High-certainty message on tranquilizing drugs	Negation message on tranquilizing drugs
Group 5		Low-certainty message on tranquilizing drugs	Negation message on tranquilizing drugs
Group 6		Control message	Negation message on tranquilizing drugs

TABLE 12.2. Grand Means * of the Six Groups in Study 1
Averaged over the Six Mental-health Concepts †

	Group 1 High-certainty message on schizophrenia		Group 2 Low-certainty message on schizophrenia		Group 3 Control	
	First testing	Second testing	First testing	Second testing	First testing	Second testing
Evaluation	5.76	5.72	5.76	5.82	5.80	5.63
Understandability	5.21	5.03	4.96	4.71	5.04	4.12
Potency	3.40	3.31	3.35	3.32	3.17	3.15
Safety	4.10	4.21	4.26	4.16	3.98	3.81
Effectiveness	6.66	5.77	5.85	5.81	6.45	5.59

	Group 4 High-certainty message on tranquilizing drugs		Group 5 Low-certainty message on tranquilizing drugs		Group 6 Control	
	First testing	Second testing	First testing	Second testing	First testing	Second testing
Evaluation	6.23	6.12	5.94	5.85	5.77	5.80
Understandability	5.37	4.88	5.32	4.95	5.18	4.70
Potency	3.57	3.30	3.22	3.08	3.18	3.18
Safety	4.92	4.86	4.72	4.68	4.60	4.31
Effectiveness	6.58	6.14	6.02	5.72	5.92	5.91

* The ratings were made on nine-point scales: 9 would mean an extremely positive rating, such as high *evaluation, understandability,* and *potency;* 1 would mean a very negative rating.
† The six concepts were: *psychiatrist, mental patient, a person who has schizophrenia, tranquilizing drugs, mental illness,* and *ways of treating mental illness.* Scores were averaged over the six concepts in order to determine whether or not the treatment conditions had over-all "good" or "bad" effects on attitudes.

"certain" at the .01 level of confidence. This lends some assurance to our interpretation that the main effects of the experiment are due to variations in message certainty.

High- versus Low-certainty Messages

Subjects who received the high-certainty messages had more favorable attitudes toward the mental-health concepts after reading the messages than did the subjects who read low-certainty messages. If the two high-certainty groups are combined and compared by *t*-test with the two low-certainty groups, the following results are obtained: subjects with high-certainty messages rate *psychiatrist* as more understandable, good, safe, and effective; *tranquilizing drugs,* as more potent and effective; *a person who has schizophrenia,* as more effective; and *me* as more "good." All of these comparisons are significant at the .05 level or beyond.

Another way of looking at the high- and low-certainty comparison is to examine the consistency with which the high-certainty messages are associated with more favorable attitudes than are the "low" messages. There are six mental-health concepts, with five scores obtained for each concept. If the high-certainty schizophrenia message is compared with the low-certainty schizophrenia message and the high-certainty tranquilizing-drugs message compared with the low-certainty tranquilizing-drugs message, a total of 60 comparisons are possible. In 44 of the 60 cases, high-certainty messages are associated with more favorable attitudes than are low-certainty messages. This proportion is significant beyond the .01 level of confidence by sign-test.

As we typically find in manipulating content variables such as certainty, message anxiety, relative solution, and others, the "good" condition (here, high certainty) not only promotes favorable attitudes toward primary concepts in the message, but also generalizes either to secondary concepts mentioned in the message or to concepts not mentioned at all in the message. This trend is exemplified in the present study by the differences between the high- and low-certainty messages in establishing favorable attitudes toward the concept *psychiatrist* and toward the self-concept (*me*). Regarding the differences in attitude toward *me*, time and again our research found that the differences in attitudes which are caused by differences in messages are reflected in momentary states of the self-concept. This finding is close to the heart of the underlying process of communication.

DESTRUCTION OF INFORMATION IN THE CONTROL GROUP. One half of the control group received the negation schizophrenia message on the second testing; the other half, the negation tranquilizing-drugs message. By looking at the attitudes expressed in the first testing session and comparing them with the attitudes expressed after the negation messages had been read, we can determine the effects of the negation messages alone. That is, we can ascertain whether telling the subjects that tranquilizing drugs are not successful cures for mental illness and that schizophrenia cannot at present be cured is associated with unfavorable attitudes toward mental-health concepts. We find that this is true. The negation messages had the effect of making the subjects' attitudes less favorable. Of the 60 comparisons between the first testing and the second testing (30 for the tranquilizing-drugs message and 30 for the schizophrenia message), 41 displayed an unfavorable change on the second testing. By signed-ranks test the difference is significant beyond the .01 level. Another experiment will be discussed in a later section of this chapter which confirms the results reported above: negation without supplying "certain" information in its place (which we refer to as "information destruction") is "bad" in that it leads to unconstructive attitudes toward mental-health concepts.

NEGATION IN THE EXPERIMENTAL GROUPS. In the first session the experimental groups read positive messages; in the second session they read messages which negated the original material. One would expect that the negation statements would create less positive attitudes toward the mental-health concepts. This comparison indicates how the subjects changed their ratings of the mental-health concepts after reading the negative messages. Of the 120 possible changes (30 for each of the four groups), 78 were in the negative direction, showing that the negative statements did indeed produce less favorable attitudes. The breakdown of 78 negative changes to 48 positive changes is significant by sign-test beyond the .01 level of confidence. (The difference is even more striking when the signed-ranks test is applied: a t value of 4.89 is obtained.)

Another question which arises concerns the relative effect on the low- and high-certainty groups. One might hypothesize that the negative message would have different effects on the two groups. The data available do not support this hypothesis. There is virtually no difference in the number and amount of negative attitude changes produced in the low- and high-certainty groups by the second message.

NEGATION EFFECTS COMPARED. Up to now we have mentioned evidence on the effects of message certainty and negative messages on attitudes. One set of our subjects received positive messages (some of high and some of low certainty) in the first session and negative messages in the second testing session. Two control groups received neutral messages in the first session and negative messages in the second session. A comparison of these two sets of subjects in the second testing session will help to answer an important question concerning the effects of the negative messages. Did the negative messages create more unfavorable attitudes in the groups that had received no previous information about the topic (the control groups) or in the groups that had received some positive information previously (the experimental groups)? The answer to this question is valuable to persons who must make decisions about disseminating information that may later turn out to be incorrect.

A significant number of the attitudes of the experimental group which received the high-certainty message are more positive than the stated attitudes of the comparable control groups. This finding is also true for the low-certainty experimental versus control groups. It seems that giving positive information and then later stating that the information is incorrect is no "worse," and evidently "better," than refuting the information initially.

In other words, at the time of the second administration of messages, the negation messages had about the same effect on both the experimental groups and the control groups: both suffered decrements in positive attitudes toward mental-health concepts, and the amount of decrement was approximately the same for both sets of subjects. On the first testing, however, the experimental groups, because they received positive messages, showed more positive attitudes toward mental-health concepts than did the control groups. Although both sets of subjects showed decrements in constructive attitudes, the relative "superiority" of the experimental groups was approximately maintained from the first to the second testing.

SUBJECTS' RATINGS OF THE CHANCES OF MENTAL ILLNESS. An incidental finding in the "certainty" study relates to a point which has puzzled us. In a number of communication experiments we asked subjects to rate the likelihood with which one of their friends would develop a mental disorder. Consistently we find that subjects who read messages about mental illness rate the odds as *less* than do subjects who read no messages or control messages. This trend occurred very markedly in the "certainty" study. Subjects were asked to rate the odds (on a seven-step scale—7 is high) of one of their personal friends developing mental illness. At the first testing the average rating for the experimental groups was 3.88, and the average rating for the control groups was 5.88—a very large difference. After reading the negation message about mental illness in the second testing, the average rating of "likelihood" by the control group dropped from 5.88 all the way down to 3.56.

There may be a number of reasons for the very different estimates of "likelihood of mental illness" by those who do and those who do not receive messages about mental illness. Our tentative interpretation relates to what has been said (and will be reiterated) numerous times in this book: mental-illness topics generally tend to create anxiety. Our hypothesis is that the individual who reads messages about mental illness defends against the anxiety with the conceptual stance that "this is not likely to happen to me, my family, or my friends." Again we see the central involvement of the "self," and the "near-self," in the reaction to communications.

STUDY 2: A REPLICATION OF STUDY 1

One of the interesting general findings of the over-all project is that relatively short, one-page messages are sufficient to produce measurable changes in attitudes toward mental-health concepts. A natural question arising from this finding asks whether or not the attitude changes are long-term or temporary. Since the "certainty" materials as described in Study 1 above had already induced significant attitude changes in previous experiments, we thought that they would be useful in studying the long-term effects of one-page messages. Using the certainty materials would also allow us partially to replicate the findings of Study 1. Consequently, we performed another study [2] using the messages developed for Study 1.

[2] The study was designed and conducted by Dr. T. R. Husek.

Experimental Materials

The messages used in Study 2 were identical to the ones used in Study 1. The Semantic Differential was used to measure attitudes, and the concepts and scales utilized were the same as in Study 1.

Subjects

The subjects were 135 high-school students, almost all of whom were juniors or seniors, who were attending a different high school from those in Study 1. They were selected to range widely in terms of their school grades and performance on the school intelligence tests.

Procedure

The subjects were tested during one school day in regular class meetings on three occasions. Five classes were tested. The entire administration of the test materials was performed by the experimenter; the teacher of the class did not participate. The instructions and administration of the first testing session were identical to those of the first study. The subjects were told they were participating in a study of writing styles, asked to read the messages, and then requested to respond to the Semantic Differential materials.

After two weeks, the experimenter returned to the high school. The subjects were asked to respond to some questions on the material they had read two weeks previously. The forms they completed contained the same Semantic Differential material that they had filled out on the first testing.

After two more months, the tester again returned to the high school. The subjects again filled out the same Semantic Differential materials. After the third, and final, testing session, the experimenter explained the nature of the study and answered questions frankly.

Results

For purposes of analysis, the subjects were placed in five groups. Group 1 received the high-certainty schizophrenia message. Group 2 received the low-certainty schizophrenia message. Group 3 received the high-certainty tranquilizing-drugs message. Group 4 received the low-certainty tranquilizing-drugs message. Group 5 received control messages which were unrelated to mental health.

Each of the five groups was tested on three occasions; on the first occasion they received the appropriate message; on the last two occasions the subjects received no messages at all. Means and standard deviations were computed for each of the five groups for each of the three testing sessions. Also, grand means were computed for five factors for each of six concepts. These are presented in Table 12.3.

The part of Study 2 that is most important for this chapter involves the replication of the findings about "certainty" which were obtained in

TABLE 12.3. Grand Means * of the Five Groups in Study 2, Averaged over the Six Mental-health Concepts †

| | Group 1 High-certainty message on schizophrenia | | | Group 2 Low-certainty message on schizophrenia | | |
	First testing	Second testing	Third testing	First testing	Second testing	Third testing
Evaluation	6.18	6.10	5.99	5.77	5.83	5.94
Understandability	5.26	5.58	5.59	4.87	5.03	5.28
Potency	3.10	3.15	3.15	3.14	3.15	3.19
Safety	4.95	4.07	5.00	4.78	4.92	5.02
Effectiveness	6.13	6.24	5.91	5.76	5.67	5.93

| | Group 3 High-certainty message on tranquilizing drugs | | | Group 4 Low-certainty message on tranquilizing drugs | | |
	First testing	Second testing	Third testing	First testing	Second testing	Third testing
Evaluation	6.08	5.97	6.17	5.86	5.83	5.75
Understandability	4.92	4.93	4.82	5.45	5.09	5.12
Potency	3.46	3.29	3.33	3.20	3.17	3.23
Safety	4.47	4.38	4.58	4.61	4.66	4.71
Effectiveness	6.51	6.07	6.02	6.24	6.12	6.02

| | Group 5 Control | | |
	First testing	Second testing	Third testing
Evaluation	5.55	5.53	5.68
Understandability	4.99	5.53	5.44
Potency	3.21	3.29	3.22
Safety	4.12	4.41	4.61
Effectiveness	5.66	5.62	5.78

* The ratings were made on nine-point scales: 9 would mean an extremely positive rating, such as high *evaluation, understandability,* and *potency;* 1 would mean a very negative rating.

† The six concepts were: *psychiatrist, mental patient, a person who has schizophrenia, tranquilizing drugs, mental illness,* and *ways of treating mental illness.*

Study 1. When we compare the results for the high-certainty groups on the first testing occasion with the results for the low-certainty groups, we find that the high-certainty condition produced more favorable attitudes. By signed-ranks test the one-tailed difference is significant beyond the .01 level.

Although the findings from the second study confirmed the findings from the first study regarding "certainty," the major purpose of the second study was to study the permanence of attitude changes toward mental-health concepts. The results relative to longevity of changes proved to be quite interesting; they are presented in Chapter 15 along with other studies concerning the permanence of attitude changes.

STUDY 3: DESTRUCTION OF INFORMATION

The research described in Study 1 and Study 2 indicates that the certainty with which material is stated affects attitudes toward the subject matter of the material. The more certain the message sounds, the more favorable the attitudes are.

Our previous research also suggests that the destruction of information about mental health results in less favorable attitudes. In other words, if you tell an individual that information about mental illness is incorrect and do not tell him what is correct, you will promote negative attitudes toward concepts like *mental patient, psychiatrist,* and *methods of treating mental patients.*

Another experiment, closely related to the problem of the destruction of information, was performed. Subjects were asked to read short written messages about mental illness. The last paragraph of the message, however, told subjects that the material reported in the message was wrong. In other words, we gave people information in the body of the message and then "destroyed" the information at the end of the message. Measures were then made of attitudes toward the mentally ill, mental-health professionals, and treatment methods. The results were compared with measurements made on control groups.

Subjects

Two experimental and two control groups, with 30 persons in each, were used in the study. Subjects were randomly assigned to the four groups. All subjects were undergraduate students at the University of Illinois.

Experimental Materials

Both experimental groups read one-page written explanations of catatonic schizophrenia. One group read a psychogenic explanation and the other group read a physiogenic explanation. The two control groups read one-page written messages about topics not concerned with mental illness. One control group read about the Great Barrier Reef and the other control group read about the use of the typewriter.

The two messages about mental illness had produced "favorable" attitude changes toward mental-illness concepts in previous studies. The full body of the physiogenic explanation is as follows:

> Some of the bizarre forms of human behavior which we refer to as insanity have been difficult for scientists to understand. A particularly baffling mental disorder is *catatonic schizophrenia*. The individual sits motionless, staring straight ahead, and is completely out of contact with his environment. He will not respond when spoken to and will not move even if the building around him is on fire. Some patients spend the rest of their lives living more like a stone than a human being.
>
> Recent scientific findings indicate how *catatonic schizophrenia* develops and what can be done to cure it. It is now known that the disease is caused by a chemical substance in the blood. A copperish substance has been found in the blood of these patients which occurs to a much less extent in normal people. When normal persons are injected with the substance, they show the catatonic reaction in a few minutes time. Their behavior is identical to real mental patients. After about an hour they return to normal.
>
> There are two important consequences of this recent discovery. First, the seemingly odd and mysterious behavior of the patient is now seen as an understandable reaction. We no longer have to invent complicated explanations of what seemed like mysterious behavior. Second, the discovery points to a cure for the disorder. The patient is given medicines to reduce the copperish substance in the blood. After several weeks of this treatment the catatonic symptoms go away. Along with the administration of drugs, the patient is given a series of therapeutic interviews. He is invited to talk over his difficulties and is advised about the problems that will be encountered on returning to society. Patients who undergo this treatment often show marked improvement. Many such persons are now back in society leading happy, productive lives. The progress that has been made with this one type of mental illness gives promise that all forms of insanity will be both understandable and curable in the decade ahead.

If we had used the two experimental messages in the form in which they were used in previous studies, they would probably have produced "favorable" attitude changes. However, we altered the two experimental messages slightly in order to provide some information relating to the hypothesis discussed above. The two experimental messages were altered in only two places. First, the two messages were introduced with the written statement: "The following article appeared several years ago in a magazine." Second, the two messages ended with the written statement:

> Research completed since this article was written tends to refute the explanation. It now seems that the cause of the disorder and the method of treatment as stated above are not as effective as was previously supposed.

TABLE 12.4. Mean Semantic Differential Ratings on the *Evaluative* Factor *

Concept	Experimental groups	Control groups
Psychiatrist	5.89	6.12
A person who has catatonic schizophrenia	4.02	3.72
Mental patient	3.87	4.22
Treatment of mental illness	5.54	5.81
Me	5.64	5.92

* Ratings were averaged over the two experimental groups separately and over the two control groups separately. There were 30 subjects in each experimental and control group. Consequently, each mean is based on 60 cases. Scales like valuable-worthless and sincere-insincere were combined to form the *evaluative* factor. The means are shown to the same scale used for the seven-step Semantic Differential ratings. A mean of 4.00 means "neutral." A mean above 4.00 indicates a positive attitude. A mean below 4.00 indicates a negative attitude.

After the two experimental and two control groups read their respective messages, a Semantic Differential form was used to measure attitudes toward mental-illness concepts. The form contained scales for the *evaluative* and *understandability* factors, and employed concepts like psychiatrist, mental patient, and others.

Results

Table 12.4 shows the mean *evaluation* ratings of mental-illness concepts and the concept *me* for the experimental and control groups. Table 12.5 shows the mean *understandability* ratings of the concepts for the experimental and the control groups. The differences between the means for both Tables 12.4 and 12.5 are small, but, with one exception, they are all in the predicted direction. The experimental groups give lower evaluations of the concepts than do the control groups. The exception is that the experimental group gives a higher evaluation of a *person who has catatonic schizophrenia,* but the difference is not statistically significant. When the four mental-illness concepts in Table 12.4 are added together, the grand means are significantly different beyond the .05 level by *t*-test.

In Table 12.5 all of the differences are in the predicted direction. The grand means on the four mental-illness concepts are significantly different beyond the .01 level by *t*-test.

Even the concept *me* follows the same pattern as the other concepts. Although the differences between experimental and control groups on *evaluation* and *understandability* are not statistically significant when treated separately, they are significant beyond the .05 level by *t*-test when averaged over both factors.

When the results of the *evaluative* and *understandability* factors are combined, the control group gives more "favorable" ratings than the experimental group in nine out of ten comparisons. Even when the com-

TABLE 12.5. Mean Semantic Differential Ratings on the *Understandability* Factor [*]

Concept	Experimental groups	Control groups
Psychiatrist	3.76	3.88
A person who has catatonic schizophrenia	2.90	3.36
Mental patient	2.16	2.53
Treatment of mental illness	2.99	3.53
Me	3.87	4.08

[*] Ratings were averaged over the two experimental groups separately and over the two control groups separately. There were 30 subjects in each experimental and control group. Consequently, each mean is based on 60 cases. Scales like understandable-mysterious and predictable-unpredictable were combined to form the *understandability* factor. The means are shown to the same scale used for the seven-step Semantic Differential ratings. A mean of 4.00 means "neutral." A mean above 4.00 indicates a positive attitude. A mean below 4.00 indicates a negative attitude.

parisons are looked at in this raw way, the difference between the two treatments is significant beyond the .05 level by sign-test.

The results from this study agree with and amplify the results reported in Study 1 and Study 2 for "negation" messages. The negation messages presented possible facts about the causes and treatment of mental illness as doubtfully true, and doubt was sprinkled throughout the message. In this study, subjects read a "certain"-sounding message but at the end they were told that "it isn't so." Both situations lead to "bad" attitudes, and in both situations the same process is at work. In both cases the individual is presented with potential information, which, if assimilated as valid information, would lead to constructive attitudes. However, the individual is not allowed to "keep" the positive information, which results in more negative attitudes toward mental-health concepts than had no information been given at all.

CONCLUSIONS

The results from studies reported in this chapter can be summarized in the following propositions.

PROPOSITION 12.1: **The more certainty with which mental-health information is stated, the more favorable will be the attitudes toward concepts related to the message.**

Direct evidence for this proposition is found in the first two experiments described in this chapter. In both of the experiments, groups which received high-certainty messages displayed more favorable attitudes toward mental-health concepts such as *psychiatrist* and *methods for treating mental patients* than did groups which read messages that were worded tentatively.

The proposition is also consistent with other research we have completed. People are relatively uninformed about the mental-health area, and it is reasonable that they should be more influenced by statements which are sure than by messages which do not seem sure. The person who does not understand an area prefers that his information be as well structured and definite as possible. Also, factual-sounding information tends to reduce the inherent anxiety engendered by mental-health communications. It is our hypothesis that reduced anxiety leads to more favorable attitudes toward mental-health concepts. Our interpretation of the differences between the attitudes resulting from high-certainty and low-certainty messages is that the former more effectively dissipate the anxiety than do the latter.

PROPOSITION 12.2: **The destruction of information about mental illness without supplying new information results in negative attitudes toward related concepts.**

We have a wealth of evidence to show that this proposition is true in a very general sense. Clear results were obtained from two different experiments reported in this chapter. Related results are also found for the solution versus no-solution (which is analogous to "certainty" versus "negation") studies of public interests reported in Chapter 9 and attitude-change studies reported in Chapter 10. More evidence for the proposition will be given in Chapters 13 and 17.

PROPOSITION 12.3: **Even if available information may turn out to be incorrect, it is better to give such information to the public than to withhold it.**

The results from Study 1 definitely support this proposition, which answers the question of whether to withhold tentative information from the public or to supply the information even if it must be rescinded later. For several reasons, however, it is best to apply caution in accepting the proposition. First, the proposition is complicated, and there are variables which we did not consider. For example, the repeated use of the build-up and later letdown procedure might have harmful effects. Second, the time between "giving" and "destroying" information is a crucial variable. In Study 1 there was a two-week interval between "giving" and "destroying." In Study 3 information was "destroyed" immediately after it was "given." In the former, the experimental group showed "better" attitudes than the control group. In the latter the experimental group showed "worse" attitudes than the control group. Consequently, if giving information and later destroying it is better than giving no information at all, people must be allowed to "keep" the information for at least a short period of time.

Evidently the proposition is complex and needs more study. However, we might have anticipated a very "bad" effect of giving information and later negating it: the subjects might have shown hostility at being "duped" and responded in kind to the persons and objects mentioned in the messages. In Study 1 (but not in Study 3), where the subjects could have conceivably felt "duped," the experimental group expressed more positive attitudes than did the control group. Consequently, there is nothing in our studies to show that giving and later destroying information is worse than giving no information at all. This should encourage those in mental-health education who would like to tell the public the best that is known, even if some of it must be rescinded later.

SUMMARY

In earlier chapters it was hypothesized that people are generally unsure of their beliefs about mental health and mental illness. Consequently, to promote favorable attitudes, it is necessary to use messages which "sound sure." Three relevant experiments were described in the chapter.

The main results from the first two studies are the same, and in both cases the effects are marked: high-certainty messages promote more favorable attitudes than low-certainty messages, and both are better than control messages. This strongly supports the hypothesis that the more certain sounding the messages, the more favorable the attitudes developed toward mental-health phenomena.

The converse of the hypothesis above is that negative messages, ones that "destroy" existing beliefs without supplying new factual information, promote *more unfavorable* attitudes than do control messages. An experiment was conducted to make the hypothesis more tenable. The results support our hypothesis: negation ("destruction of information") leads to unfavorable attitudes toward mental-health concepts. The combined results of the three experiments demonstrate the bad effects that are obtained from communicating in an unsure, hesitant manner, and the even worse effects that are obtained by telling people only what does *not* cause mental disorder and what does *not* cure mental disorder. Our hypothesis is that lack of sureness tends to create anxiety, and, as was shown in Chapter 10, anxiety is one of the major factors in determining public attitudes toward mental-health phenomena.

13

Other Variables of
Effective Communication

THIS CHAPTER will be used as a catch-all for three experiments dealing with communication variables not discussed in other chapters. The first experiment is concerned with the effects on information and attitudes of "contact" with the mentally ill; the second, with the differential effect of "personal" versus "impersonal" messages; and the third, with relationships between changes in information and changes in attitudes. Some other communication variables were considered in each of the three studies. Also, some of the findings from the three studies help confirm and clarify results reported in previous and subsequent chapters of the book.

STUDY 1: CONTACT

It is often supposed that if people had more face-to-face contact with the mentally ill and with those who have recovered from mental illness, much of the stigma associated with mental illness would be removed. For this reason, some people have proposed that the general public be encouraged to visit mental hospitals and meet the patients at first hand. Does contact actually have the desired effect?

The first experiment [1] described here concerns one aspect of the "contact" issue: the differential effectiveness of messages when the sources are identified as former mental patients and when the sources are identified as "normal" persons. A standard talk was delivered to different groups of subjects; in some groups the speaker was identified as a "former mental patient"; in other groups the speaker was not so identified. In addition, some of the messages were keyed to a personal approach and others were keyed to an impersonal approach. Tests were then made to determine the differential effectiveness of the various presentations.

[1] The study was conducted by Dr. T. R. Husek.

Experimental Procedure

The subjects' view of the study was rather simple. One day, a Friday, a young woman came into their class in high school and gave a twenty-minute talk on mental health. On the following Monday, someone else came into class and gave tests.

The experimental design was more complicated. Two different women were used as communicators. The speaker may or may not have said that she was a former mental patient, and if she did claim to be one, she may have said it at the beginning of the talk or at the end of the talk. In addition, the talk may have been presented in a personal or an impersonal manner.

Classes in two high-schools were used (480 students). They were tested one week apart. The communicators told the subjects that they were from a "state organization" and were visiting some high schools giving talks on mental health. They made the presentations during regular class sessions. Then, on the following Monday a different person came to the class and said he was making a survey for the "university." He passed out the testing materials during the regular class meetings. In this way it was hoped that the test materials would be disassociated from the talks given earlier.

On both occasions the teachers of the classes participated only by introducing the experimenters; during the session they sat in the back of the room and merely watched. The experimenters answered questions about the instructions for the test materials but not about the content and purpose of the tests.

On the day after the testing (Tuesday), the experimenter returned to the classes, explained the nature of the experiment, and answered frankly any questions the subjects had, both about the experiment and the talk.

THE TALK. A twenty-minute talk was composed which attempted to promote favorable attitudes toward some mental-illness concepts and to correct some common misconceptions about mental illness. The content of the talk ranged widely over topics concerning mental illness, mentioning such items as the shortage of hospital beds, the fact that a vacation is not a cure for mental illness, and the fact that mental patients are not just pretending to be sick. Here is a short section of the presentation which was intended to promote favorable attitudes:

> Patients in a mental hospital seem to behave in a confused manner. But when you get to know the patients in the hospital and understand what's wrong with them, you find that their behavior is not so strange after all. The doctors in the hospitals have to understand why the patients be- have the way they do in order to cure them. The way a person develops an emotional disturbance is closely related to his personality, history, and en- vironment. And when you understand more about him, his behavior doesn't seem so strange any more; for the way that a patient acts follows from

the kind of a person he is and the problem he has. Most of you in this room, given enough time to study the problem, could understand why mentally ill people act the way they do.

Here is a part of the talk which attempted to impart some information about mental illness:

> Let's discuss the idea that a mental illness will clear up if a person is helped with his financial and social problems, or can just "get away from it all." If things get bad, avoid them, and they'll go away. Well, sometimes if a person is overworked and overtired, he will show symptoms of mental illness. In these few cases a trip or a rest may help. But in most cases it will just not work. A trip or help with financial problems will lessen some of the pressures on a disturbed person. It may keep him busy and get his mind off the problems for a while. But the problems of an emotionally disturbed person are not so trivial that they'll blow away with the wind if you ignore them. No one would ever suggest that somebody with cancer or appendicitis should go on a trip if he wants to feel better. In the same way, a trip or some help with financial and social problems is not a cure for mental illness.

COMMUNICATORS. The talk was presented orally. Because the communicator is usually an important factor in oral communications, two female speakers were used in the study. They were about the same age and their backgrounds were similar.

Although the speakers did not memorize the talk, they were able to present the material only occasionally glancing at their notes. They practiced for several weeks and watched each other's presentation with a view to standardizing the talk as much as possible.

THE CONTACT VARIABLE. For one third of the presentations, the speaker mentioned at the beginning of the speech that she was a "former mental patient." For another third of the presentations, the point was made at the end of the talk. For the last third no mention was made about the background of the speaker. (Neither speaker had actually been a "mental patient.")

At each of the two high schools, the role of each of the two speakers was held constant. That is, for all of the classes tested in one high school, one of the speakers played the role of the former mental patient (sometimes announcing the fact at the beginning of the talk and at other times announcing the fact at the end of the talk). In that high school, the second speaker consistently made no mention of being a former mental patient. Roles were reversed in the other high school.

The Personal versus Impersonal Variable

Half of the talks were presented in an impersonal manner; the other half were made as personal as possible. Here is a section from the personal-treatment version:

Right now 9,000,000 people in this country are suffering from mental illness or a personality disturbance. What does this mean to you? It means that on the average two people in this class here today would be expected to have some kind of mental illness or personality disturbance. It means that on the average, every one of you might have one close relative suffering from a mental illness or a personality disturbance right now.

Here is the impersonal treatment for the same section:

It is estimated that right now there are about 9,000,000 people in the United States suffering from mental illness and personality disturbances. This counts only the people who have trouble right now. One out of every 12 people in the United States will spend some time in his life in a mental institution.

The Experimental Design

There were two communicators, three variations of contact, and personal and impersonal treatments. The complete design is outlined in Table 13.1.

Attitude and Information Measures

A form of the Semantic Differential was used to measure attitudes, and 20 items from the information questionnaire (see Ch. 2) were used to measure information. A list of the Semantic Differential concepts and scales used in the experiment is found in Table 13.2.

The information questionnaire contained items such as "The best way to mental health is by avoiding morbid thoughts" and "Nervous breakdowns seldom have a physical origin." The subjects marked the amount of their agreement or disagreement with the items on a seven-point scale.

Results

Semantic Differential results were obtained for the concepts *me, psychotherapy, neurotic people, mental hospital,* and *ex-mental patient.* Scores were obtained for the *evaluation* factor and for the scales predict-

TABLE 13.1. Experimental Design for Study 1

Variable	Treatment		
Communicator	Miss *X*	Miss *Y*	
Contact	Early contact	Late contact	No contact
Personal versus impersonal styling	Personal	Impersonal	

TABLE 13.2. Mean Scores on the Semantic Differential
for the "Contact" Treatments *

Scales	Early contact	Late contact	No contact
Evaluation (worthless-valuable, dirty-clean, insincere-sincere, foolish-wise)			
Me	5.83	5.97	5.93
Psychotherapy	5.72	5.81	5.71
Neurotic people	3.64	3.67	3.77
Mental hospital	5.72	6.04	6.03
Ex-mental patient	5.35	5.55	5.53
Grand means	5.26	5.41	5.40
Unpredictable-predictable			
Me	4.42	4.79	4.61
Psychotherapy	4.03	4.46	4.00
Neurotic people	2.07	2.28	2.37
Mental hospital	4.02	4.23	4.15
Ex-mental patient	4.30	4.54	4.46
Grand means	3.77	4.06	3.92
Sick-healthy			
Me	6.18	6.33	6.26
Psychotherapy	4.00	4.34	4.22
Neurotic people	1.79	2.11	2.02
Mental hospital	2.82	3.50	2.64
Ex-mental patient	5.01	5.50	5.16
Grand means	3.96	4.36	4.06
Dangerous-safe			
Me	5.95	6.17	6.19
Psychotherapy	5.57	5.78	5.63
Neurotic people	3.20	3.45	3.47
Mental hospital	5.14	5.34	5.37
Ex-mental patient	5.32	5.43	5.37
Grand means	5.04	5.23	5.21

* The means are restricted to the range of 1.00 to 7.00. The higher the mean, the more "positive" the attitude—that is, higher means are associated with ratings of higher *evaluation*, more predictability, more health, or more safety.

able-unpredictable (which related prominently to *understandability*), sick-healthy, and dangerous-safe.

Means were obtained for each of the four scale groups for each of the five concepts for the three contact treatments. These results are presented in Table 13.2. The following results are found when the 20 variables for the early-contact, late-contact, and no-contact groups are compared. By signed-rank test, late contact results in more favorable attitudes than early contact beyond the .01 level of confidence. Late contact is better than early contact for all of the 20 possible comparisons. If a communications program on mental health requires that a former mental patient be the communicator, the results indicate that the announcement of the past treatment is better made after the communication than before.

The no-contact treatment is also better than the early-contact treatment, beyond the .01 level of confidence by signed-rank test. In addition, the late-contact treatment is slightly better than the no-contact treatment; the difference between the two treatments is significant by the signed-rank test at about the .05 level of confidence.

The results should be a warning to anyone who supposes that contact with the mentally ill necessarily promotes favorable attitudes. Of course, we investigated only one way in which contact might be employed. If contact is to be employed by the communicator, then it is important how that contact is handled. Our results indicate that if the speaker is to identify himself as being or having been mentally ill, it is better for him to do so after he has delivered the substance of his message. If the identification is made at the start of the talk, it may have a harmful effect on attitudes toward the mentally ill. Our hypothesis is that early identification allowed the subjects to discount the speaker and, hence, to offset the influence of the talk on their attitudes toward the mentally ill.

On the basis of these results, we offer the following proposition:

PROPOSITION 13.1: **If the source of a message is to be identified as being, or having been, mentally ill, it is better for the identification to be made after the substance of the message has been imparted.**

The above findings, however, must be qualified. The speaker himself is a very important element if contact is to be employed in a communication. We performed analyses of variance on the 20 variables listed in Table 13.2. For eight of the analyses, the interaction between the speaker variable and the contact variable was significant at or beyond the .05 level of confidence. The variables which show significant interaction are listed in Table 13.3. The statistical significance of the interaction terms indicates that the contact variable does not have the same effect for one speaker as it does for the other. Even though, over-all, late contact is better than no contact and both are better than early contact, the person of the speaker is very important.

TABLE 13.3. Variables Which Displayed a Significant Interaction between the "Contact" Variable and the Communicator Variable

Concept	Semantic Differential Scales
Mental hospital	health
Neurotic people	evaluation; predictableness; health
Ex-mental patient	evaluation; safety
Psychotherapy	evaluation; predictableness

TABLE 13.4. Mean Scores on the Semantic Differential for the Personal and the Impersonal Treatments *

Scales	Personal	Impersonal
Evaluation		
Me	5.95	5.88
Psychotherapy	5.74	5.76
Neurotic people	3.67	3.72
Mental hospital	6.02	5.84
Ex-mental patient	5.58	5.38
Unpredictable-predictable		
Me	4.60	4.62
Psychotherapy	4.04	4.29
Neurotic people	2.13	2.34
Mental hospital	4.01	4.25
Ex-mental patient	4.54	4.33
Sick-healthy		
Me	6.30	6.22
Psychotherapy	4.33	4.04
Neurotic people	1.89	2.06
Mental hospital	3.08	2.90
Ex-mental patient	5.29	5.15
Dangerous-safe		
Me	6.18	6.03
Psychotherapy	5.57	5.75
Neurotic people	3.26	3.48
Mental hospital	5.47	5.11
Ex-mental patient	5.55	5.20

* The means are restricted to the range of 1.00 to 7.00. The higher the mean, the more "positive" the attitude—that is, higher means are associated with ratings of higher *evaluation*, more predictability, more health, or more safety.

Personal versus impersonal treatments apparently had little, if any, effect on attitudes. The means for the two treatments for the Semantic Differential scales and concepts are presented in Table 13.4. An examination of the table indicates that the two treatments did not produce different attitudes. More findings about the personal versus impersonal variable will be presented in the next section of this chapter.

The results in general for the information questionnaire were not as clear as those for the attitude measures. There were nine items which were directly mentioned in the talk. There were no consistent differences between the various "contact" groups in terms of the information they acquired from the talks. There was a slight difference between the personal and impersonal treatments. There was an impersonal and personal treatment for the early-contact groups, for the late-contact groups, and for the no-contact groups. Considering nine items for each pair of groups, this allows us to make 27 comparisons between the personal and impersonal treatments. In only seven of these comparisons was the impersonal treatment more successful than the personal treatment in terms of moving the groups in the direction advocated by the message. This difference between treatment groups is significant by sign-test at the .05 level of confidence.

STUDY 2: PERSONAL VERSUS IMPERSONAL TREATMENTS

In numerous places so far in this book we have mentioned the message variable which concerns the personal versus impersonal treatment of topics. Topics can be discussed in such a way as to enlist the active identification of the audience, or they can be discussed in such a way as to let the audience feel remote from the events. We had thought that the variable would play an important part in the communicative effectiveness of messages designed to promote favorable attitudes toward mental-health concepts. In comparing personal and impersonal treatments, however, we have consistently found negative results. An experiment will be described which principally concerned the differential effectiveness of personal and impersonal messages.[2] Because the experiment serves only to add further negative evidence regarding the variable, it will be summarized briefly.

Design

Two versions of the same message were composed. One version was made as personal as possible; the other was made as impersonal as possible. One month before the messages were given to the subjects, the subjects were tested on a Semantic Differential form measuring attitudes toward various mental-illness concepts (mental patient, cured mental patient, and others) and toward various "normal" concepts. After the subjects read the messages, the Semantic Differential measures were administered again. Analyses were made of the amounts of attitude change produced by the messages and of the different amounts of change induced by the two versions of the message.

Messages

The personal version of the message described how the reader would react and how he would be treated if he were mentally ill. The impersonal version described how other people behave and how they are treated when they become mentally ill. The differences are illustrated by the

[2] The study was designed and conducted by Dr. Edward E. Ware.

following paragraph as it appeared in the personal and impersonal versions.

PERSONAL VERSION

Have you ever thought how it would be if you were mentally ill? How would you behave? Two of the major types of mental illness that you might have are neuroses and psychoses. A neurosis is a type of emotional illness which interferes with your happiness and efficiency. The psychoses are more severe mental illnesses. As a neurotic person you might feel that you are not loved; you might feel guilty, inferior, and inadequate without reason; you might have an almost constant sense of dread and fear. Some of the symptoms you might show are: extreme fears, like fear of high places or closed-in places; tiredness or nervous tension; excessive shyness; sleeplessness; constant fear of physical illness; inability to get along with people. Let us suppose you become psychotic instead of neurotic. In this case you might lose touch with reality and go back to childish behavior. As a pychotic you would generally be placed in a mental hospital for treatment, whereas as a neurotic you would probably be able to continue your daily business while receiving treatment.

IMPERSONAL VERSION

What is mental illness like and how do mentally-ill people behave? Two of the major types of mental illness are neuroses and psychoses. A neurosis is a type of emotional illness which interferes with a person's happiness and efficiency. The psychoses are more severe mental illnesses. Neurotic people feel that they are not loved; they feel guilty, inferior, and inadequate without reason; they have an almost constant sense of dread and fear. Some of the symptoms shown by neurotics are: extreme fears, like fear of high places or closed-in places; tiredness or nervous tension; excessive shyness; sleeplessness; constant fear of physical illness; inability to get along with people. How does the psychotic differ from the neurotic? The psychotic has lost touch with reality and goes back to childish behavior. The psychotic is generally placed in a mental hospital for treatment, whereas the neurotic generally is able to continue his daily business while receiving treatment.

Subjects and Procedures

High-school students were randomly divided into two groups corresponding to the two treatment conditions. The Semantic Differential measure was first applied alone. One month later, the experimenter returned, presented the messages, and re-administered the Semantic Differential form. For the impersonal version of the messages, 37 subjects participated in both the first and second testings. For the personal version, 34 subjects participated in both testings.

Analysis and Results

The Semantic Differential contained scales to measure *evaluation* and *understandability*. In addition, clusters of scales were used to measure "anxiety" and "safety." Means were obtained for each treatment group and for each scale applied to each concept, separately for the two testing occasions. Before-after differences were computed in order to determine the amounts of attitude change. Finally, tests of statistical significance were made on the observed differences.

Both versions of the message produced "favorable" attitude changes which were statistically significant. This was no surprise—most of our experimental messages produced favorable changes.

The important point of the experiment was to determine whether the personal and impersonal treatments produced different amounts of attitude change. The answer is clearly "no." In order to make a thorough test, we applied Hotelling's T statistic, a simultaneous test over all scales and concepts relating to mental illness. The result was not significant. The same statistic was applied to the "normal" concepts employed in the Semantic Differential form: *me, my parents,* and *most people.* Again the statistic was not significant.

On the basis of these results we offer the following proposition:

> PROPOSITION 13.2: **Personal versus impersonal treatments are not importantly related to the effectiveness of communications that are designed to promote favorable attitudes toward mental-health concepts.**

Ordinarily we do not reach major conclusions on the basis of negative results. In testing personal and impersonal treatments, however, we found negative results in a number of experiments. In the first experiment reported in this chapter personal and impersonal treatments made no significant difference in the amounts of attitude change. Moreover, this variable has little, if any, effect on the public's interest in mental-health topics (see Ch. 9). If personal and impersonal treatments have an important influence on communicative effectiveness, it is certainly difficult to demonstrate in controlled experiments. It may be that, as was suggested by the results of the "contact" study, the variable influences *information transmission* (amount of learning); but when the major experimental concern is with the variables that influence *attitudes,* as ours is here, it apparently makes little or no difference whether personal or impersonal styles are used.

STUDY 3: INFORMATION AND ATTITUDE CHANGE

The primary method of changing attitudes is to supply people with information. For example, you tell people, as we have done in some of our experiments, that schizophrenia is caused by X and is cured by Y. Then you sit back to see whether the new information has a good or a bad effect on attitudes toward the mentally ill and related concepts. Of course the problem is more complicated than that: it is necessary to determine which kinds of facts, presented in which ways, produce which kinds of attitude changes.

In this experiment,[3] an effort was made to learn some of the relations between kinds of information changes and kinds of attitude changes. Four short written messages, each supplying some correct information about one of the ten information factors discussed in Chapter 2, were distributed to our subjects. After reading one of the messages, each subject completed questionnaires measuring (1) information about mental illness and (2) attitudes toward mental-illness concepts. Analyses were made of the amounts and kinds of information and attitude changes, and comparisons were made between attitude changes and information changes.

Messages

The four messages concerned the factors *look and act different* (I), *will power* (II), *avoidance of morbid thoughts* (IV), and *hopelessness* (VI). These four factors were chosen because they are ones on which experts (psychologists and psychiatrists) are in good agreement. Predominant expert opinion disagrees with the factors. (The "incorrect" pole of each factor was purposely made the high end of the item score. See Ch. 2. Most of the factors could have easily been reversed, for example, "hopefulness" instead of hopelessness.) Two of the four messages are as follows:

HOPELESSNESS (FACTOR VI)

Mental illness has become an important health problem. Mental illness is a name covering several sicknesses of the mind which affect the way a person thinks, feels, and behaves. There are several misconceptions or mistaken beliefs about mental illness and the mentally ill. Some misinformed people still believe that mental illness is a hopeless condition. The experts, psychiatrists and psychologists, agree that this is not true. Mental illness is not a hopeless condition. Today tens of thousands of patients are being treated successfully. In those hospitals with good facilities where patients are given the best and latest treatments, as many as seven to eight out of ten leave the hospital recovered or definitely improved. With less severe mental disturbances not requiring admission to a mental hospital, the recovery rates are, of course, much higher.

---

[3] The study was designed and conducted by Dr. Edward E. Ware.

WILL POWER (FACTOR II)

Mental illness has become an important health problem. Mental ill-ness is a name covering several sicknesses of the mind which affect the way a person thinks, feels, and behaves. There are several misconceptions or mistaken beliefs about mental illness and the mentally ill. Some mis-informed people still believe that mental illness is caused largely by lack of will power. The experts, psychiatrists and psychologists, agree that this is not true. People do not become mentally ill because they have little will power. Some of the strongest-willed people become mentally ill. Tell-ing a mentally ill person to use his will power to cure himself is like telling a person with a fever to use his will power without giving him medical help. Will power alone will not cure mental illness. Most mentally ill people are incapable of controlling their thoughts and feelings. They need scien-tific treatment in order to get well.

Measures

The amount of information the subjects obtained from the messages was measured by our revised information questionnaire. (The revised questionnaire grew out of our standard 50-item information questionnaire which was described in Ch. 2. The revised form is presented and de-scribed in Appendix 2.) Two of the questionnaire items were used to measure each of the four factors. For example, to measure the *hopeless-ness* factor, the following two items were used: "There is not much that can be done for a person who develops mental disorder" and "Mental disorder is not a hopeless condition." Questionnaire items that were not related to any of the four factors were used to test for generalization of information.

To measure attitudes, a Semantic Differential form was used. Scales were employed to measure the factors of *evaluation* and *understandabil-ity,* and groups of scales were combined to measure "anxiety" and "dan-gerousness." Six concepts relating to mental illness were used: mental patient, mental hospital, cured mental patient, insane person, psychiatrist, and methods for the treatment of mental patients.

Subjects and Procedures

The subjects were 330 high-school students, randomly divided into five groups. Four groups read one of the four messages; the fifth, a control group, received no message. The numbers of subjects in a group ranged from 63 to 71.

Our routine experimental procedure was applied. Students were supplied with self-explanatory test booklets. For four of the five groups, the first section of the test booklet contained one of the four messages about mental illness. For the control group, the test booklet introduced the student directly to the information questionnaire and the Semantic Differential form.

Analysis and Results

INFORMATION. As we were sure they would, the messages affected information as evidenced on the information questionnaire. Differences between the four experimental groups and the control group were all in the predicted direction. Three of these were statistically significant either at or beyond the .05 level by *t*-test. The difference for the message pertaining to the *hopelessness* factor was not significant. (In the analysis of results we discovered an "end effect" for the *hopelessness* factor: the students as a whole disagreed so strongly with the factor that there was little room for improvement.)

Information pertaining to any one factor did not generalize to information pertaining to other factors. For example, the students who read the message pertaining to the *look and act different* factor did perform differently from the control group on items pertaining to that factor; but they did not perform differently from the control group on items pertaining to other factors represented in the information questionnaire. The failure for any generalization to occur is what we expected. The items principally concerned knowledge about mental illness, and consequently, generalization is not expected. (In contrast we expect and usually find generalization of changes in attitudes. For example, in one study we found that a message about the treatment of schizophrenia generalized to the improvement of attitudes toward psychiatrists, who were not mentioned in the message.)

ATTITUDES. Mean Semantic Differential ratings were obtained for each group of scales for each concept. As we expected, the messages about mental illness resulted in different attitude ratings than those found in the control group. Some of the statistically significant differences are shown in Table 13.5.

Table 13.5 contains an interesting finding: the messages did not always have "good" effects on attitudes. For example, the message pertaining to the *will power* factor had an over-all "bad" effect on attitudes toward the concept mental patient. This demonstrates that correct information can sometimes defeat the purpose of the communication by bringing about unfavorable changes in attitudes.

We think we know why the messages about mental illness had some "bad" effects on attitudes. The messages were not well controlled for content variables such as anxiety, solution, certainty, and destruction of information. Our principal oversight in this study (we think) was to "destroy" information, which, as is shown clearly in Chapter 12, promotes unfavorable attitudes toward mental-illness concepts. For example, in the message concerning the *will power* factor (quoted previously) we told

TABLE 13.5. Attitude Changes Occurring in Response to Messages
Concerning Information about Mental Illness *

Message concerning factor	Attitude changes induced by message
I. Look and act different	*Psychiatrist* rated more anxious.
II. Will power	*Mental patient* rated lower on *evaluation* and predictability and higher on anxiety. *Mental hospital* rated more predictable and less dangerous. *Insane person* rated more anxious. *Methods for the treatment of mental patients* rated less dangerous.
III. Avoidance of morbid thoughts	*Mental patient* rated less predictable. *Mental hospital* rated less dangerous.
IV. Hopelessness	*Mental hospital* rated more predictable and less dangerous. *Cured mental patient* rated more predictable and less anxious.

* Attitude changes are defined as differences from a control group which were statistically significant beyond the .05 level.

students that "will power" was not the answer but we supplied them with no positive information to replace what was "destroyed." Consequently, although the information in the four messages was correct, the failure to control for important content variables led to some unfavorable changes in attitudes. The notable exception is the message relating to the *hopelessness* factor, where we did supply positive information. For that message, the attitude changes are predominantly favorable.

Although more clear-cut results in other respects might have been obtained from this study had we more carefully controlled some of the important content variables, the results here serve to illustrate a common mistake in applied programs of communication. It is commonly assumed that as long as the communication is about an important issue and as long as the audience "learns" something from the communication, favorable attitudes develop toward related concepts. As the results here illustrate, however, this is not always an effective communication strategy. Even if the information in the communication is correct and even if the audience actually learns the information, the failure to control for important content variables may induce unfavorable attitudes. Thus we are able to come to the following conclusion:

PROPOSITION 13.3: **If important content variables are not controlled, correct information sometimes produces unfavorable changes in attitudes.**

This point will be pursued more fully in Chapter 17, where it will be shown that the converse holds: false information can be very effective in promoting favorable attitudes if content variables are properly manipulated.

SUMMARY

This chapter reported experimental studies which tested for the importance of three variables in communicative effectiveness: "contact" with an identified source, personal versus impersonal styling of messages, and the relationship between changes in information and changes in attitudes.

The first experiment tested for the effect of "contact" with a former mental patient on attitude change. When we compared the effectiveness of three different approaches—no contact, early contact, and late contact—we found that, if used at all, contact (in this case, identifying the source of a message as a former mental patient) is better made *after* the body of the message has been delivered.

A number of studies reported in this book dealt with a potentially important message-treatment variable: personal versus impersonal styling. In none of the studies did this variable produce differences in amount and kinds of attitude change. Differences in attitudes attributable to the personal versus impersonal styling of verbal communications were examined as an incidental aspect of the first experiment discussed in this chapter, and no significant differences were found. The second experiment discussed here was specifically designed to test the effect of personal versus impersonal styling. The results were uniformly negative and support our earlier results. Although personal and impersonal styling may influence the acquisition of *information,* or retention, and some results from our experiments suggest that this is so, such differences in treatment apparently have very little effect on *attitude* change.

The third experiment reported here explored the correlations between changes in information and changes in attitudes. Our major finding sustained our hypothesis: changes in information do not generalize beyond the information factor relating to the message. This is in contrast to changes in attitudes, where generalization usually occurs.

This experiment yielded a surprising discovery. Some of the "correct" information contained in the messages led to some *unfavorable* changes in attitudes toward mental-health concepts. We attributed this to our failure to control for several important content variables. This finding illustrates a common fallacy about the effectiveness of communications: even correct information may not effect the desired change in attitudes.

14

Stylistic Features

of Messages

A MAJOR CONCERN of our studies has been with those variables which affect the "meaning" of messages, for example, the effects of manipulating anxiety and of providing solutions. In addition to differing in meaning, messages also differ in style, such features as vocabulary, grammar, and sentence structure. These stylistic variables may have an important effect on the public's reactions to mental-health communications.

As part of our over-all research plan, we studied the stylistic features of written messages. Since early results indicated that stylistic features probably are not as important as other variables in mental-health communications, the study was relegated to a modest position in our program. Consequently we will only summarize our research, filling in the gaps of our investigations with results from other studies.

DIMENSIONS OF STYLE

Studies of written material have examined many stylistic features. In most cases stylistic features are measured by simple counts, such as the number of adjectives per 100 words, the average length of sentences, and the average number of letters in words. Some studies have used more complex measures, such as the ratio of the frequency of nouns to the frequency of adjectives, the variation in sentence length, and the average number of words between pronouns and their antecedents. In a few cases, stylistic features have been measured by the subjects' reactions, such as subjects' ratings of the interestingness of written material and measures of reading comprehension. The most widely used measures of stylistic features are the "readability" formulas, which measure the simplicity of written material and employ such indices as sentence length and word length.

182 /

In spite of the number of studies of stylistic features and the potential usefulness of such studies, little has been done to discover the basic dimensions of style. This was the purpose of our investigation.

Stylistic Variables

The first step in the investigation was to assemble a list of stylistic variables that had proved useful in previous studies. To this list we added a number of new variables. The final list contained 56 measures of stylistic variables, ten of which are printed below:

1. The Flesch readability score (a count of average sentence length in words and number of syllables per 100 words)
2. Number of similes and metaphors
3. Number of words expressive of negative evaluation such as *no, don't, horrid,* and *dislike*
4. Average number of sentences per paragraph
5. Number of qualification words such as *however, but, except,* and *if*
6. Interestingness (a measure obtained from the ratings of 20 judges)
7. *Cloze* score (a test of reading difficulty. Every fifth word was deleted from the messages and subjects filled in the blanks. The average number of correctly inserted words provided an "easiness" score.)
8. Type-token ratio (the total number of different words in a message divided by the total number of words)
9. Thorndike-Lorge word count (a measure of the frequency of occurrence of words in everyday usage)
10. Number of allness terms such as *nobody, always,* and *never*

Messages

Ideally the 56 variables should have been applied to either a random or systematic sample of everything ever written. As an approximation of this ideal, we applied the 56 variables to a highly diverse collection of 70 one-page messages collected from a wide variety of sources. Ten of these are listed below:

1. An article on sun glasses from *Consumer Reports* (1954)
2. A selection from *Triumph and Tragedy* by Winston Churchill
3. An excerpt from the New Testament
4. A personal letter
5. A section from an article describing the functions of a child-guidance clinic
6. A section from a manual on typewriter maintenance
7. An article on an election turnout from the Chicago *Tribune*
8. A statement by the late Senator Joseph McCarthy on "the Communist-ridden Truman-Acheson regime"
9. A travel pamphlet on Starved Rock State Park, Illinois
10. A section from a textbook on probability theory

Each message was limited to one double-spaced typewritten page. In most cases the selection was chosen to meet the one-page space requirement.

Measurements

The third step in the investigation was to apply the 56 measures to the 70 messages. Most of the 56 measures were objective counts of stylistic characteristics, and these measures were made accurately and fairly rapidly. Such high agreement was found among counts on the same messages by different workers that only one "counter" was used for most measurements. A group of 20 college students measured those variables which involved subjective judgments, such as "interestingness" and the *Cloze* score.

Analysis

The data consisted of scores on each of the 56 variables for each of the 70 messages. All possible intercorrelations of the stylistic variables were made. The correlations were then factor analyzed by the centroid method, and ten factors were extracted. Communalities were estimated with the highest coefficient in each column. The ten factors accounted for 62 percent of the total variance. (For those who are not familiar with the technical aspects, factor analysis is simply a means of finding groups of variables, the members of which tend to measure the same underlying attribute. Each factor can be thought of as a more general variable. Because it is more general than any single stylistic measure, it may prove to be an important dimension of writing style.)

The ten centroid factors were rotated in various ways. Analytic procedures were used on the digital computer at the University of Illinois, using first the Quartimax method and then the Varimax method. Because neither method produced the statistically neat and meaningful factors that were desired, the final rotations were done "by hand." Orthogonal rotations were used.

Results

Of the ten factors which entered the rotations, four factors, which were strong enough and meaningful enough to be given serious consideration, emerged. Of the remaining six factors, some were strong enough (had high enough loadings) but were not interpretable; the loadings of the others were too small to be useful. The four factors and the stylistic variables which load most strongly for each of them are listed below.

FACTOR 1. WORD DIFFICULTY

Loading	*Variable*
.89	Average number of one-syllable words
.87	Flesch readability score (described on p. 183)
—.78	Average word length in letters
—.77	Average number of three-syllable words
.75	Thorndike-Lorge word count (described on p. 183)
—.72	Dale-Chall readability score—average sentence length and number of words not on a list of familiar words. (In contrast to the Flesch measure, a high score on the Dale-Chall measure means difficult reading.)
—.71	Average number of words with four or more syllables
—.68	Variance of word length, obtained from the frequency distribution of lengths of words for messages
.66	Number of first- and second-person pronouns
.58	*Cloze* score (described on p. 183)

Factor 1 is concerned with the complexity, abstruseness, and difficulty of the individual words in written messages. The positive pole of the factor is oriented toward easiness of words and the negative pole is oriented toward difficulty of words.

FACTOR 2. SENTENCE DIFFICULTY

Loading	*Variable*
.84	Average sentence length in words
.72	Average sentence length in syllables
.62	Average number of words before the main verb
—.59	Number of simple sentences
.44	Variation of sentence length before the main verb

As Factor 1 is concerned with the difficulty of individual words, Factor 2 is concerned with the difficulty of sentences. Whereas on Factor 1 a high loading means "easy" for words, on Factor 2 a high loading means "difficult" for sentences.

Factors 1 and 2 show that there are two almost distinctly different elements of "reading ease." A message may employ simple words and thus be "easy" on that score; but the same message may weave the simple words into long, complex sentences and thus be difficult on that score. It is interesting that the Flesch and Dale-Chall readability formulas load heavily on Factor 1, particularly so for the Flesch formula, and that neither has a substantial loading on Factor 2. Intuitively, it would seem that a more comprehensive readability formula would place substantial weight on Factor 2 as well as on Factor 1.

FACTOR 3. NEGATIVE VERSUS POSITIVE TONE

Loading	*Variable*
.71	Number of words expressive of negative evaluation (described on p. 183)
.64	Discomfort-relief Quotient (The number of units expressive of displeasure, tension, and unhappiness, and of pleasure, relief, and happiness. DRQ = number of discomfort units ÷ number of relief units + number of discomfort units.)
.62	Evaluative common-meaning terms (a subjective count of all words that have a "good" or "bad" connotation for everyone)
—.50	Fries class III words (similar to a count of adjectives)

Whereas Factors 1 and 2 are clearly interpretable, and Factor 4 will be shown to be interpretable also, the meaning of Factor 3 is not clear. Apparently it has something to do with the pleasantness and unpleasantness of the message content. Perhaps a magazine horror story would epitomize the factor. The two most highly loaded variables concern negative feelings expressed in the message. However, the interpretation is complicated somewhat by the appearance of the other two variables which load prominently.

The count of "evaluative common-meaning terms" was admittedly subjective. The count was made by one psychologist only, and it was included mainly as a "marker variable" to help clarify the more objective measures. Included in the count were all adjectives, nouns, verbs, and adverbs which implied to the rater either "good" or "bad" states of being, words like *sickness, pretty, war, hunger, love, steal,* and *harshly.*

Considering the composition of the count for evaluative common-meaning terms, a near balance of "good" and "bad" things for all messages would be expected. The loading of the variable, .62, with Factor 3, however, tends to indicate that a preponderance of the elements counted were "bad" things. One explanation may be that the rater found it easier to identify the "bad" elements. Or it may be that, in fact, evaluation in messages is more often negative than positive.

The interpretation of Factor 3 is complicated further by the loading of —.50 of Fries class III words (which is much like a count of adjectives). If the factor interpretation is correct, then evidently adjectives are more often "positive" than "negative." Conversely, negative tone is more often expressed with nonadjectival forms, such as nouns (*war*) and verbs (*distrust*). Is the association of pleasant tone with adjectives an artifactual property of our study, or does it reflect a more basic property of our written language? Clearly, Factor 3 should be investigated further before sure interpretations are made. The most that can be said now is that the factor in some way concerns the pleasantness and unpleasantness of message content.

FACTOR 4. READERSHIP APPEAL

Loading	Variable
.71	How well liked in general
.71	Interestingness of subject matter
.69	How well written

Factor 4 is a factor only in a restricted sense. All of the highly loaded variables were rated by the same subjects—a group of 20 college students. For example, they rated how well they liked each of the messages in general, and the mean rating for each message constituted a score. The loadings above show that there is a strong factor, or cluster, of "appeal."

In this study, the three variables that define Factor 4 correlate very little with the variables that define Factors 1, 2, and 3. (More evidence on this point will be given in the next section of this chapter.) Because of the particular kinds of subjects (college students) used to define Factor 4, however, it is unsafe to say that "appeal" is not generally related to Factors 1 through 3. For example, if ratings of "appeal" were made by persons with little formal education, such ratings might correlate negatively with the degree of word difficulty and sentence difficulty. Although from this study we cannot reach generalized conclusions about the relationship of "appeal" to stylistic variables, except for college students, the results leave little doubt that a factor of general appeal exists.

Factor Scores

In the factor rotations, the axes were kept orthogonal, and, consequently, the factors per se are uncorrelated. Before using the factors either in new research or in practical work, we had to estimate factor scores for messages. Although precise estimates can be made if time and resources permit, it is usually necessary to employ relatively simple approximations. Approximate factor scores for Factors 1 through 4 were obtained by simply averaging scores over some of the variables on each factor. There are several standards that should be employed in choosing the variables to be used in estimating factor scores. First, the variables to be chosen should load heavily on the particular factor. Second, the variables to be chosen should have negligible loadings on factors other than the one to be estimated. Third, after considering points 1 and 2, the variables to be chosen should be easy to measure. For example, we did not use *Cloze* scores to estimate Factor 1 because they are difficult and time-consuming measures to apply. The variables which were used to estimate factor scores are as follows:

FACTOR 1. WORD DIFFICULTY

Average number of one-syllable words
Average word length in letters (measure inverted)
Thorndike-Lorge word count
Average number of words with four or more syllables (inverted)

FACTOR 2. SENTENCE DIFFICULTY

Average sentence length in syllables
Average sentence length in words
Number of simple sentences (inverted)
Average sentence length before the main verb

FACTOR 3. NEGATIVE VERSUS POSITIVE TONE

Number of words expressive of negative evaluation
Discomfort-Relief Quotient
Evaluative common-meaning terms

For the reasons discussed previously, future studies may show that it was a mistake to include "evaluative common-meaning terms" in the group of variables used to estimate factor scores. If so, either the remaining two variables above should be used alone, or the two should be augmented by other variables which prove to be related to the factor.

FACTOR 4. READERSHIP APPEAL

Interestingness of subject matter
How well written
How well liked in general

Although the orthogonal factors, by definition, are uncorrelated, factor estimates usually correlate to some extent. The correlations between the four sets of estimated factor scores for our 70 messages are presented in Table 14.1. If, as we suggested, scores for the factors are estimated as described above, the correlations between the sets of factor scores are worthy of inspection.

The results in Table 14.1 show that the correlations for Factor 3 are too small to be of practical or theoretical importance. Factor 3 is almost totally unrelated to the other three factors. Consequently, if Factor 3 is an important dimension of writing style, it is interestingly unrelated to the other dimensions found in the study. Because Factor 4 is based on judgments, and because all the judges were college students, the correlations between the estimates for Factor 4 and those for the other three factors should not be taken seriously as indicating the usual relationships to be found in samples of readers. For this particular group of college students, the correlations show that more difficult words and more difficult sentences tend to raise "readership appeal." As was mentioned previously, the reverse may be true for people with only a small amount of formal schooling.

The most important piece of information in Table 14.1 is the correlation of —.41 between word difficulty and sentence difficulty. Because Factor 1 is oriented toward word easiness, it can be said that "difficulty" in words and in sentences correlates positively to the amount of .41. It is interesting that the correlation is not larger. As was said previously, the two do not necessarily go together.

Results from Other Studies

The results from two other studies of stylistic variables are worth discussing in the context of this chapter. Stolurow and Newman performed a study similar to our own in 1959. Their analysis was made on data which had been collected earlier by Gray and Leary (1935), who had applied 44 stylistic measures to 48 paragraphs and computed correlations among all the stylistic variables. Stolurow and Newman weeded out what appeared to be duplicating variables from the list, retaining 23 of the 44 variables. Their factor analysis of the 23 by 23 correlation matrix revealed only two strong and clearly interpretable factors. Their first factor, concerning the "relative difficulty of words" is very much like our Factor 1. Their second factor, a "difficult versus easy sentence" factor, is very much like our Factor 2.

Another study (Carroll, 1958) also relates importantly to the discussion in this chapter. As in our study and the Stolurow and Newman study, Carroll performed a factor analysis of stylistic variables. Carroll's study differs principally in that a large share of the stylistic measures consisted of ratings and reactions by judges to the message content. Employing Semantic Differential ratings, he required judges, for example, to rate messages as relatively good versus bad, pleasant versus unpleasant, abstract versus concrete, and so on. In all, the judges applied a broad col-

TABLE 14.1. Correlations between Estimates of Factor Scores

		Factor			
		1	2	3	4
Factor	1	—	—.41	—.07	—.40
	2	—.41	—	—.08	.31
	3	—.07	—.08	—	.15
	4	—.40	.31	.15	—

lection of 29 Semantic Differential scales to each message. To these subjective measures were added 39 objective measures, confined almost entirely to counts of various parts of speech found in the messages. The 68
measures were applied to a diverse collection of 150 written samples, each
300 words long.

Because Carroll placed major emphasis on subjective ratings and
because most of his factors are dominated by those ratings, his results
serve more to augment rather than to validate our factors. The most
prominent factor found by Carroll concerns scales such as good-bad,
pleasant-unpleasant, and interesting-boring. The factor which he tentatively named "general stylistic appeal" is clearly related to the "readership-
appeal" factor which we found.

In addition to the "stylistic-appeal" factor, Carroll found two other
relatively clear factors which are dominated by subjective ratings. One
is tentatively designated "seriousness" and is characterized by ratings like
earnest-flippant, serious-humorous, and profound-superficial. Another
factor is tentatively designated "ornamentation" and is characterized by
scales like florid-plain, wordy-succinct, and lush-austere.

One of Carroll's factors, tentatively designated "personal appeal," is
determined primarily by objective measures rather than by Semantic
Differential ratings. The two most heavily loaded variables are the
number of pronouns and the number of personal pronouns. The meaning
of the factor is clarified by the fact that high loadings also occur for the
Semantic Differential scales personal-impersonal and intimate-remote.

In our analysis we detected signs of a "personal versus impersonal"
factor, although we could not document it clearly enough to offer it as part
of the results, possibly because our study had an insufficient number of
variables relating to "personal appeal." The clear-cut findings by Carroll,
and common sense, strongly support the existence of a "personal-appeal"
factor in written material. (We assumed the existence of such a factor in
some of the experimental studies reported in previous chapters.)

COMPARISONS OF DIFFERENT KINDS OF MESSAGES

One way to learn about and judge the importance of stylistic variables
is to apply them to different kinds of written material. We performed
three such small studies with our four factors. As a small exploratory
study, Factors 1, 2, and 3 were applied to samples of the content of three
magazines: *Time, Newsweek,* and *U.S. News and World Report.* To control for content, write-ups of the same stories and events were selected
from the three magazines. Only one small difference among the magazines
was found: they differ slightly on Factor 1, "word difficulty."

More important than the differences among the magazines is the fact
that they received very similar ratings on the factors. Perhaps writers and

editors of the three have, in a sense, taken such stylistic factors into account and have tried to achieve ideal levels.

A more substantial study was made to compare the stylistic features of suicide notes with personal letters. A collection of suicide notes and personal letters was available from another communication study. Ten of each were chosen, with the writers approximately matched for sex and age. Factors 1, 2, and 3 were applied. (Factor 4 was not applied because it requires the use of judges and is thus too time consuming.)

The results from the study help to clarify the meanings of our factors. Suicide notes are higher on Factor 3, indicating that they have higher "negative tone"—a classic example of "construct validation." Suicide notes are less "difficult" on both Factors 1 and 2, which tends to indicate that when people are under stress, they resort to highly "readable," simple forms of writing. (Some implications of this point for mental-health communications will be discussed later.)

A third small study was performed with the 70 one-page messages used in the factor-analysis study. Seventeen of the 70 messages were intentionally chosen to represent topics relating to mental health and illness (for example, the description of a child-guidance clinic, a section from a textbook on mental hygiene, and a pamphlet about treatment facilities in mental hospitals). To provide some suggestions about the stylistic features of mental-health messages, on each of our four stylistic factors the 17 mental-health topics were compared with the 53 topics which were not related to mental health. Significant differences were found on two of the factors: "word difficulty" and "negative versus positive tone." The mental-health topics had more "difficult" words and more "negative tone." Because of the size of the sample of messages and the way in which the sample was obtained, the comparison could not provide firm conclusions. Nevertheless, the results suggest that messages relating to mental health and illness tend to be prolix and essentially negative in tone. This tends to support two points which were made in previous chapters: (1) there is a "terminological barrier" between mental-health professionals and the public, and (2) messages about mental illness tend to create anxiety.

AN EXPERIMENTAL STUDY OF STYLISTIC EFFECTS

A rather complex experiment was undertaken to determine the effects of stylistic factors.[1] Some of the factors used in the study were not the same as those reported earlier in the chapter, because some rotations were performed after the experiment was undertaken. Only two factors were used: Factor 1, "word difficulty," and Factor 3, "negative versus positive tone."

A direct way to explore the meaning of our stylistic factors is to vary

[1] The study was designed and conducted by Dr. T. R. Husek.

the factors in a controlled manner and to determine the different effects on readers. The purpose of the experiment was to answer such questions as: How will readers' reactions vary if the "word difficulty" of a particular message is increased? Will the message be more interesting, or more difficult to comprehend? If word difficulty is increased, will it affect attitudes toward characters portrayed in the message, for example by engendering more favorable attitudes toward mental patients.

Messages

Three of the 70 messages used in our factor analysis were employed in the experiment. All three messages were about mental-health problems, concerning marital adjustment, the treatment of emotional problems, and child-guidance clinics. The three messages were near average on "word difficulty" and "negative versus positive tone." Four additional versions of each message were made. Two versions were composed for "word difficulty," one high and the other low. ("Word difficulty" was manipulated by substituting some difficult words for easier ones where difficulty was to be increased, and vice versa where difficulty was to be decreased.) Similarly two versions of each article were written for "tone." ("Negative versus positive tone" was manipulated by substituting some "negative" terms for "positive" terms and vice versa.) The factor measures were applied to the new versions, all of which were at least two standard deviations in the desired direction from the mean on the respective factors. This shows in a direct way that the altered versions accomplished their purposes. There were, then, 15 messages, five for each topic: the original (or average) version and the high and low versions for each of the two stylistic factors.

Subjects and Procedure

Each of the 15 messages was administered to eight students at the University of Illinois. The students were told only that they were "to participate in a study of writing styles." After they had read their respective messages, various measures were applied. Students answered a comprehension test concerning information stated or implied in the message. A different test was used for each of the three topics, the same one being used for the five versions of each topic. After the comprehension test, a Semantic Differential measure was applied. The form used two concepts: (1) "the message you have just read" and (2) a concept relating to the subject matter, for example, "family life" for the marital-adjustment topic. The first concept was more concerned with the style of the message; the second, with the content of the message. Subjects were also asked to rate the extent to which they would or would not like to read more about the material in the messages.

Analysis and Results

Corresponding to each "effect" measure used in the study was a 3 by 3 by 2 analysis-of-variance design (three topics, three factor levels, and two factors). Separate analyses were made for the comprehension test and for the question concerning "reading more." For the Semantic Differential results, 30 separate analyses of variance were made, one for each of 15 scales for each of two concepts. The complete results are far too bulky and not important enough in the present context to be presented in detail. Consequently, only the outstanding results will be mentioned. Before these are cited, a warning should be given: because of the large number of statistical analyses that were made, some of the apparently "significant" results may be due to "taking advantage of chance."

High "word-difficulty" and high "negative-tone" versions of both topics tended to receive "good" ratings. For example, the versions with more difficult words were rated as more intelligent, powerful, and smooth. The versions with high "negative tone" were rated as more interesting and rated more highly on the "read-more" scale. In summary, high "word-difficulty" and high "negative-tone" messages were generally liked better than the other versions.

In contrast to the findings from the "word-difficulty" factor, the three versions of the "negative-versus-positive-tone" factor produced differences in comprehension-test scores. The students seemed to comprehend less from the high negative versions than from the average and low versions. Perhaps the negative tone distracted the readers from the factual content of the messages.

One confirming piece of evidence was found for the interpretation given for Factor 3 ("negative versus positive tone"): the high negative versions were rated as more tense on the tense-relaxed scale of the Semantic Differential.

There is a cardinal limitation to the specific findings reported in the experiment: the results are probably somewhat particular to college students. The over-all results tend to indicate that the students like difficult and disturbing messages. Some of our studies of the general population show different trends (see Ch. 9).

Regardless of the limited generality of particular results from the study, a very general finding occurred which may transcend samples of subjects and may have important implications. As was mentioned previously, subjects were required to rate two concepts on the Semantic Differential: one pertaining to the message as written material and the other pertaining to the central character or the central theme of the subject matter (such as "family life" in one of the three topics). The finding is that much larger differences occur (in response to factor variations) for the message itself than for ideas or characters in the messages. To test this finding, an over-all analysis of variance was done for "the message you have just read," simultaneously considering all 15 scales, all three topics, both factors, and all three levels on each factor. The same type of analysis was made for concepts relating to the subject matter. The results of the former are highly significant (beyond the .0005 level by F-ratio test). The results from the latter are not statistically significant (.45 level).

CONCLUSIONS

The results indicate that our stylistic factors influence reactions to *how* messages are written but do not appreciably influence reactions to the ideas and characters portrayed in the messages. This is one of the reasons why stylistic variables are probably not as important as content variables in the communication of mental-health information. For such content variables as relative certainty, anxiety, and solution, different treatment levels do influence reactions to the ideas and characters portrayed in messages. For example, a high-anxiety message induces readers to rate ideas and persons in the message (such as treatment of mental patients and psychiatrists) as more tense and anxious, and as less safe (see Ch. 10).

Regarding their influence on public attitudes toward mental-health concepts, stylistic variables are probably important to the extent that they interact with content variables. The amount of "negative tone" (Factor 3) probably correlates with the amount of message anxiety and, to the extent that it does, negative tone may influence the meanings of mental-health concepts. When negative tone is high and/or the topic is anxiety-provoking, difficult words and difficult sentences may accentuate the inherent anxiety associated with the topic. This conclusion comes in part from the study of suicide notes, where it was found that, because of the stressful situation, the writers chose simple words and simple sentences. The difficulty of both words and sentences may correlate with the amount of "solution" and the conceived "certainty" in mental-health messages, and, if so, these two stylistic factors may indirectly affect the meaning of mental-health concepts.

Some implications of our studies for public-information programs are relatively clear. As was made explicit in Chapter 11, there is a terminology barrier between mental-health experts and the public. Moreover, the public is relatively uninformed about mental-health issues. Yet, we found that mental-health messages tend to have relatively high "word difficulty." In information programs intended for the public at large, therefore, it would probably be wise to make messages as "easy" as possible by lowering both word difficulty and sentence difficulty.

Regarding Factor 3, "negative versus positive tone," there is some evidence to indicate that high negative tone in mental-health messages tends to make readers somewhat anxious. But if the communications are to increase public interest in mental-health and to engender more positive attitudes, a high level of message anxiety is generally "bad" (see Chs. 9 and 10). Consequently, it would probably be wise to diminish the amount of negative tone in messages intended for wide public consumption.

Mental-health messages should be written to obtain high "readership appeal" (Factor 4). Although our analyses show that a general factor of appeal exists (similar results were found by Carroll), the results unfortunately provide no concrete techniques for increasing readership appeal. After messages have been composed, however, it is a sound practice to measure the amount of appeal; only appealing messages should be transmitted to the public.

Although the studies in this chapter, taken individually, do not have important implications for communicating mental-health information, the total results suggest four rules (which we call "propositions") for dealing with stylistic variables:

> PROPOSITION 14.1: Stylistic variables are important determiners of attitudes toward mental-health concepts only to the degree that they interact with content variables such as message anxiety, relative solution, and relative certainty.

> PROPOSITION 14.2: Mental-health messages aimed at the general public should have relatively low "word difficulty" and "sentence difficulty."

> PROPOSITION 14.3: Mental-health messages aimed at the general public should usually have low "negative tone."

> PROPOSITION 14.4: Mental-health messages should be tested for "readership appeal" before they are used in public-information programs.

SUMMARY

In this chapter were described some studies which attempted to determine (1) some of the basic dimensions of stylistic characteristics of written messages and (2) the influence of stylistic factors on information transmission and attitude change. The major finding was that stylistic factors do not have an important direct effect on attitude change, but they do have some important indirect effects. Stylistic factors may be important to the extent that they interact with content characteristics such as anxiety, relative solution, and relative certainty, because these do have a direct effect on attitudes. Also, stylistic factors have definite effects on the readability and interest value of messages, and these are very important variables to consider in their own right.

15

The Permanence of Information

and Attitude Change

MOST OF THE EXPERIMENTS reported in this book are short-range investigations of information and attitude change. In a typical study, high-school students were asked to read short written messages about some aspect of mental illness. The messages were structured to determine the effects of high-anxiety versus low-anxiety treatments and other content variables. Immediately after reading the messages, the effects of the messages were measured by questionnaires.

The real purpose of our research is to discover principles that work effectively not only in the short run but also in the long run. Ideally, all of our experiments should extend over a period of years, with follow-up investigations of the same subjects at regular intervals. Such long-range studies, however, are impractical at the present stage of communications research.

It has been necessary for us to perform many different studies in order to weave a net of interconnected findings. Only in this way can the short-comings in particular experimental designs be overcome and broad principles of communications be devised. Consequently, it was more important for us to try many variations on the same theme than to study exhaustively the impact of one or two sets of experimental procedures and messages. For example, we explored the effect of "solution" versus "no solution" in four different studies performed on different kinds of subjects, and all of the results point to the conclusion that no-solution messages are "bad" in most communications about mental illness. We regard such a multifaceted approach as more meaningful at the present stage of communications research than a longitudinal study employing only one experimental design.

One way to think about the longevity of communication effects is to regard each communication as a "dose." We usually employed small doses of communication, with each dose compounded of known content characteristics. Our small-dose experiments can be contrasted with our studies using high-school students in psychology and mental-hygiene courses. (The studies are outlined in Chapter 16 and are described in more detail in Chapter 17.) During the four-month duration of the psychology courses, the students read about and discussed various topics concerning mental illness, adjustment, and personality development. The students received much larger doses of communication in their psychology courses than in our communication experiments.

Not only did the doses differ in size, they differed in degree of control. Whereas the doses employed in our experiments were controlled in the sense that some content variables were deliberately manipulated and others were held constant, the doses in the studies conducted in high-school courses were not well controlled—different teachers and texts were involved; some students studied more than others; and other uncontrolled variables were present.

The contrast between the amounts and kinds of communication doses in the high-school studies and in our experiments provided us with an opportunity to learn about the permanence of attitude and information change. Two relevant studies will be discussed in this chapter.

CHANGES AFTER PARTICIPATING IN PSYCHOLOGY COURSES

The purpose of the studies of high-school students in psychology and mental-hygiene courses was to discover some principles of change which transcend the particularities of communication situations. In these studies we were not so much interested in what makes people change but in *how* people change. By combining results obtained from different schools and from different sections in the same school, we were able to devise some general principles concerning the change of mental-health information and attitudes toward mental-health concepts. The principles are discussed in Chapters 16 and 17.

In all of our studies of high-school psychology courses, a standard procedure was employed. At the beginning of the semester, two major measuring instruments were administered—the information questionnaire and a Semantic Differential measure of attitudes toward mental-health concepts. At the end of the semester, the same measures were re-applied. Students were told only that the instruments were part of a survey of public opinion being conducted at the University of Illinois. They were not told that repeat measures would be made later.

In order to study the permanence of information and attitude change, some of the high-school classes were followed up. Students from two high schools were used in the study. In high school A, 36 students from three sections of a psychology course were given repeat measures one year after the course was completed. In high school B, 67 students from four sections of a psychology course were given repeat measures six months after the course was completed. The measures were given in the schools for those students who were still in attendance; they were mailed to those who had completed high school by the time of the follow-up.

For comparison purposes, the same measures were applied to a control group of 58 students in art courses in school A. The measures were administered at the beginning of the semester and repeated at the end of the semester. The control group was not followed up after the end of the semester. (Because of some results which will be described in the following sections, we now wish that we had made repeat measures six months or one year later.) It is important to emphasize that the same information questionnaire and Semantic Differential form were administered on all occasions to all groups.

Analysis and Results

In the analyses of results, comparisons were made of the responses of the *same* students at different times. As is inevitably the case, some of the students who participated at the first testing session were not available at later testing sessions. These students were not included in the analyses.

INFORMATION. Only part of the results obtained from the information questionnaire are important to the present discussion. Ten of the information items form a "test" of correctness of information, which is scored in terms of ratings given on the same items by psychologists and psychiatrists. Mean scores on the test were obtained for each group at each testing time. The results are presented in Table 15.1.

Table 15.1 shows average combined results for the psychology classes in schools A and B. A low score on the test means "correct" information; the minimum (good) score is 2.33 and the maximum (bad) score is 46.95. The trend is for psychology students to improve over time, although the differences in "correctness" scores over time are not large in an absolute sense. (Even if the movement toward correct information was not large, it should not be assumed that changes on the information-questionnaire items were small. As will be shown later, changes on individual items

TABLE 15.1. Mean Scores of High-school Students
on Mental-health Information Test *

Group	Beginning of semester	End of semester	Six months to one year later
Psychology courses ($N = 103$)	7.24	6.70	6.36
Nonpsychology courses ($N = 58$)	7.37	6.80	not tested

* A low score implies "correct" information.

were usually large, although not always toward more correct information.)

Table 15.1 shows an interesting result: the control group improved approximately the same amount as the groups participating in the psychology courses. For several reasons, it is not wise to make extensive interpretations about the results shown in Table 15.1. First, the information "test" should not be taken too seriously as a measure of learning. It was intended only as a gross measure of differences between samples of subjects. (Studies show that the test correlates well with years of schooling and intelligence-test scores.) Second, the differences shown in Table 15.1 are not striking enough to support major conclusions. Third, the relationships between amounts and kinds of information change and attitude change are complicated. As was shown in Chapter 13, correct information sometimes leads to "bad" attitude changes. As will be shown in Chapter 17, false information sometimes leads to "good" attitude changes.

ATTITUDES. Because the complete results of the Semantic Differential test are bulky and some of them are not relevant to the immediate issue, they have been relegated to Appendix 8. Some of the over-all results are presented in Tables 15.2 and 15.3. Five concepts relating to mental illness were used in the Semantic Differential form: insane people, neurotic people, ex-mental patient, psychotherapy, and mental hospital. In addition, the following "normal" concepts were used: me, my parents, most people, and old man. In Table 15.2, average ratings are shown for all five mental-illness concepts combined. Mean ratings are shown separately for the factors of *evaluation* and *understandability* and for the scales tense-relaxed, sick-healthy, and dangerous-safe. The table is arranged so that a large mean indicates "good" ratings.

Looking at the results for the combined psychology courses in Table 15.2, several findings are apparent. The students developed more favorable attitudes during the semester, and they apparently continued to "improve" during the six-month to one-year interval between the end of the course and the follow-up test. Surprisingly the control group also tended to develop more favorable attitudes toward mental-health concepts.

The trends toward more favorable attitudes are shown more directly in Table 15.3. There, mean ratings are obtained for the five mental-illness concepts over the three scales where change would be considered "desirable"—*evaluation, understandability,* and the scale dangerous-safe. (There is no compelling reason why the mental-illness concepts should be rated as more relaxed or more healthy.)

Table 15.3 shows the same trends noted in Table 15.2. The students in psychology courses underwent favorable changes in attitudes from the beginning to the end of the semester. Of the 30 differences between individual means (three scales, two high schools, and five concepts) only two of the "after" means are lower than the "before" means. Also, six months to one year later, the students who participated in the psychology courses continued to develop more favorable attitudes. By the type of comparison mentioned above, the means at final testing are significantly greater than the means at the end of the semester (beyond the .01 level by signed-ranks test). Taken by themselves, these are very encouraging findings. They indicate that psychology courses in high school can bring favorable changes in attitudes toward mental-health concepts and that even more favorable attitudes grow after the course is completed. There is one large fly in the ointment: the control group also developed more favorable attitudes during the one-semester period (differences significant beyond the 0.5 level by signed-rank test), improving by exactly the same amount as the psychology students.

The finding that the control group improved as much as the psychology students raises some serious questions about the methodology of the study. There are two reasonable explanations for the "improvement" shown by the control group. First, they may have profited sufficiently by the four months of maturing (during the time the "experimental" groups were participating in psychology courses) and by continuing their general education to develop "better" attitudes toward mental-health concepts. Or, the apparent trend toward more favorable attitudes and more correct information may have been conditioned by the impact of our questionnaire instruments.

It is doubtful that the first possible explanation is correct. We might have expected the control group to learn slightly more correct information, as was shown in Table 15.1. Correctness of information does cor-

TABLE 15.2. Mean Semantic Differential Ratings of Five Mental-health Concepts by High-school Students in Psychology Courses and High-school Students Not in Psychology Courses

	Students participating in psychology courses (N = 103)			Students not participating in psychology courses (N = 58)	
	Beginning of semester	End of semester	Six months to one year later	Beginning of semester	End of semester
Rating: *					
Evaluation	5.08	5.30	5.48	4.66	5.04
Tense-relaxed	3.08	3.42	3.35	3.22	3.42
Understandability	3.23	3.52	3.62	3.40	3.56
Sick-healthy	3.49	3.61	3.83	3.44	3.58
Dangerous-safe	4.50	4.78	4.84	4.10	4.32
Column means	3.88	4.13	4.22	3.76	3.98

* High means indicate "good ratings." Thus means of 7.00 would imply highest evaluation, understandability, and completely "relaxed," "healthy," and "safe."

TABLE 15.3. Mean Semantic Differential Ratings of High-school Students Averaged Over Five Mental-health Concepts, Over the Factors of *Evaluation* and *Understandability,* and the Scale Dangerous-Safe

Group	Beginning of semester	End of semester	Six months to one year later
Psychology courses ($N = 103$)	4.27	4.53	4.65
Nonpsychology courses ($N = 58$)	4.05	4.31	not tested

relate positively with years of schooling; and between the first and second administration of the information questionnaire, all of the students had completed a half-year of high-school study. However, there is little reason to expect changes in *attitudes* as large as those reflected in the Semantic Differential results. As was shown in Chapter 4, attitudes toward mental-health concepts are affected very little by education.

The most reasonable explanation of the apparent tendency for the control group to develop more favorable attitudes is that the mere administration of our questionnaires tends to promote more favorable ratings of mental-health concepts. If this is so, an important question is whether the more favorable ratings engendered by the questionnaires alone are real changes in feeling or only artifactual properties of the measuring instruments. This point will be discussed more fully after the results from another study are presented.

THE PERMANENCE OF ATTITUDE CHANGE IN A CONTROLLED EXPERIMENT

We did not think that experiments using small communications doses (one-page messages, for example) would have lasting effects on subjects. Our hope was to create a temporary mood in each experiment which would indicate small effects of different treatments of messages. For example, when the amount of anxiety was varied in different versions of a message, our only hope was that the relative states of anxiety would last long enough to show their effects on questionnaire instruments administered immediately afterwards. However, we are no longer sure that small doses of communication have only small and temporary effects. As the experiment will show, the attitude changes brought about by one-page written messages are relatively large and can last for at least two and one half months, and perhaps indefinitely.

To study the permanence of attitude change, we chose a content variable which has definite effects on attitudes—"certainty," the degree to which the message is stated in a sure versus an unsure manner. Message certainty was discussed in detail in Chapter 12, where it was shown that the higher the certainty, the more favorable the attitudes engendered toward mental-health concepts.

The experiment to be discussed here used the same experimental materials employed in the first two studies discussed in Chapter 12; however, we also administered follow-up measures two weeks and two and one half months later to determine the permanence of the effects of the experimental treatments.

Messages

Two one-page messages about mental illness were used in the study—one about the treatment of schizophrenia and the other about tranquilizing drugs. For each of the two messages, a high-certainty version and a low-certainty version were composed. The two versions differed only by the substitution of a few words and phrases. (A more complete description of the messages is given in Ch. 12.) As a basis of comparison for the messages about mental illness, two control messages were used, neither of which dealt with mental illness.

Subjects and Procedures

In the study we followed the routine procedure which we employed in experiments with high-school students. We randomly assigned 135 students to one of the six message treatments (two versions of two messages about mental illness, varied for certainty level, and two control messages). The students were told only that they were "participating in a study of writing styles."

Immediately after reading their respective messages, students were asked to fill out a Semantic Differential form. In the form, the *evaluation* and *understandability* factors and other groups of scales were applied to the following concepts relating to mental illness: psychiatrist, mental patient, a person who has schizophrenia, tranquilizing drugs, mental illness, and ways of treating mental illness.

After the students completed the Semantic Differential, the experimenter thanked them and left without mentioning that repeat measures would be made later. The teachers also did not know that repeat measures would be made later.

Two weeks later, the experimenter returned and administered the same Semantic Differential form used previously. The students were asked "to respond to some questions about the material you read previously." Again the students were given no suggestion that the experimenter would return later. Two months later, the Semantic Differential form was administered again.

Analysis and Results

Mean Semantic Differential ratings were obtained for the high-certainty, low-certainty, and control messages on each of the three testing occasions. The most meaningful way to look at the results is in terms of the over-all effect of the different message treatments. This is done by adding together the mean ratings given to all the mental-illness concepts. To do this, we left out the concept *mental illness* when averaging over the *evaluation* factor, because there was no reason to expect that high-certainty messages should make students regard mental illness as "good." (Nevertheless, the present study reaches the same conclusions whether *mental illness* is included or left out. As a matter of fact, the trend is so stable that it is apparent even when each concept is considered separately or when concepts are added together in different combinations.)

Figure 15.1 shows the mean evaluations of the five mental-health concepts on each of the three occasions for each of the three message treatments (135 students participating). As was shown in Chapter 12, on the first testing occasion a high-certainty message promotes more favorable attitudes than does a low-certainty message, and both do better than control messages. The important question here is "How do the differences hold up over time?" The results shown in Figure 15.1 indicate that the differential effects of the three treatment conditions were maintained over the two-and-one-half-month span.

The results shown in Figure 15.1 make a very severe test of the permanence of attitude changes. Some of the five mental-illness concepts, *psychiatrist,* for example, were not mentioned in the two messages about mental illness. Figure 15.1 shows not only attitude changes toward specific concepts mentioned in the messages but also the amount of generalization to concepts not mentioned in the messages. (We usually find that the differential effects of message variables generalize to concepts not mentioned in the messages.) A more meaningful comparison is made in Figure 15.2 which compares the results for the two concepts which were mentioned directly in the two mental-illness messages—*a person who has schizophrenia* and *tranquilizing drugs.*

After looking at the results shown in Figure 15.2, there is little doubt that (1) a high-certainty message is better than a low-certainty message, (2) both are better than control messages, and (3) the effect is lasting. On each of the three testing occasions, the differences between each of the three message treatments were significant at the .05 level or beyond. Even after two and one half months, the high-certainty message maintained its superiority over the low-certainty message, and both remained superior to the control messages. Before discussing the importance of these findings in detail, let us look at an unexpected finding from the study.

The first study discussed in this chapter showed that the attitudes

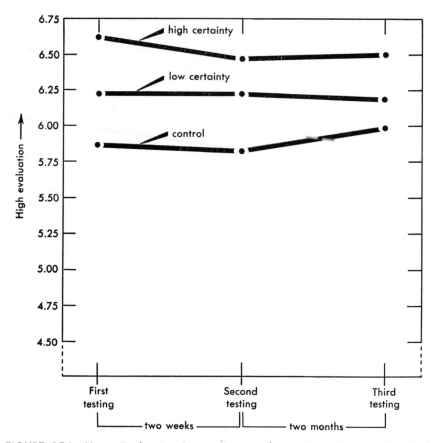

FIGURE 15.1. Mean *Evaluation* Scores Averaged over Five Concepts for Each of Three Treatment Conditions on Each of Three Occasions

and information of control groups improved over time. The second study tends to show the same thing. The apparent trend is for the control groups to develop more favorable attitudes over the two-and-one-half-month period (see Figs. 15.1 and 15.2). The mean difference between first and third testing is significant beyond the .05 level. If the trend had been found in only one study, we would not seriously consider it. Because we find similar results in two studies, an explanation is required.

We are not sure why control groups tend to "improve" over time. As was said previously, there are several reasons why the "improvement" is probably not due to the time lapse alone. Our hypothesis is that our measuring instruments, by themselves, induce people to change. We think that our subjects, after filling-out the information questionnaire and Semantic Differential form, were stirred to think about mental illness, treatment methods, and the "mental" professions. We hypothesized earlier

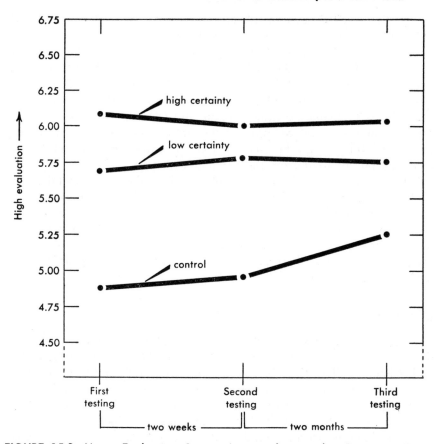

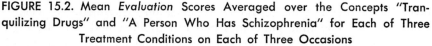

FIGURE 15.2. Mean *Evaluation* Scores Averaged over the Concepts "Tranquilizing Drugs" and "A Person Who Has Schizophrenia" for Each of Three Treatment Conditions on Each of Three Occasions

that people do not often think about problems relating to mental illness, do not discuss the subject frequently, and do not actively seek information about it. It simply may be that when people are stimulated to think about problems relating to mental illness, they develop more constructive attitudes.

Unfortunately, only during the last days of our research did we become aware of the tendency for control groups to "improve" over time. Otherwise, we would have studied the problem in more detail. An interesting study would be to provoke people to think about mental illness by asking them questions (either on printed forms or in interviews) like, "What do most people think about the mentally ill?," "How does mental illness develop?," and "How does the community treat mental patients who are returning to society?" Perhaps that approach would prove to be an effective way to induce people to learn about and develop more favorable attitudes toward mental-illness concepts.

The results for the control groups relate to a methodological point discussed in Chapter 1. There it was said that we found fault with the before-after experimental design for communications studies. The before-after design consists of (1) applying measures of attitude and/or information, (2) giving a communication, and (3) measuring the effect of the communication by re-applying the initial measures. We were suspicious of this design because "before" measures may affect "after" measures purely apart from the communication.

In the early phases of our research, we chose the experimental versus control design for general use. In this design, no "before" measures are made. The effect of the experimental communication is determined by comparison with a control group, either a group which receives no message or a group which receives a "neutral" message. Because subjects are tested only once, there is no chance for results to be contaminated by influences from "before" measures.

DISCUSSION

In none of our studies do we show that control groups improve during very short periods of time, such as one day or two weeks. In the high-school studies, the change was detected only after about four months. In the experiment discussed above, the "improvement" of the control group was observable only after two and one half months. However, the demonstration that "before" measures *can* have a pronounced effect on later measures should lend additional caution to those who favor the before-after design for communication experiments, especially if a relatively long time intervenes between the first and later testings.

Aside from the interesting questions raised by the behavior of control groups in communications studies, both studies reported in this chapter show that (1) attitudes toward mental-health concepts can be improved and (2) the improvement lasts. In the high-school studies some questions remain as to whether or not the participation in psychology courses had anything to do with the favorable changes in attitudes. In the experiment reported in this chapter, the results are clearer: although the control group "improved," the two experimental treatments continued to be "superior."

The "certainty" experiment shows that our small-dosage communication studies are more powerful than we had thought in two ways. First, their effects were more than ephemeral. Second, the small doses of communication used in our experiments produced as much, or more, attitude change as the larger doses given in high-school mental-hygiene and psychology courses. We have additional data obtained from college subjects in abnormal-psychology courses and from other studies to show that the improvement in attitudes is statistically significant and systematic, but the improvement in such classroom studies is small in absolute size. The improvement found in college courses in psychology is even smaller in most cases than that found in high-school courses in psychology.

The relative size of the attitude changes of students in the high-school courses and in the "certainty" experiment can be seen by comparing the results shown in Tables 15.2 and 15.3 and Appendix 8 with the results shown in Figures 15.1 and 15.2 and Chapter 12. The one-page messages about mental illness in the "certainty" study promoted more favorable attitudes over-all and for separate concepts than were promoted by four-months participation in high-school and college courses in psychology, mental hygiene, and abnormal psychology.

Although in some of our studies (actually only two) one-page messages about mental illness failed to produce substantially different attitudes from those found in control groups, the important point is that short messages, when properly compounded, can have marked effects. An experiment discussed in Chapter 17 will show that even incorrect one-page messages can produce marked changes.

Results such as those mentioned above have taught us that the size of the communication dosage is not necessarily an index of the power to persuade. A short message may induce considerable change if it is carefully structured in terms of the known effects of relevant content variables. In contrast, if people are bombarded with a heavy and continual dosage of communications, in which content variables are not correctly compounded, then either small changes in the desired direction or "bad" changes can result.

The following proposition summarizes the major findings reported in this chapter:

> PROPOSITION 15.1: Short messages, which are compounded in such a way as to take advantage of the differential effects of relevant content variables, can produce substantial and lasting changes in attitudes.

SUMMARY

This chapter described two studies concerning the permanence of information and attitude changes. In the first study, measures were made of the amounts of information and attitude change that occurred among students in high-school psychology courses. Measures were taken at the beginning of the semester, at the end of the semester, and six months to one year later. As a control, measures were also taken on students participating in nonpsychology courses. It was found that the attitudes of students in psychology courses "improved" during the semester and were continuing to "improve" six months and one year later. A surprising finding was that the attitudes of the control group apparently "improved" as much as those of the psychology students. The second study discussed in the chapter followed up this finding.

In designing our communication experiments, we had guessed that our relatively small communication "doses" (for example, one-page messages) would have only transitory effects on subjects. The second study tested for the permanence of such effects in follow-up measures administered to students who participated in a communication experiment. Measures of attitude change were made two weeks after the experiment and again two and a half months after the experiment. It was found that the "favorable" attitude changes induced in the experiment did *not* diminish over the two-and-a-half-month period, and that small communication "doses" can have relatively large effects on attitudes. Thus to change attitudes, the length of the message is not nearly as important as the way in which the message is structured.

Like that in the first study, the so-called "control" group in the second study developed more favorable attitudes toward mental-health concepts. It was hypothesized that such changes in control groups were due to the impact of our measuring instruments. If true, this hypothesis suggests some methods for promoting interest in mental-health topics and for developing more favorable attitudes toward mental-health concepts.

16

Individual Differences

in Mental-health Conceptions

ONE MAJOR PURPOSE of our research is to find principles of communication that apply to all people. We are most gratified when we find that communication strategy *A* is more effective than communication strategy *B* with *all* subjects. One communication strategy is seldom better than another in all cases, however, and we must be satisfied with finding that communication strategy *A* is more effective than communication strategy *B* with more, or with most, subjects. This is another way of saying that there are individual differences in the reactions to communication variables.

There are two kinds of individual differences to study in our research. First, individuals have different types of information about and attitudes toward mental-health concepts before they participate in experiments or before other efforts are made to change them. The second concerns individual differences in reaction to communication variables. The two kinds of individual differences are not necessarily related. For example, initial individual differences in information and attitudes may be large but they may not correlate with the amounts and kinds of reactions to communication variables.

Although only a few of our studies were aimed at finding individual differences, measures of some individual differences were included in most of them. Consequently, we have a wide variety of data to interpret. Most of the results reported in this chapter are borrowed from the studies reported in earlier chapters or in Chapter 17.

INITIAL INFORMATION AND ATTITUDES

This section discusses individual differences in conceptions that exist before any effort is made to change people's attitudes and information. The most direct evidence comes from the surveys reported in Chapters 2 and 4, respectively concerning information and attitudes held by the public.

The two most important dimensions of individual differences on information are age and years of education (see Ch. 2). Both variables correlate with some of our ten information factors. Age tends to correlate positively with all of the factors, which means that older people are somewhat less correct in their information than are younger adults. *Years of education* tends to correlate negatively with the ten factors, which means that, as would be expected, people with more education have more correct information about mental-health phenomena.

On the average, women have slightly different information than men on several of the information factors (see Ch. 2). Although the differences are statistically significant, they are too small to suggest that sex is a prominent dimension of individual differences relating to mental-health conceptions.

Chapter 4 discussed studies of public attitudes toward mental-health concepts. Amount of education is found to relate to attitudes, the more highly educated people having more favorable attitudes toward most mental-health concepts; but the differences between high- and low-education groups are small. We would have come to the same general conclusions about public attitudes if we had studied only college graduates rather than broader segments of the general public. Even smaller differences were found between attitude ratings made by men and women. No other important relationships between attitudes and other individual-difference variables were found.

Other sources of information about individual differences are the studies which we made of the attitude changes among students in high-school courses in psychology and mental hygiene. The purpose of the studies was to discover some principles of information transmission and attitude change which later could be investigated in controlled experiments. In the psychology courses, we administered our information questionnaire and a Semantic Differential form at the beginning of the semester and again at the end of the semester. Analyses were made of the amounts and kinds of changes in information and attitudes. The procedure and results will be discussed in more detail in Chapter 17. Here we will discuss only those results concerning individual differences in responses to our measures.

Because the subjects in our high-school studies were relatively homogeneous in terms of age and years of education, two major dimensions of individual differences were not at work. This provided an opportunity for other individual-difference variables to emerge.

In the high-school studies we had available as measures of individual differences the sex of each subject, intelligence-test scores, measures of various "response-set" tendencies, and some measure of personality. Only intelligence proved to be an important determiner of initial information about mental illness. From the information questionnaire, a ten-item test was composed. The ten items were ones on which the experts were in sound agreement and on which a wide range of responses was obtained from the public. Each subject was given a "correctness" score based on the difference between his score and the score of experts on the items. (The test is described in greater detail in the next chapter.) A low score on the test indicates "correct" information and a high score indicates "incorrect" information. In one high school (101 students participating) the test correlated —.42 with intelligence-test scores. In another high school (98 students participating), the information test correlated —.39 with intelligence-test scores. In other words, more intelligent students tend to have more correct information about mental health and mental illness.

The correlation between intelligence-test scores and "correctness" scores further supports our hunch that running through the responses to the information questionnaire is a general dimension of "sophistication." Sophistication is represented partly by amount of schooling and, holding years of schooling constant, partly by intelligence-test scores.

In contrast to the correlations between intelligence-test scores and correctness of information, correlations between intelligence-test scores and Semantic Differential ratings of mental-health concepts are nil. Persons who scored high on intelligence tests gave about the same ratings to concepts like *former mental patient, neurotic person, mental hospital,* and *psychotherapy* as did people who scored low on intelligence tests. This supplements the findings reported in Chapter 4 which show that years of education is also not a potent differentiator of attitudes toward mental-illness concepts. In addition, it adds further support to our contention that mental-health information and attitudes behave in very different ways and, consequently, must be studied separately.

In the high-school studies no substantial differences were found between the attitudes and information held by boys and girls. On both the information questionnaire and the Semantic Differential, a few differences were statistically significant; however, these might have been due to "taking advantage of chance." Moreover the differences were all small in an absolute sense. This supports what was found in studies of broad segments of the public: sex makes very little difference in attitudes and information held about mental health.

Response-set Tendencies

Because most of our studies employed questionnaires of one form or another, we worried about the extent to which results were influenced by "response-set" tendencies. Numerous response sets have been found in questionnaires, such as the tendency of some people to agree with everything, the tendency to use only the extreme positions on rating scales, the tendency to give only "acceptable" responses, and others.

To gauge the influence of response-set tendencies in our questionnaires, two measures of response sets were included in one of our high-school studies (69 students). One set of measures tested for the tendency to mark extreme positions on rating scales. Separate measures were made on the information questionnaire and the Semantic Differential. Each measure consisted of the number of 1 and 7 (the extreme) ratings made by each person.

The second measure of response sets was closely related to "acquiescence," the tendency to agree with questionnaire statements of all kinds. The measure consisted of the sum of scores on 20 items in the information questionnaire. The 20 items were made up of ten pairs of items, each pair representing one of our ten information factors. For each factor, one item loaded positively on the factor and the other item loaded negatively. If a person agrees with one of the items for a factor, he should, logically, disagree with the other. To the extent that he tends to agree with *both* statements pertaining to the same factor, he is being acquiescent. An acquiescent person would tend to agree with all of the statements and thus obtain a high score.

Neither of the two measures of response-set tendencies substantially correlated with initial information and attitudes or with amounts of changes in information and attitudes during the period of the psychology course. These results lessened our worries about response-set tendencies in our questionnaires.

Personality Variables

Some quasi-personality variables were also included in our studies of students in high-school psychology courses. These concerned the self-concept, relations between the self-concept and the "perception" of other people, and conceptions of family roles.

On both the information questionnaire and the Semantic Differential, "atypicality" scores were obtained for each student. In each case this consisted of the sum of absolute differences between the rating made by each student on each scale and the mean rating obtained from the total group of 69 students. Students who obtained a high score on the atypicality index were very different from the average in information and attitudes. We had assumed that atypical persons would tend to change their information and attitudes to conform to group averages. If this had been the case, it would have explained some of the changes that occurred during the psychology course.

To measure the self-esteem of each student, we subtracted the mean *evaluation* score on the Semantic Differential for the concept *average man* (*average woman* for girls) from the mean *evaluation* score for the concept *me* for each student. Similar difference scores were obtained for the concept pairs of *father* and *mother,* and *insane man* and *neurotic man.* None of the personality-type variables produced substantial correlations (nearly all were below .20) with initial or change measures of information and attitudes. The few correlations which were individually "significant" might have been due to chance.

The only personality-type variable which correlated consistently with initial attitudes (none do with information) is the self-concept, measured by Semantic Differential ratings of the concept *me.* Some of the statistically significant relations are listed in Table 16.1. In general, students who have "good" attitudes toward themselves tend to have "good" attitudes toward mental-health concepts such as *ex-mental patient* and *mental hospital.* Although the coefficients which are individually "significant" are too numerous to be ignored, they are not large, averaging about .25.

There are two reasonable explanations of the tendency for high self-evaluations to go with high evaluations of mental-health concepts. The first is that a high self-evaluation represents good personal adjustment, and it might be expected that the well-adjusted person would have a tolerant attitude toward mental illness and related concepts. An equally reasonable explanation is that the correlations are due to a type of response set, a "Pollyanna" attitude, which induces the individual to give favorable ratings to everything.

The results of our research project do not tell us which of the two explanations is correct, but they do offer some clues. If the correlations between self-evaluations and evaluations of mental-health concepts were due only to a response set, self-evaluations should correlate significantly with the evaluations of all concepts. This is not the case. For example, the correlation between evaluations of *me* and evaluations of *most people* is only .20. Also, self-evaluations do not correlate significantly with all of the mental-health concepts. For example, the correlations with *insane people* and *neurotic people* are .08 and —.03 respectively. Another point against the response-set argument is that self-evaluations generalize to scales and concepts which are not obviously related to an over-all Pollyanna attitude. For example, the student who rates himself high on the *evaluation* factor tends to rate mental hospitals as more *understandable.* The individual who rates himself high on *potency* tends to rate *insane people* as relatively safe rather than dangerous. Other generalizations of self-attitudes to attitudes toward mental-health concepts are shown in Table 16.1.

Another argument against the response-set hypothesis is that there are some "significant" negative correlations between "good" attitudes toward the self and "good" attitudes toward mental-health concepts. For example, the student who places a high evaluation on himself tends to

TABLE 16.1. Statistically Significant (Beyond .05 Level) Relationships between Ratings of Self (Me) and Ratings of Mental-health Concepts

---

1. *Me* high on *evaluation* related to:
   a. *Ex-mental patient* high on *evaluation, understandability,* and safety.
   b. *Psychotherapy* high on *evaluation* and safety.
   c. *Neurotic people* low on safety.
   d. *Mental hospital* high on *evaluation* and *understandability.*
2. *Me* high on *understandability* related to:
   a. *Ex-mental patient* high on *understandability.*
   b. *Mental hospital* high on *understandability* and safety.
3. *Me* high on *potency* related to:
   a. *Insane people* high on *understandability* and safety.
   b. *Mental hospital* high on safety.
4. *Me* high on *activity* related to:
   a. *Ex-mental patient* high on *evaluation, understandability, potency, activity,* and safety.
5. *Me* high on *safety* related to:
   a. *Insane people* low on *activity.*
   b. *Mental hospital* high on *evaluation.*

---

regard *neurotic people* as relatively dangerous, and the student who rates himself high on "safety" tends to rate *insane people* as low on *activity.*

REACTIONS TO COMMUNICATIONS

Most of the results reported in this section also come from the studies of the changes in information and attitudes of students in high-school psychology and mental-hygiene courses. Here the results are uniformly negative. None of the following variables correlates significantly with information changes and attitude changes (101 students participating):

1. Intelligence-test scores
2. Sex
3. Self-ratings on the Semantic Differential
4. Response-set ratings (the two measures described previously)
5. Personality ratings (those mentioned previously)

Supporting evidence is found in some of our communication experiments. An experiment concerning the "interest value" of differently styled messages is reported in Chapter 9. The study was performed on our opinion panel, which is an approximate miniature of the United States population in terms of sex ratio and distribution of age, income, and education. None of the demographic variables correlated significantly with the influence of "anxiety," "solution," or personal versus impersonal styling.

In most of our communications experiments some information about individual differences was available—intelligence-test scores, sex, comprehension tests, self-ratings with the Semantic Differential, and others.

No striking correlations were found between the measures of individual differences and measures of attitude and information change for any of the experimental variables investigated. Seldom were any of the correlations as large as .20.

SUMMARY AND CONCLUSIONS

The results reported in this chapter can be summarized in terms of several propositions:

PROPOSITION 16.1: **The correctness of initial information about mental-health phenomena corresponds strongly to general sophistication, sophistication being represented by years of formal schooling and intelligence-test scores.**

As we hypothesized earlier, the kinds of questionnaire material which we refer to as "information" are open to learning; and learning about mental-health phenomena evidently occurs in much the same way that people learn about history, current events, art, and other aspects of the culture.

PROPOSITION 16.2: **The favorableness of initial attitudes toward mental-health concepts is unrelated, or only weakly related, to prominent dimensions of individual differences such as age, sex, education, intelligence-test scores, some response sets, and some measures of personality.**

Evidently the dislike and fear of the mentally ill and the partial distrust of mental-health treatment methods are general to most segments of our culture. There are some small differences, for example, those due to amount of education, but the differences are slight in comparison to the over-all tendency to degrade mental-health concepts. The stigma is all pervasive, and it is not easily changed by schooling and other cultural influences. This point is dramatized most fully by the attitude ratings given by a group which is high in intelligence, schooling, and socio-economic status—general practitioners in medicine, whose attitudes were discussed in Chapter 8. Their attitudes correspond strongly with those of the general population (see Ch. 4): the mentally ill are regarded as dirty, worthless, and dangerous.

PROPOSITION 16.3: **Individual differences in reaction to communications about mental illness are not strongly related to major dimensions of individual differences such as intelligence, age, sex, some response-set tendencies, and some measures of personality.**

Both the meaning and the implication of the above proposition should be clarified. Individual differences are large in initial ratings made on our information questionnaire and on the Semantic Differential. We know this is so because the standard deviations on the rating scales are usually large. (Typically we find standards of about 1.00 for seven-step scales.) When subjects are placed in communication experiments and "after" measures are made, individual differences are still large. In such situations, simpler principles are obtained if all people tend to increase their ratings by about the same amount. Of course, this is an ideal which seldom occurs: some people change to more positive attitudes and some change to more negative attitudes, some people change by large amounts and some people change by small amounts.

It is important for us to learn whether individual differences in amount and kind of change are systematic tendencies or merely random error. If they are systematic, we would expect to find substantial correlations between change-scores and some other important measures of individual differences, such as sex and intelligence. We find that change-scores correlate very little, or not at all, with a variety of potentially important dimensions of individual differences. Consequently, the implication is that individual differences in reaction to our communication variables are mainly due to random error induced by the unreliability of the measuring instruments and the lack of control in experimental situations.

If, as the results indicate, the variance of change-scores is mainly the result of random error, methods of reducing variance can be devised. Variance can be reduced primarily by increasing the reliability of information and attitude measures by appropriate techniques or by more fully standardizing the communication situations. One of the primary approaches to standardizing the communication situation is to give heavier communication "doses." We have relied mainly on short written messages in our experiments. If we had used five-page messages (holding content variables constant), we might have lowered the variance of change-scores. Although no one has formulated the problem in this way, it is probable that the length of a communication works like the length of a test—the longer the communication, the more reliable the results. (However, it is important to keep in mind a point made in Chapter 15: a heavy dose of communication which is not properly controlled for content variables may be less effective than a small dose which is properly controlled for content variables. Here we are considering the relative effects of small and large doses both of which are compounded of the *same* levels of content variables such as amount of anxiety, interest, and certainty.)

Of course, we are glad to find that change-scores do not correlate substantially with prominent measures of individual differences. If they did, a number of our propositions about the relative effectiveness of different communication strategies would be weakened. In that case it would be necessary to make statements like "strategy *A* should be used with group *X*, but strategy *B* should be used with group *Y*," which would complicate our business considerably.

17

Characteristics of Information
and Attitude Change

THE EXPERIMENTAL STUDIES reported in the preceding chapters employed a variety of communication techniques, messages, and population samples. The communication techniques ranged from the use of one-page written messages to the use of a fifteen-minute lecture. The message content of the studies ranged from general discussions of neurosis to descriptions of particular treatment techniques. The experiments were performed on college students, high-school students, special groups in the general population, and broad segments of the general population. In spite of the diversity of communication techniques, messages, and population samples, some general principles are evidenced in all of the results. Because of their generality, these principles are the major "pay dirt" of our experimental program.

Some evidence for the general principles comes from the experimental results described in preceding chapters. In addition, a number of studies were undertaken specifically to clarify the principles, and these will be described in the course of this chapter. To provide a background for the principles, some studies of "naturalistic" communication situations will be described.

CLASSROOM STUDIES

Over a period of several years, studies were made of the typical changes that occur in the information and attitudes of students in psychology courses. One class of college students (91 students) and nine different groups of high-school students in three schools were studied. The students were taking courses variously labeled as Mental Hygiene, Abnormal Psychology, and Personal Psychology. Although the courses differed widely in content, the texts and the lectures all had much to say about mental-health problems.

As standard procedure for studying all of the classes, information and attitude measures were made at the beginning of the semester. Information about mental-health issues was measured by the 50-item form described in Chapter 2. Attitudes toward mental-health concepts were measured with Semantic Differential forms of the kind illustrated in Chapter 4 and in subsequent chapters. Concepts were chosen to represent various forms of mental illness (*mental patients, neurotic people,* and so forth) and, for purposes of comparison, "normal" concepts were employed (*my father, most people, me, psychiatrist,* and others). Semantic Differential scales were chosen to represent the four factors of *evaluation, potency, activity,* and *understandability.*

The instruments were introduced to the students as being part of a "university study of public opinion." Aside from the explicit instructions for completing the forms and an effort to obtain the frank cooperation of the students, the purpose of the study was not disclosed. On the first testing, the students were given no hint that they would be tested again later. Close to the end of the semester, all students were retested with the same information and Semantic Differential forms.

The classroom studies cannot be thought of as experiments in the proper sense of the word because the communication content and method of presentation were not the same for all classes. In these studies, however, we were interested not in *what* produces particular kinds of changes but in *how* people change when they do change. From the studies we learned the kinds of attitude and information changes that occur most often, the correlations between changes in attitudes and changes in information, and the correlations between changes in both and individual difference variables such as intelligence, sex, and personality characteristics. The major purpose of the classroom studies was to generate hypotheses for testing in controlled experiments, some fruits of which were shown in Chapters 9 through 16. As a bonus, we found some common trends in all of the classroom studies, the results of which will be described in this chapter.

TRENDS

PROPOSITION 17.1: It is relatively easy to transmit mental-health information effectively.

Propositions 2.1 and 2.2 (p. 21) stated that public information is both "unstructured" and "uncrystallized." From this it was hypothesized that people will readily accept new mental-health information and forsake their old ideas. The experimental studies in previous chapters clearly demonstrate that communications bring about large changes in opinions (information). For example, in an experiment described in Chapter 13, a fifteen-minute lecture was sufficient to alter opinions markedly. In all of the classroom studies, students shifted their opinions markedly from the beginning to the end of the semester. Table 17.1, showing some results for our first classroom study, illustrates the kinds of changes in information that were found. In that study, 32 of the before-after mean differences in item scores were significant beyond the .01 level by *t*-test. Of the remaining 18 differences, ten were significant beyond the .05 level. In other words, mean changes were significant on most of the 50 items, and many of the changes were quite large. On a seven-interval scale, one third of the mean differences were as large as one whole scale unit, which, in practical terms, indicates very large shifts. These are typical of the results found in all of the classroom studies.

TABLE 17.1. Illustrative Changes in Information during One-semester High-school Courses in Mental Hygiene *

Information statement	Before mean †	After mean
1. Most of the people in mental hospitals speak in words that can be understood.	4.06	3.63
2. More women than men have nervous breakdowns.	4.41	4.11
3. Books on "peace of mind" prevent many people from developing nervous breakdowns.	4.67	5.19
4. Men worry more than women.	4.09	3.17
5. Most clergymen will encourage a person with a mental disorder to see a psychiatrist.	5.56	4.43
6. If a person concentrates on happy memories, he will not be bothered by unpleasant things in the present.	3.59	3.20
7. Physical exhaustion does not lead to a nervous breakdown.	4.18	3.67
8. The adult who needs a great deal of affection is likely to have had little affection in childhood.	3.27	4.28
9. Feeble-minded children are less obedient than normal children.	4.08	4.16
10. Physical rest will not prevent a mental disorder.	5.01	3.95
11. The brains of the feeble-minded are smaller than those of normals.	3.51	3.13
12. The main job of the psychiatrist is to recommend hobbies and other ways for the mental patient to occupy his mind.	3.19	4.44
13. There is not much that can be done for a person who develops a mental disorder.	4.26	3.37
14. Adult problems are less important in causing emotional disorders than the individual's childhood experiences.	2.62	2.84
15. Most people who "go crazy" try to kill themselves.	3.69	3.51

TABLE 17.1. Illustrative Changes in Information during
One-semester High-school Courses in Mental Hygiene * (continued)

Information statement	Before mean †	After mean
16. Few of the people who seek psychiatric help need the treatment.	4.74	3.59
17. Most people can recognize the type of person who is likely to have a nervous breakdown.	3.51	3.73
18. If a child is jealous of a younger brother, it is best not to let him show it in any way.	4.79	4.48
19. The main job of the psychiatrist is to explain to the patient the origin of his troubles.	4.41	5.39
20. Psychiatrists have to have a good sense of humor in order to help their patients.	3.28	3.48

* The 20 information statements shown here were the first 20 items appearing in our questionnaire. Of the 50 items in the questionnaire, 32 of the before-after differences were significant beyond the .01 level.

† A mean of 7.00 indicates an average complete agreement with the statement. A mean of 1.00 indicates an average complete disagreement with the statement. A mean of 4.00 indicates an average neutrality about the truth of the statement. Three classes at the same high school were used in this study. The "before" means are based on the responses of 78 pupils and the "after" means are based on 75 pupils.

What our findings indicate is that the public is not emotionally invested in its opinions about mental health to the point where it resists new ideas. Instead the public is apparently hungry for more and better information and will gobble it up when presented. Consequently, diverse methods of communication and presenting material may all be successful in improving public understanding. (What is needed is for the experts to derive a more solid body of facts to communicate to the public.)

PROPOSITION 17.2: **It is more difficult to change attitudes toward mental-health concepts than to increase knowledge of mental-health phenomena.**

It is relatively easy to increase people's knowledge, or to alter opinions, but it is relatively difficult to change people's feelings, or to alter attitudes. This is the case in the mental-health area. For example, although we found large changes in information during one-semester courses in mental hygiene, we found relatively small, even if consistent, changes in attitudes toward concepts like *mental patient, psychotherapy, psychiatrist,* and *neurotic person* (see Table 17.2). Our experimental studies showed much larger changes in information than in attitudes. These findings indicate that it will be a more difficult job to

TABLE 17.2. Illustrative Changes in Attitudes During One-semester Courses in Mental Hygiene * (Average Semantic Differential Rating at the Beginning and End of the Semester †)

	Concepts								
	Neurotic woman		Insane man		Psychiatrist		Average man		
Scales	Before	After	Before	After	Before	After	Before	After	
Foolish	2.42	2.95	2.34	2.32	6.18	6.45	5.44	5.44	Wise
Ignorant	3.28	3.68	2.86	2.93	6.42	6.70	5.54	5.73	Intelligent
Sad	2.98	3.01	2.81	2.89	5.10	5.67	5.91	5.94	Happy
Passive	3.76	3.71	3.31	3.26	5.80	6.23	6.20	6.14	Active
Insincere	3.20	3.41	2.96	2.92	6.18	6.52	6.11	6.04	Sincere
Poor	3.62	3.84	3.70	3.71	5.59	5.69	4.20	4.45	Rich
Unpredictable	2.66	2.53	1.92	1.78	4.98	5.15	5.09	4.89	Predictable
Weak	2.61	3.10	3.41	3.78	5.38	5.77	5.96	6.07	Strong
Slow	3.20	3.32	3.41	3.56	4.71	4.90	5.32	5.51	Fast
Delicate	3.71	3.51	4.54	4.78	4.26	4.59	5.30	5.66	Rugged
Cold	3.80	3.70	3.36	3.29	5.24	5.81	5.69	5.64	Warm
Dirty	4.39	4.93	4.36	4.27	6.42	6.67	6.21	6.44	Clean
Dangerous	3.39	3.89	2.35	2.71	6.15	6.56	6.02	6.10	Safe
Tense	2.36	2.62	2.36	2.18	5.85	6.37	5.08	5.63	Relaxed
Worthless	3.56	4.29	3.81	3.97	6.36	6.64	6.04	6.44	Valuable
Sick	2.35	2.56	1.66	1.68	5.78	5.99	5.81	5.86	Healthy
Bad	3.64	4.30	3.70	3.64	6.06	6.59	6.02	6.23	Good

* The same three classes were used in this study as were used in the study shown in Table 17.1. "Before" means are based on 78 cases, and "after" means are based on 75 cases. Note that mean differences here for attitudes are generally smaller than those shown in Table 17.1 for "information." Whereas about two thirds of the "information" differences were significant beyond the .01 level, differences of that significance among "attitudes" are the exception rather than the rule.

† A mean rating of 1.00 indicates an average response which is like the adjective on the left. A mean response of 7.00 indicates an average response completely like the adjective on the right. A mean response of 4.00 indicates neutrality between the two polar adjectives. For example, *neurotic woman* is rated "before" at 2.42 on the foolish-wise scale, which indicates an average response of somewhat foolish. The mean response changed to 2.95 on the "after" ratings, and, consequently, the change is toward viewing *neurotic woman* as less foolish.

establish effective communication programs for changing attitudes than for increasing popular knowledge.

PROPOSITION 17.3: **Favorable changes in attitudes can be obtained with diverse messages.**

Whereas the messages we used in different studies said different things about mental health and some of them gave conflicting explanations, they all tended to produce the same kinds (but not amounts) of attitude change. The attitude changes were in the direction of higher evaluations of the mentally ill, the people who treat them, and the treatment methods. For example, different types of communications—written messages, short lectures, high-school courses in mental hygiene—all tended to make the individual rate a concept like *mental patient* as more predictable and sincere and as less worthless, dirty, and dangerous. This is a case in which "all roads lead to Rome," although some roads (communication strategies) are faster than others.

Another way of phrasing the proposition is that *kinds* of information change and *kinds* of attitude change are relatively independent of each other. This point is best illustrated by a comparison of the attitude and information changes in psychology classes in two different high schools. The classes in the two schools were taught by different teachers, using different texts; and, from our observations, it seemed that subject-matter emphases varied widely. In both schools we found large changes in information on the 50-item questionnaire of the kind illustrated in Table 17.1, and small but significant attitude changes of the kind illustrated in Table 17.2. An analysis was made to see if the same kinds of attitude changes occurred in both schools. Mean changes in Semantic Differential ratings from "before" to "after" in the two schools were correlated over all scales over the concepts pertaining to mental-health issues (*psychiatrist, neurotic woman, insane man,* and so forth). We found a correlation (Spearman's *Rho*) of .73, which shows that similar kinds of changes occurred in the two schools. The mean difference in the over-all amount of change in the two schools was not statistically significant, showing that approximately the same *amount* as well as *kind* of attitude change occurred in the two schools. The attitude changes were in the direction of viewing psychiatrists as more valuable, strong, and effective, and of regarding persons with mental disorders as less foolish, dangerous, dirty, and worthless. (As was mentioned previously, the same pattern of attitude changes tends to occur in all of our studies.)

In spite of the similarity of the attitude changes found in the two schools, very different kinds of information changes occurred, as measured by the 50-item questionnaire. Although in both schools large changes were found on individual items from "before" to "after," the changes in the two schools were different. The correlation between the two sets of change scores is only .16, which is not statistically significant.

Whereas changes in attitudes fit a definite and meaningful pattern, changes in information at neither of the two schools conformed to any meaningful pattern. Although mean information changes were large on individual items (many being larger than one scale interval), changes on the item factors (described in Ch. 2) were generally very small. In other words, when the changes on the items belonging to a factor are added together, some are positive and some are negative, and they tend to cancel one another. This offers one type of circumstantial evidence to indicate that information changes were not "systematic." A more direct type of evidence to show that changes were not systematic will be described in the next section, where it will be shown that overall changes were not toward more *correct* viewpoints.

Another type of evidence more strongly indicates that attitude changes toward mental-health concepts are largely independent of information changes. If particular kinds of information changes led to particular kinds of attitude changes, we would expect to find substantial correlations between change scores on the information factors and change scores on the Semantic Differential factors (*evaluation, understandability,* and so forth) applied to the mental-health concepts. The mean absolute correlation between the two sets of measures is only .18, which shows that even if some of the correlations are "real," on the average they are near zero. Consequently, the conservative conclusion is that there are no substantial correlations between information changes and attitude changes in the study.

The evidence indicates that information in the two schools did not change in any systematic manner; rather, it seems that information was largely *scrambled.* Whatever students believed at the beginning of the semester, they believed something different at the end of the semester, and the shifts were large. Out of the seemingly chaotic changes in information and different changes in different schools came a meaningful pattern of attitude changes in all schools. The results of our experimental studies give further supporting evidence. In different experiments the subjects were given different kinds of information, yet similar kinds (but not amounts) of attitude changes occurred in most.

PROPOSITION 17.4: **Favorable attitudes toward mental-health concepts develop when people think they know something about the phenomena, regardless of whether or not their information is actually correct.**

The proposition follows from the results of the experimental and classroom studies described above. Supporting evidence was also obtained from an experiment which will be described later in the chapter.

Previously it was said that large changes in information occurred in our experimental studies, and particularly large changes were found among students in psychology courses. In the classroom studies the kinds of information changes that occurred in different schools and in different classes at the same schools were correlated. The correlations proved to be very low, yet in all settings a similar set of "constructive" changes in attitudes occurred. For example, whereas students in one class moved to a higher agreement with the information item "Most people in mental hospitals speak in words that can be understood," students in another class moved to a lower agreement with the item, and so on for the other items. Then either the textbook, the teacher, or something about the total communication situation induced changes in information, and the influences were evidently different in different classes. An inevitable conclusion is that "incorrect" informational changes were as effective in promoting "constructive" attitudes as "correct" changes. Whenever "before-after" changes on an information item were large and whenever different classes changed in different directions, at least some of the classes were moving toward less correct viewpoints.

In order to determine more carefully the correctness of information changes in the classroom studies, a special test was used. The test consists of ten of the information items. The items are those on which the experts generally agree (see Ch. 3), on which the mean expert responses are clearly to one side or the other of the neutral, or 4, point on the scale, and on which there is considerable dispersion of popular opinion (see Ch. 2). The ten test items, with the mean expert responses, are shown in Table 17.3. A person's score on the test is obtained by summing the absolute differences between his item scores and the mean expert scores. A low score indicates good agreement with the expert means, and a high score indicates large disagreement with the expert means. Because the ten items appeared in all of our information forms, all of the subjects could be given a score indicating the relative correctness of their information. Previous studies showed that the test correlates with years of education and with socioeconomic status. In a group of 189 high-school students, scores on the test at the beginning of the psychology courses correlated —.39 with intelligence-test scores (re-

TABLE 17.3. Mean Responses of 176 Experts on the Ten-item Mental-health Information Test (86 psychologists and 90 psychiatrists)

Item	Mean
1. There is not much that can be done for a person who develops a mental disorder.	1.26
2. Most of the people in mental hospitals speak in words that can be understood.	5.85
3. Mental health is largely a matter of trying hard to control the emotions.	2.36
4. If a person concentrates on happy memories, he will not be bothered by unpleasant things in the present.	2.69
5. Almost any disease that attacks the nervous system is likely to bring on insanity.	2.21
6. X-rays of a head will not tell whether a person is likely to become insane.	5.88
7. Psychiatrists try to teach mental patients to hold in their strong emotions.	2.76
8. The main job of the psychiatrist is to recommend hobbies and other ways for the mental patient to occupy his mind.	2.19
9. The insane laugh more than normals.	2.40
10. A change of climate seldom helps an emotional disorder.	5.09

member that a high score indicates "ignorance" of mental-health issues).

The importance of the information test here is that it shows something about the correctness of the information changes in the classroom studies. Changes in scores on the test were determined for the two classes discussed above. The mean change in one class was —.52 showing that the class as a whole learned slightly more "correct" information during the semester. The mean change for the other class was 1.44, showing that they learned slightly less "correct" information during the semester. More important than the direction of the mean changes is the fact that the mean changes are very small in both cases, supporting our earlier contention that essentially information was *scrambled* during the psychology courses.

Primarily what happened to the "psychology" students was that they *changed* information, not that they actually learned more correct viewpoints. Consequently, it is reasonable to conjecture that the very act of changing information leads to "constructive" attitude changes toward mental-health concepts. Although it cannot be proven directly from our data, our hypothesis is that on changing information the students *thought* that they had learned a considerable amount about the phenomena, and that this in turn reduced the fear of mental illness and the distrust of the mentally ill and the people who treat them.

PROPOSITION 17.5: **False information can serve a useful purpose on occasion.**

Following from the previous discussion, if false information sometimes leads to "constructive" changes in attitudes, it raises the possibility that false information presently held by the public might, in a sense, serve a useful purpose. Although it is difficult to test this hypothesis directly, an experiment was designed to make it more plausible. The experiment also provides some supporting evidence for other statements made in this chapter.

"Knowledge dispels fear" is an assumption often implicitly held in public-information programs about anxiety-provoking issues. Consequently, such programs often aim their efforts at negating false beliefs. However, this may not always produce the desired effect. Merely negating false ideas can serve to increase popular fears when no effort is made to replace incorrect information with new positive information or when there is no correct information available to give (see Ch. 12). Conversely, false information may sometimes serve a useful purpose by reducing the perceived threat related to anxiety-provoking situations.

THE EXPERIMENT

The purpose of the experiment was to provide an illustration of some points made above: (1) people are highly gullible when presented with authoritative-sounding information; (2) consequently they will accept even grossly oversimplified and patently false explanations; and (3) if those explanations are properly compounded in terms of relevant content variables (for example, "certainty"), favorable attitudes will develop.

Messages

Six written messages, all approximately one single-spaced typewrit ten page in length, were used. Four of them concerned explanations of catatonic schizophrenia. The remaining two were control messages concerned with topics other than mental illness: the Great Barrier Reef near Australia and the use of the typewriter. Two of the "catatonic" messages offered psychological-type explanations (one of these was plausible in terms of current thinking, the other was false). The other two "catatonic" messages gave physical-type explanations (again, one was plausible and the other false). The four messages on catatonic schizophrenia were the same except for the substitution of several sentences which changed them from "psychological" to "physical" and from relatively correct to relatively incorrect explanations.

The first paragraph of all four messages concerning catatonic schizophrenia read as follows:

> Some of the bizarre forms of human behavior which we refer to as insanity have been difficult for scientists to understand. A particularly baffling mental disorder is *catatonic schizophrenia*. The individual sits motionless, staring straight ahead, and is completely out of contact with his environment. He will not respond when spoken to and will not move even if the building around him is on fire. Some patients spend the rest of their lives living more like a stone than a human being.

The second paragraph of all four of the messages began with the following sentence: "Recent scientific findings indicate how *catatonic schizophrenia* develops and what can be done to cure it." From that point on the four versions gave four different explanations. The physical-plausible message explained that the disorder is associated with a characteristic substance in the blood. The psychological-plausible message explained that, because of strong rejection by his parents, particularly the mother, the child gradually withdraws. Although, as is characteristic of "experts," we were not sure of the validity of our "plausible" versions, we had little difficulty in composing versions that are far less plausible. The physical-false version explained that the disorder was caused by the blocking of an artery in the brain and the subsequent deficiency of the hormone, "thymadrone" (a name we invented). The psychological-false explanation was that catatonic schizophrenia is caused by a *personna phobia* (also an invented term), an intense fear reaction to a particular person. Each of the four versions, after explaining how the disorder is caused, discussed possible "cures." The "plausible" versions described accepted methods (for example, psychotherapy) and/or potentially useful ones (chemical therapy). The "false" versions discussed methods which, in all likelihood, would not be effective (for example, injections of "thymadrone" and hypnotic suggestion).

All four versions attempted to present "solutions" and to sound "certain," two message characteristics which promote favorable attitudes (see Chs. 10 and 12). All four versions ended with the following two sentences:

> Many such persons are now back in society leading happy productive lives. The progress that has been made with this one type of mental illness gives promise that all forms of insanity will be both understandable and curable in the decade ahead.

Subjects

The subjects were 192 undergraduate students at the University of Illinois. The messages were systematically ordered to insure a random pairing of messages with students within each class. Each student was given one of the six messages to read. The students were instructed that they were "to participate in a study of writing styles." Each student first read the message assigned to him, and then made attitude ratings and answered questions about the message.

Test Materials

A form of the Semantic Differential was used to measure attitudes toward mental illness, the mentally ill, and persons who treat the mentally ill. Ratings were made of the following concepts: mental illness, a person who has catatonic schizophrenia, mental patient, insane person, psychiatrist, and me. Scales were chosen to represent the four factors discussed in Chapter 4.

In addition to the Semantic Differential form, a short questionnaire was employed to obtain some additional reactions to the messages. Those subjects receiving one of the messages about catatonic schizophrenia were asked whether or not they thought the treatment described in the message they had read would work. All subjects were asked to rate the message according to whether or not they thought it was dull or interesting, simple or complicated, convincing or unconvincing. They were also asked what they thought the odds were that one of their friends would become mentally ill.

Results

The results indicate that the four explanations about catatonic schizophrenia were all relatively convincing. With a maximum convincingness rating of 7.0, the mean rating was 4.9 for the physical-false message, 5.7 for the physical-plausible message, 5.4 for the psychological-false message, and 5.2 for the psychological-plausible message. When asked whether or not they thought the treatment procedures described in the message would work, the percent answering "yes" was 88 for the physical-false message, 87 for the physical-plausible message, 83 for the psychological-false message, and 75 for the psychological-plausible message. These findings support what was said earlier: people (at least college students) are unsure of what they think about mental-health problems and will readily gobble up any factual-sounding information. We had thought that college students would be somewhat more resistant to accepting the oversimplifications and patent falsities in the messages, but evidently that is not the case. (Similar results are found in the "certainty" studies discussed in Ch. 12.)

The second step in the analysis was to determine whether or not the four messages concerning catatonic schizophrenia elicited different attitude ratings than the two control messages. Separate analyses were made for each concept on each of the four attitudinal factors. Estimates of factor scores were obtained by averaging scores over the scales representing each factor.

The results for the concept *a person who has catatonic schizophrenia* are summarized in Table 17.4. The primary observation about these results is that all of the messages concerning catatonic schizophrenia produced markedly different attitudes toward the concept *a person who has catatonic schizophrenia* than did the control messages. The subjects receiving the "catatonic" messages rated the concept as more *valuable,* less *potent,* less *active,* and more *understandable* than did the subjects receiving the control messages (all significant beyond the .01 level by *t*-test).

TABLE 17.4. Mean Ratings of Semantic Differential Factors for the Concept
A Person Who Has Catatonic Schizophrenia *

	Evaluation	Potency	Activity	Understandability
Catatonic messages				
Physical-false	4.77	3.16	2.13	3.42
Physical-plausible	4.16	2.55	1.73	3.69
Psychological-false	3.95	2.06	2.06	3.16
Psychological-plausible	4.22	2.30	1.91	3.03
Control messages				
The Great Barrier Reef	3.37	3.64	3.72	2.66
Typewriter maintenance	3.81	3.31	4.39	2.54

* The mean ratings are restricted to the range 1 through 7. A mean rating of 7 would indicate that the concept is regarded as completely valuable, potent, active, or understandable; and a mean rating of 1 would indicate that the concept is regarded as completely worthless, impotent, passive, or nonunderstandable. A mean of 4 indicates a neutral reaction.

The differences in attitude ratings produced by the "catatonic" messages and the control messages generalized somewhat to the concept *mental illness,* with the difference between the two being significant beyond the .01 level on the *potency* and *activity* factors. Also, there was a generalization on the *understandability* factor to the concept *psychiatrist* ($p = .05$), the concept being rated as more understandable by the experimental groups.

A third analysis was undertaken to determine whether the various messages concerned with catatonic schizophrenia produced different attitude ratings. Analysis of variance showed no significant differences between "physical" and "psychological" messages or between "false" and "plausible" messages. Consequently, there was no evidence to indicate that these factors influence attitudes. It was our hypothesis that the effectiveness of messages would not be influenced by their relative correctness.

It might be argued that the only reason that the "catatonic" messages elicited different attitude responses than the control messages was that the subjects had never before heard of catatonic schizophrenia. This may be a partial explanation of the results. If subjects had no attitudes toward *a person who has catatonic schizophrenia,* one would expect to find "neutral" ratings (means near 4 on the seven-step scale) for subjects receiving control messages. Instead, it is seen from Table 17.4 that the control groups viewed *a person who has catatonic schizophrenia* low on the *evaluation, potency,* and *understandability* factors. More important, subjects who read messages about catatonic schizophrenia, when compared with subjects who read the control messages, showed significant attitude differences not only for the concept *a person who has catatonic schizophrenia* but also for the concepts *mental illness* and *psychiatrist.*

In order to understand these results it is necessary to consider the message content which concerned mental illness. Previous research has shown that mental illness is a topic which tends to create anxiety (see Ch. 10). People usually associate mental illness with pain, embarrassment, and danger. Coupled with the "threatening" nature of the topic, people tend to have "uncrystallized" beliefs about mental illness. They do not know very much, and they are unsure of their information. Apparently, the consequence of these two factors is that people eagerly accept almost any authoritative-sounding information about the causes and treatments of mental illness. Further, it may be that the fear and stigma attached to the mentally ill are reduced when people feel that they have some knowledge about mental illness. The results of this study suggest that the popular fear of mental illness and the mentally ill will be reduced if plausible-sounding information is given—whether or not this information is really correct. Much of the mental-health information now given to the public is concerned with explaining what does *not* cause mental illness, how the mentally ill do *not* act, and what does *not* cure mental illness. Because there is still so much to be learned about mental illness and so much of what is known is complex and difficult to explain to the public, the public is frequently not provided with intelligible information.

We are not suggesting that the public be provided with incorrect information in order to promote favorable attitudes. The wisdom of destroying false beliefs when there are no correct beliefs to give in return, however, is questionable. False beliefs and superstitions may have a temporary functional value in that they make the individual feel less insecure in threatening situations.

The results of this study may apply to other "threatening" topics such as cancer, atomic warfare, natural disasters, and economic recessions. False beliefs in these areas may also serve to reduce feelings of being "threatened."

The third experiment discussed in Chapter 12 bears on the present discussion. In the experiment, "negation" messages were compared with control messages. In the body of the "negation" messages, subjects were given some seemingly factual information about the causes and treatment of mental illness. This portion of the messages had been used in previous studies and had produced "constructive" attitude changes. In the "certainty" study, however, a short paragraph, appended to the end of the message, said that the information given in the message was incorrect. In other words, we gave information and then took it away. The "negation" messages produce "nonconstructive" attitudes, tending to increase fear and distrust of the mentally ill. This demonstrates the effect of telling people what does *not* cause mental illness, how the mentally ill do *not* act, and how cures are *not* brought about.

DISCUSSION

The general characteristics described in the chapter tie together in such a way as to provide an over-all picture of public attitudes toward and information about mental-health issues. In previous chapters it was shown that the public fears and devalues the mentally ill and is skeptical of the professionals and the treatment methods which they use. Our studies show that these attitudes can be changed. In the short communications used in our experimental studies, attitude changes are not large, but they are statistically significant and follow a consistent pattern.

In comparison to the changing of public attitudes, our experimental studies and the classroom studies produced surprisingly easy and surprisingly large changes in public information. In spite of their size, however, the changes suggested that information merely had been *scrambled* rather than rearranged in some systematic manner. Although the changes in information, and the different changes in different studies, were apparently chaotic, there was a consistent set of attitude changes.

The fact that kinds of information changes are largely independent of kinds of attitude changes, does not mean that different communication *strategies* are equally effective. In Chapters 9 through 13 it was shown that the communication strategy used (for example, whether the message is made more or less anxiety-provoking) will be an important influence on the amount of attitude change. What the findings indicate is that different message *contents* lead to similar kinds of attitude changes. For example, a message about psychotherapy can bring favorable changes in attitudes toward psychotics, even if psychotics are not mentioned in the message. A message which states that physiological factors determine mental disorders produces the same kinds and about the same amount of "constructive" attitude change as a message which ignores physiological factors and stresses the importance of childhood experiences.

People are evidently unsure of their information about mental-health issues. Consequently, they will accept almost any seemingly authoritative and factual-sounding information. The acceptance of new information, regardless of its validity, reduces the fear of mental illness and the mentally ill. As was demonstrated experimentally, even grossly oversimplified and false information can produce "constructive" changes in attitudes. Conversely, it was reasoned that existing false information about mental-health issues may serve a useful function to the public. Unless a valid and understandable body of information can be given in return, it is probably unwise to destroy existing public misinformation.

Whereas it was found in our studies that people change their information markedly after only small doses of persuasion and the mere changing (*scrambling*) apparently promotes favorable attitudes, such results would probably be found only with topics such as ours: where the public's information is "unstructured" and "uncrystallized," and where, because of the anxiety associated with the phenomena, there is a strong need to know.

18

An Interpretive Overview

THE READER who has faithfully followed our research to this point is probably asking himself, "What does it all mean?" We will try to give at least a partial answer to that question. Because of the number, diversity, and bulk of the studies, a complete summary of the results would consume too much space. Instead, this chapter will present what we believe to be some of the most important implications of the total research.

It is hoped that in previous chapters we stuck fairly close to the actual research results and did not overly interpret the meaning of particular findings. Here we will let our hair down and make some broad interpretations; such interpretations should be considered mainly as food for future studies.

THE PUBLIC

Information

In studying what the public knows and thinks about mental-health problems, we could foresee only two possible results: (1) the public is *misinformed*, in the sense that the "average man" holds numerous misconceptions about mental illness, or (2) the public is *uninformed*, in the sense that the average man has little information, correct or incorrect, about many of the problems. It was, and is, inconceivable to us that the average man could be *well informed*. If he were, it would present a curious paradox: because so much is yet to be discovered, even psychologists and psychiatrists are not well informed in the absolute sense.

Our results show clearly that the average man is not grossly misinformed. That is, it is difficult to document specific misconceptions which are widely held by the public. Consequently, the major job in future communication programs will be to fill in the voids where people are uninformed.

Partially because of the anxiety associated with mental-health topics and partially because of the lack of semantic referents for his terms (for example, "neurotic"), the average man does not systematically learn about mental-health phenomena from daily experience. What information he has exists largely as an abstract system. Although the average man swims in a sea of mental-health phenomena, he usually does not catalogue them as such. Consequently, the abstract system is neither confirmed nor denied.

The average man is relatively unsure of his opinions about mental-health phenomena. Consequently, he eagerly looks to experts for "the answers." We found that people do not resist new information, even when that information is plainly incorrect. In general, we found that people will accept almost any seemingly factual and authoritative-sounding information on mental health.

Attitudes

It is commonly asserted that people attach a stigma to the mentally ill. Our research results leave little doubt that the stigma exists. The most important finding from our studies of public attitudes is that the stigma is very general, both across social groups and across attitude indicators. There is a strong "negative halo" associated with the mentally ill. They are considered, unselectively, as being all things "bad." Some of the "bad" attitudes that people have toward the mentally ill are partially supported by the facts—for example, the mentally ill sometimes *are* unpredictable and dangerous. However, the average man generalizes to the point of considering the mentally ill as dirty, unintelligent, insincere, and worthless. Such unselectively negative attitudes are probably due in part to a lack of information about mental illness and a failure to observe and learn about mental-illness phenomena in daily life.

Our research suggests some of the dynamics of public attitudes toward the mentally ill. One of the cornerstones of public attitudes is the feeling that the mentally ill are highly unpredictable. The mentally ill are thought to be people who do not go by the "rules" and who, because of their erratic behavior, may suddenly embarrass or endanger others. The feeling is like that of sitting next to a temperamental explosive which may detonate without warning. Consequently, most people are very uncomfortable in the presence of someone who is, or is purported to be, mentally ill.

Public attitudes toward psychologists, psychiatrists, and other mental-treatment specialists are evidently not as "bad" as is commonly suspected. The public holds moderately high, favorable attitudes toward mental specialists *as individuals*. What is "wrong" with public attitudes is a moderate distrust and devaluing of mental-treatment methods and institutions. Consequently, the emphasis in information programs should be on improving attitudes toward the tools and methods used by mental specialists.

Interests

Public interest in mental-health topics varies considerably with the topic and with the way in which the topic is treated in communications. Most of the interest is not due to intellectual curiosity, as it is, for example, with information about space flight. Instead, the interest is motivated by a somewhat panicky "need to know." The public is mainly interested in information about mental health of a kind that will relieve immediate personal threats. The public will reject (e.g. not continue to read) messages that raise anxiety and do not supply "solutions." One of the difficulties in preparing a program of public information is designing messages that contain reasonably simple facts about mental-health phenomena and how-to-do-it rules for handling problems; but this is what the public wants.

THE EXPERTS

If experts had a more definitive body of knowledge about mental-health problems, and if they could agree on particular points, the job of communicating with the public would be immensely simplified. We found reasonably good agreement among experts about some things that should be said in a program of public information about mental-health problems. In our studies, however, we dealt only with the relatively narrow range of ideas with which the public is presently familiar. What is needed now is to determine what *new* things can be told to the public. One approach to this problem would be to ask psychiatrists and psychologists to compile a list of facts, or near-facts, that can be communicated to the public about the causes, symptoms, treatment, and social effects of mental-health problems. Such a list might provide many new things to tell the public, or it might prove to be embarrassingly short.

General practitioners of medicine play an important role in the treatment of mental-health problems. They act as "gatekeepers" between the public and the mental specialists. It is often the general practitioner who determines whether or not a patient sees a mental specialist, and if so, what type of specialist he consults. Equally important as the number of referrals that they make are the number of mental cases that general practitioners treat themselves. It remains to be determined what kinds of cases general practitioners treat and what kinds of treatment they give. One of our most important findings was that the younger, better-informed physicians tend to have "better" attitudes toward mental patients; and it is this type of general practitioner who is more likely to treat mental problems instead of referring them to mental specialists.

THE MASS MEDIA

If the average man uncritically accepted the information contained and implied in mass-media presentations, he would indeed be misinformed. In those cases where media presentations are specifically designed to enlighten the public and where expert advice and cooperation are available, the results are often quite good. Such presentations, however, comprise only a minute proportion of the total "information" relating to mental-health phenomena carried by the media. Most of the information is obliquely woven into dramatic presentations, for example, the suggestion that a healthy person can be driven insane after a rather short exposure to a frustrating or frightening situation.

Evidently, presentations of mental-health problems in the mass media have been stylized to fit the requirements of fiction and drama. The symptoms of mental illness are exaggerated, the causes and treatment are greatly oversimplified and often erroneous, and mental illness usually appears in a context of "horror," sin, and violence. The "cognitive," or informational, implications of such presentations are either so amorphous and contradictory, or so obviously incorrect, that the average man is not particularly affected—he knows better. The affective, or attitudinal, implications may be strong, however, because they closely match the attitudes that the public holds toward the mentally ill.

Mass-media personnel are not to be "blamed" for the nature of presentations relating to mental-health problems. Their primary business is not to educate the public but to entertain, in the broad sense of the word, and that must be done at a profit. Because of the subtle way in which mental-health "information" is woven into programs, and because of the many hands that shape such presentations, even if the media tried to "control" they would find it very difficult. When media personnel try to promote "better" presentations, they often obtain confusing and contradictory advice from mental experts, and the experts are often loathe to cooperate.

We are not sure what should, or could, be done to utilize more effectively the mass media in programs of mental-health information. Because of the faddism that dominates the media, it is doubtful that any sustained drive will be exerted by the media personnel unless they are encouraged and helped by professional societies and other organizations concerned with mental-health problems. We did come up with one solution, though half in jest: Some organization might finance a "good" soap opera, to be produced cooperatively by experts and media personnel and specifically intended to enlighten the public about mental-health problems as well as to be entertaining. Many such programs, in forms suitable to the different media, might go a long way toward providing the public with better information and developing better attitudes toward mental-health phenomena.

COMMUNICATION STRATEGIES

The Topic

The topic itself constitutes an important variable in selecting communication strategies. Thus, very different strategies might be needed in order to communicate about labor-management relations than about mental illness. This does not mean that no general science of communication is possible and that communication strategy is chaotically dependent on particular topics. Communication strategy in general consists of promoting interest, satisfying human needs, providing desired information, verbal conditioning, and so on. Before strategies for communicating about a particular topic can be established, it is necessary to determine where that topic presently resides in a nexus of psychological variables. For example, does information about the particular topic supply a pertinent human need? In this section will be summarized some research results which serve to index mental-health information in terms of its communicative properties.

Some of the points relating to this section were mentioned in earlier sections of this chapter. To reiterate: (1) People know very little, and are unsure of what they think; (2) people want to obtain more information about mental health, but their interest is largely restricted to learning ways to meet or avoid threatening situations; (3) people do not systematically gather information from their daily experiences or do not catalogue their experiences as pertaining to mental health, and (4) people want authoritative answers but seldom get them from mass-media presentations, nor do they obtain "closure" from what the experts say.

Another important feature of mental-health topics is that they tend to generate anxiety. People are uneasy when they hear or read about emotional disturbance, neurosis, mental hospitals, hallucinations, psychotherapy, and many other related matters. The reduction of that anxiety is a primary route to increasing public interest and promoting favorable attitudes.

Mental-health topics are beset by a "language" problem. In Chapter 11 were presented some research results which indicate that a number of things are "wrong" with the available terminology: (1) there is a shortage of terms, (2) the terms bear strong negative connotations, and (3) the terms suggest misleading explanations of mental-health phenomena. These "language" problems limit the effectiveness of some communication strategies. For example, in our experiments we found it nearly impossible to promote more favorable attitudes toward the concept *insane man*. When we translated the term to *mental-hospital patient*, however, we obtained favorable changes in attitudes. Until more is done to develop a suitable terminology, it will be very difficult to undertake effective large-scale programs of public information. We need a lexicon for communicating about mental-health problems, one that is based on agreement among experts and on research evidence concerning the suitability of particular terms.

Information Transmission

Apparently it is very easy to get people to accept new facts about mental-health problems. People will gobble up any seemingly factual and authoritative-sounding information. Indeed, we were surprised to learn the extent to which explanations could be oversimplified and distorted, and still accepted as true. Among high-school students in psychology courses, we were surprised to find huge changes in information (expressed opinions) during the semester. Consequently, for the purpose of transmitting new information, strategy is not an important consideration. In that case, strategy largely concerns rhetorical skill, journalistic niceties, and the maintainance of interest. However, the type of information given to people will very much affect the *attitudes* that they hold, and, consequently, the choice of information to communicate becomes an important aspect of attitude-change strategy.

Attitude Change

In many communication experiments, the effort is to *convince* people to hold opinions (information) that are different from those which they held initially. As was said above, there is little difficulty in convincing people to hold new ideas in the mental-health domain. The widespread "bad" attitudes are not held *because* of existing information, but rather because of the *lack* of it. Early in our research, we hypothesized that to relieve the threat associated with mental-health problems the important ingredient is for people to *think* that they have a valid system of information regardless of its real validity. Our research results tended to bear out this hypothesis. We found that the mere act of *changing* from one set of opinions to another (scrambling information) promoted favorable attitudes toward the mentally ill and toward treatment specialists and methods. This was so even though the new "information" was in many cases less correct than what had been believed initially. Although we do not know how long people can be "fooled" in this way, the results illustrate the comfort that people obtain from having, or thinking they have, mental armament against anxiety-provoking problems.

It should not be implied that *any* communication will have the desired effect. Messages must actually contain information—understandable statements about factual or potentially factual matters. According to this definition, many messages contain little or no information. Instead, they (1) say little that people can understand, (2) ask questions rather than give answers, (3) "destroy" what information people have rather than provide new information, or (4) make exhortative appeals for people to develop better attitudes. Even if messages actually do contain information, that information must have certain optimum properties before it will produce the desired effect. It should usually be related to some problem-solving aspect of mental health. That is, it should help people in some way to cope with mental-health problems. Much of the information currently given to the public does not serve that function; for example, telling people that half the hospital beds in this country are filled with mental patients raises anxiety but does not help them to deal with the problem.

In toto our studies show that the factual content of messages is important largely to the extent that it induces a proper *emotional state*. A message will promote favorable attitudes toward mental-health concepts if (1) the concepts are visible in the message (directly mentioned) or associated with visible concepts (generalization), (2) the message has a high interest-value, (3) the message is thought to come from an authoritative source (e.g., a university or a psychiatrist), and (4) the message makes the reader feel *secure* by sounding certain, by providing solutions, by presenting an understandable explanation, and by reducing anxiety in other ways. If these content characteristics are present, people will develop more favorable attitudes and will be more open to continued learning about mental-health phenomena. If these characteristics are not present, no amount of sermonizing, haranguing, or factual presentation will work; and it would be better not to communicate at all.

APPENDIX

Three kinds of materials are presented in the Appendix: (1) data too bulky to be presented in the body of the book, (2) results from studies which relate only indirectly to the central topic of the book, and (3) questionnaires and other measuring instruments. The findings reported in the Appendix could be subjected to a variety of analyses which were not undertaken. It is hoped that readers will explore such possibilities.

One of the major purposes of our project was to develop measuring instruments for general use in the mental-health area. Consequently, it is hoped that readers will borrow the instruments freely for their own research.

1

The Preliminary 240-item

Information Questionnaire

FOLLOWING IS THE complete 240-item information form used with the 349 subjects of the Champaign-Urbana sample (see Ch. 2) and the frequencies of response to the agree-disagree categories for each item.

NATIONAL HEALTH STUDY

You are being asked to participate in a study of health problems. The study is being done at the University of Illinois under contract from the U.S. Public Health Service. Your participation will supply valuable information to those responsible for the nation's health.

On the following pages you will find 240 statements about health problems. We want to know how much you agree or disagree with each of the statements. To the right of each statement you can find a rating scale as follows:

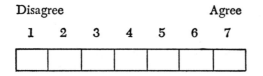

The points along the scale (1, 2, 3, . . . 7) can be interpreted as follows:

1. Completely disagree
2. Mostly disagree
3. Disagree more than agree
4. Agree and disagree equally
5. Agree more than disagree
6. Mostly agree
7. Completely agree

The use of the scale can be illustrated with the following statement:

"Smoking causes lung cancer."

If you agreed completely with the statement, you would place a mark in column 7. If you agreed slightly with the statement, you would place a mark in column 5. If you mostly disagreed with the statement, you would place a mark in column 2. In this manner you can indicate the extent to which you agree or disagree with each of the statements on the following pages.

Like everyone else, you will probably feel that you do not know the answers to many of the statements. When this occurs, please make the best guess that you can.

Please make your marks inside the agreement and disagreement boxes of the scales. Do it like this:

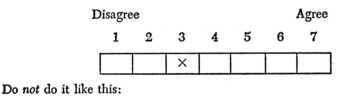

Do *not* do it like this:

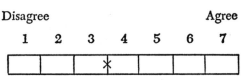

Please make sure that you make a mark for each statement. Leave none of the statements blank and make only one mark for each. You should not spend more than a few seconds marking each statement. If it is difficult for you to make up your mind, make the best guess that you can and go on to the next one.

We do not want to know your name for this study. *Please do not write your name anywhere on this form.* However, it would be very helpful if you would supply us with the following information.

1. Age at nearest birthday _____ 2. Male _____ Female _____
3. Please circle the number of the last year of education you completed on the following line.

Elementary	H. S.	College	
1 2 3 4 5 6 7 8	9 10 11 12	13 14 15 16	17 18 19

4. What is your major occupation? _____.
   (If you are retired, please list your former occupation. If you are gainfully employed less than four hours a day please write in the word such as "student" or "housewife" that would apply to your case.)
5. What is the occupation of the major wage earner in your household?

_____

   (If you are the major wage earner, your answer to this question will be the same as your answer to Question 4.)

6. Married _____ Single _____ Widowed, divorced, or separated _____

7. What is your religious preference?

Protestant _____   Jewish _____

Catholic _____   None of these _____

8. If you do not mind, would you check the group in which your total household income fell in 1954. (Income of husband, wife, children, and any other sources.)

under $1,200 _____ $6,001–8,400 _____

$1,201–3,600 _____ $8,401–10,800 _____

$3,601–6,000 _____   over $10,801 _____

After you have answered the questions above, please turn the page and start indicating the extent to which you agree or disagree with each of the statements.

1

	Disagree						Agree
	1	2	3	4	5	6	7
a. The insane have facial expressions like those of normals.	60	46	52	52	45	52	42
b. Mentally retarded people smile less often than people of normal intelligence.	59	45	52	54	55	50	45
c. No matter how hard feeble-minded children work in school, they cannot do as well as normal children.	13	5	13	10	27	78	203
d. Normal people cannot suddenly become insane.	84	37	50	28	33	45	72
e. Short men are less likely to have feelings of inferiority than men of average height.	143	76	55	38	11	15	11
f. A nervous breakdown will grow into insanity if help is not given.	18	18	29	50	71	76	87
g. People usually look much older after recovering from a mental disorder.	35	34	43	72	48	52	65
h. Few of the people in mental hospitals require special diets.	25	15	38	68	56	58	89
i. A person can rid himself of unpleasant memories if he tries hard enough to forget them.	47	48	47	34	54	50	69
j. The brains of the insane are the same size as those of normals.	9	6	15	54	36	65	164
k. Highly educated people are more likely to "lose their minds" than other people.	81	41	44	56	54	31	42
l. Most of the people in mental hospitals are able to recognize the members of their family.	16	17	28	60	59	85	84

1

	Disagree						Agree
	1	2	3	4	5	6	7
m. It helps most mental hospital patients to have regular visits from their families.	13	18	23	44	56	77	118
n. The brains of the feeble-minded are smaller than those of normals.	129	45	42	66	21	19	27
o. People of average intelligence are usually more popular than people of high intelligence.	41	20	23	44	52	61	108

2

	Disagree						Agree
	1	2	3	4	5	6	7
a. Good emotional habits can be taught to children in school as easily as spelling can.	41	50	45	30	54	61	68
b. People who lose their memories have things that they want to forget.	67	59	40	54	46	50	33
c. Few mental-hospital patients are kept in padded cells.	13	7	12	26	58	77	156
d. Insanity comes about gradually.	12	17	21	57	68	85	89
e. Women have the same kinds of mental disease that men do.	18	14	28	65	54	69	101
f. Most of the insane can remember their past lives.	31	38	56	78	55	39	52
g. People who go from doctor to doctor with many complaints know that there is nothing really wrong with them.	84	50	61	38	40	33	42
h. Becoming overweight will not affect the mind.	20	31	51	44	43	57	103
i. Emotionally healthy people do not try to hold back their emotions.	48	52	42	47	55	49	56
j. If a person says that he is "going crazy," there is little chance that he will do so.	15	12	34	61	66	77	84
k. An only child is more likely to grow into a neurotic adult.	66	31	29	48	79	55	41
l. There are not enough mental hospitals to take care of the patients.	16	8	8	20	43	52	202

2

	Disagree					Agree	
	1	2	3	4	5	6	7
m. Forgetfulness is not a sign of insanity.	11	8	20	18	32	70	190
n. Most of the people who have nervous breakdowns have had more real problems than normal people.	100	58	46	38	34	40	33
o. It is harmful to a person's mental health to let others dominate him.	15	13	17	32	68	93	111

3

	Disagree					Agree	
	1	2	3	4	5	6	7
a. Nervous breakdowns usually come after a person has had some personal tragedy.	26	23	39	54	86	63	58
b. Children can have nervous breakdowns.	11	8	16	28	59	76	151
c. Feeble-minded children appear less often among the poor.	120	52	66	76	8	9	18
d. The insane are able to walk as well as normals.	18	23	49	49	58	68	84
e. Psychiatrists need to be a bit mentally unbalanced themselves in order to work with their patients.	250	38	19	19	8	6	9
f. If a person dreams that all of his teeth have fallen out, it is a sign that he is afraid of going to a dentist.	201	57	27	31	19	4	10
g. A child cannot inherit fears directly from his mother.	43	24	25	32	17	47	161
h. Good schooling can make a feeble-minded child as smart as any other.	219	41	42	18	11	7	11
i. Normal men do not become mental cases in the stress of battle.	94	57	41	43	35	31	48
j. The best way to get over a fear of high places is to gradually get used to them.	30	16	25	36	55	72	115
k. Insanity is not brought on as a punishment for sins.	23	8	1	10	15	37	255
l. It may help the mental patient if he shows his anger to the psychiatrist.	33	13	21	66	41	65	110
m. People who are likely to have a nervous breakdown pay little attention to their personal appearance.	56	52	51	62	45	39	44

3

	Disagree						Agree
	1	2	3	4	5	6	7
n. Feeble-mindedness is not caused by the mother being frightened during pregnancy.	14	2	10	18	14	43	248
o. There is little chance that a feeble minded child will develop into a normally intelligent adult.	19	7	15	33	37	61	177

4

	Disagree						Agree
	1	2	3	4	5	6	7
a. People who have been reared in prosperous environments enjoy adult life more than those who have been reared in poor circumstances.	103	61	42	50	42	29	22
b. There are indications that a person's mind will break before it happens.	13	17	20	47	83	90	79
c. People who seldom smile are likely to have a nervous breakdown.	97	45	47	58	50	32	20
d. Mental dullness is inherited.	52	42	34	56	58	51	56
e. People with college educations have less trouble solving their emotional problems.	71	55	38	41	51	58	35
f. If a child receives a hard blow on the head, he may become insane later.	55	43	44	79	54	30	44
g. Physical rest will not prevent a mental disorder.	29	43	56	59	53	47	62
h. Handsome children are seldom the most intelligent ones.	123	55	35	65	23	24	24
i. If a child is not taught things when he is young, his intelligence will still develop normally.	62	63	65	40	32	37	50
j. There is no way of telling from a child's behavior whether or not he will become insane later in life.	30	30	46	53	42	58	90
k. The brain cannot grow smaller from lack of use.	35	14	14	42	25	42	177
l. Children may develop a strong attachment for animals because they are not given sufficient love by their parents.	15	15	12	36	66	71	134
m. Financial worries are seldom the cause of nervous breakdowns.	110	100	55	25	19	18	22

	Disagree						Agree
4	1	2	3	4	5	6	7

n. In middle age more women than men develop mental disorders.

23	21	35	69	53	69	79

o. Books on "peace of mind" prevent many people from developing nervous breakdowns.

38	41	37	**76**	76	37	44

	Disagree						Agree
5	1	2	3	4	5	6	7

a. The main job of the psychiatrist is to recommend hobbies and other ways for the mental patient to occupy his mind.

66	54	35	52	40	40	62

b. Early training will not make the child's brain grow faster.

37	32	41	33	31	37	138

c. People who belong to clubs and social organizations are more likely to develop mental illness than those who do not.

169	74	48	30	10	10	8

d. A change of climate seldom helps an emotional disorder.

29	32	38	64	50	60	76

e. A child will not develop a liking for people unless he is taught.

115	71	40	34	33	21	35

f. Children usually forget about frightening experiences in a short time.

83	75	57	22	36	34	42

g. If a mother is nervous and upset when pregnant, it may make the child emotionally unstable.

127	51	39	43	34	23	32

h. Many people under twenty-one go to mental hospitals.

64	31	48	70	50	38	48

i. Ulcers are most frequently found in unaggressive-acting people.

145	64	40	56	21	12	11

j. People in mental hospitals prefer to be with normals rather than with other mental patients.

31	32	43	102	49	41	51

k. A normal person could live among the insane in a mental hospital without becoming insane himself.

13	11	20	42	48	64	151

l. Almost any disease that attacks the nervous system is likely to bring on insanity.

90	50	45	55	54	24	31

m. It would be difficult for a psychiatrist to treat a patient if they were close friends in private life.

62	35	30	47	47	65	63

	Disagree						Agree
5	1	2	3	4	5	6	7
n. A lack of vitamins will bring on a neurotic condition.	52	23	38	68	68	53	47
o. One severe fright does not make a person "nervous" for the rest of his life.	14	10	18	23	58	88	138

	Disagree						Agree
6	1	2	3	4	5	6	7
a. Helping the mentally ill person with his financial and social problems will not cure his disorder.	24	48	67	37	55	56	62
b. A confession of sins will not prevent insanity.	6	17	35	41	65	69	116
c. People of below normal intelligence like to mix socially as much as the normally intelligent do.	39	46	39	29	45	68	83
d. "Insanity" is found more often among women than men.	58	29	32	124	35	42	29
e. People who have one nervous breakdown seldom have another one.	102	86	81	42	15	15	8
f. Financial trouble is the most frequent cause of nervous breakdowns.	43	42	64	77	46	50	27
g. A girl who is taken advantage of sexually is usually left with a lasting fear of sexual relations.	22	20	32	58	84	64	69
h. There is a range of severity in mental illness between the normal and the insane.	13	6	18	71	30	55	156
i. Few of the people who go to mental hospitals are able to return to work in society again.	117	67	58	22	31	31	23
j. Shyness is not inherited.	31	28	37	46	31	58	118
k. A job promotion is usually helpful in curing a person's inferiority complex.	18	20	24	22	78	84	103
l. Alcohol can damage the brain.	16	10	8	17	43	64	191
m. The insane are people who have been cursed by the devil.	301	23	8	6	0	2	10
n. Intelligent people have as many strong fears as people of average intelligence.	27	22	30	31	34	78	127

6

	Disagree						Agree
	1	2	3	4	5	6	7
o. The insane are easily disturbed by noise.	25	29	27	106	60	51	51

7

	Disagree						Agree
	1	2	3	4	5	6	7
a. Normal people are more changeable in their attitudes than are insane people.	48	35	33	55	46	58	74
b. Most people who go to see a psychiatrist get shock treatments.	135	59	59	48	16	16	16
c. Most of the time psychiatrists have difficulty in telling whether or not a patient's mental disorder is curable.	54	52	46	70	51	42	34
d. Most of the people in mental hospitals are likely to commit violent acts.	104	80	61	36	24	25	19
e. If a person has more than the average amount of sexual relations, it can drive him insane.	134	47	45	44	35	15	29
f. Dreams do not foretell the future.	13	9	15	19	25	47	221
g. Children become tense when their parents are upset.	3	2	2	10	23	85	224
h. A nervous breakdown can often be avoided by moving to a different city.	71	45	40	63	65	37	28
i. The adult who needs a great deal of affection is likely to have had little affection in childhood.	28	19	24	42	59	82	95
j. Psychiatrists make less money than other doctors.	87	48	41	105	27	18	23
k. Few mental-hospital patients are kept in bed.	10	16	19	37	59	94	114
l. A person with a nervous breakdown feels more nervous in a darkened room.	30	21	24	114	60	52	48
m. Some people are born with the kind of nervous system that makes it easy for them to become emotionally disturbed.	25	24	18	39	68	71	104
n. "Immorality" can cause permanent damage to the brain.	109	41	27	45	44	35	48
o. Few of the people who seek psychiatric help need treatment.	82	74	60	49	33	26	25

8

	Disagree						Agree
	1	2	3	4	5	6	7
a. Most of the people in mental hospitals would prefer to be on the outside again.	19	29	36	69	42	67	87
b. Psychiatrists, as a group, are older than other doctors.	108	57	51	66	24	15	28
c. Most people can recognize the type of person who is likely to have a nervous breakdown.	130	59	43	45	36	16	20
d. People who have little sexual desire are less likely to have a "nervous breakdown" than are other people.	106	50	34	83	25	28	23
e. People of low intelligence are more superstitious than normals.	21	21	14	26	50	82	136
f. If a child is jealous of a younger brother, it is best not to let him show it in any way.	110	57	47	44	23	20	48
g. There is a shortage of well-trained doctors in mental hospitals.	10	4	3	23	25	55	229
h. Most mental disorders can be cured by drugs.	196	75	29	24	12	2	11
i. The children in a family can be quite different in terms of intelligence.	7	7	6	19	22	63	225
j. People who attend church regularly are as likely to end up in a mental hospital as those who do not.	96	50	35	24	21	40	83
k. It is injurious to a person's mental health to think a great deal about any one problem.	45	27	27	34	59	60	97
l. People who are in good physical condition seldom have emotional upsets.	49	51	46	35	45	62	61
m. Anger is never simply forgotten—it comes out in one way or another.	27	24	30	40	67	66	95
n. Children who move from city to city are more likely to develop an emotional disorder than those who grow up in one neighborhood.	37	19	22	57	69	67	78
o. Parents can build self-confidence in a child by complimenting him a great deal.	15	14	27	35	69	71	118

9

	Disagree						Agree
	1	2	3	4	5	6	7
a. It would improve anyone's mental health to spend a certain amount of time each day thinking over his emotional problems.	67	41	33	56	62	48	42
b. The blood of the insane is not as red as that of normal people.	233	26	21	54	6	2	7
c. Showing a great deal of affection to a child can prevent him from developing independence.	103	64	36	30	36	41	39
d. Feeble-minded people can work better with their hands than normals can.	162	53	29	46	27	15	17
e. Psychiatrists try to show the mental patient where his ideas are incorrect.	53	31	26	57	46	59	77
f. Psychiatrists teach the patient to live for the future instead of the present.	62	40	25	76	42	45	59
g. People of low intelligence are usually retarded in all of their mental abilities.	55	38	49	31	45	61	70
h. "In-law" trouble is the largest cause of divorce.	88	63	40	55	40	36	27
i. Most of the insane have little regard for their own safety.	37	37	50	48	46	64	67
j. Jealousy is a sign of feelings of inferiority.	20	13	15	30	68	99	104
k. People remember unpleasant events longer than pleasant ones.	59	39	26	46	40	52	87
l. Most clergymen will encourage a person with a mental disorder to see a psychiatrist.	16	24	24	69	52	64	100
m. You can tell a person's intelligence from the shape of his head.	241	44	18	18	10	8	10
n. Feeble-minded adults like to play children's games.	12	22	25	68	68	65	89
o. People usually leave mental hospitals thinner than when they were admitted.	86	50	34	97	29	20	33

10

	Disagree 1	2	3	4	5	6	Agree 7
a. If a person concentrates on happy memories, he will not be bothered by unpleasant things in the present.	63	38	47	37	63	50	51
b. If you try acting as though you like someone, you will learn to like him eventually.	20	21	33	41	97	69	60
c. When a person is recovering from a mental illness, it is best not to discuss the treatment that he has had.	21	25	40	50	49	65	99
d. Most of the insane realize that something is wrong with them.	37	39	46	47	63	55	62
e. When a person starts losing his mind he keeps going down hill, getting worse and worse.	18	29	42	66	87	51	56
f. There are more psychiatrists in the U.S. than heart specialists.	73	31	53	119	25	17	31
g. Boys are more likely to develop a "nervous disposition" if they have no father rather than no mother.	70	32	46	96	51	29	25
h. A facial twitch is seldom caused by an injured nerve.	55	38	52	75	42	40	47
i. "Nervousness" is not a sign of oncoming insanity.	14	18	22	29	70	73	123
j. Men worry more than women.	75	48	52	101	29	25	19
k. Boys and girls who start dating at an early age are less likely to develop emotional disorders.	58	40	46	86	55	32	32
l. There is less research being done on mental disorder than on cancer.	20	14	27	70	44	70	104
m. Beautiful women are more likely to have a nervous breakdown during the change of life than are less attractive women.	92	35	33	81	52	25	31
n. If a girl has sexual relations before she is mature, it can lead to a mental disorder.	51	31	48	75	63	38	43
o. Older people have a less difficult time recovering from a nervous breakdown.	71	66	59	56	28	29	40

11

	Disagree						Agree
	1	2	3	4	5	6	7

a. Vacations do not help people recover from nervous breakdowns.

94	86	68	24	24	25	28

b. It is not likely that a person will recover from a nervous breakdown overnight.

9	10	6	3	21	62	238

c. The insane talk about the same things that children do.

82	52	49	68	45	28	25

d. The insane live longer than normal people.

126	64	39	81	18	9	12

e. Most of the people in mental hospitals speak in words that cannot be understood.

124	65	61	45	24	16	14

f. Mental disorders are more widespread now than they were twenty years ago.

35	26	22	40	49	66	111

g. Most suicides occur because of rejection in love.

107	71	52	55	30	18	16

h. If a person's mind is going to "crack," nothing can prevent it.

135	69	73	36	11	6	19

i. Most social workers go into their field because of their own misfortunes in life.

158	68	34	42	25	14	8

j. Brain operations cannot cure feeble-mindedness.

24	13	39	61	34	41	137

k. Affection is less important to the child's emotional development than financial security.

252	44	12	6	5	7	23

l. The feeble-minded usually have keener sight than normal people.

141	50	34	91	15	10	8

m. Few people who have nervous breakdowns go to mental hospitals.

24	25	59	38	71	61	71

n. An emotional shock in childhood is seldom responsible for adult mental disorder.

64	69	56	55	43	30	32

o. Mental disorders have their beginnings in childhood.

33	33	39	69	66	52	57

12

	Disagree 1	2	3	4	5	6	Agree 7
a. Women are more likely to commit suicide than men.	119	61	47	82	13	13	14
b. The brain can be overworked to the point of insanity.	58	35	20	33	53	65	85
c. Many nervous breakdowns could be prevented if people changed to jobs that fit them better.	2	9	11	13	55	102	157
d. People are more capable of skillful action when they are angry.	180	82	29	26	9	10	13
e. Venereal disease is responsible for much of the insanity.	26	24	35	58	66	65	75
f. An emotionally upset person will become calmer if he talks about his problems.	8	11	12	36	71	85	126
g. More people develop insanity than tuberculosis.	36	17	33	76	49	63	75
h. Most of the people who sleep a great deal are in need of vitamins.	83	36	46	71	49	26	38
i. Psychiatrists do not advertise in newspapers.	19	7	17	62	31	55	158
j. Most of the recoveries from insanity are brought about by brain surgery.	165	75	47	38	11	4	9
k. If a person is very much afraid of fire, it probably came from a serious burn in childhood.	67	40	40	65	62	43	32
l. Nearly all nightmares result from eating too much at bedtime.	99	63	41	44	39	34	29
m. Disappointments do not affect children as much as they do adults.	130	62	37	24	29	28	39
n. Psychiatrists are successful in treating most of their mental patients.	23	23	44	81	84	53	41
o. The feeble-minded usually have keener hearing than normal people.	121	42	42	89	20	15	20

		Disagree					Agree
13	1	2	3	4	5	6	7

a. Psychiatrists have to have a good sense of humor in order to help their patients.

13	16	25	57	61	73	104

b. Emotionally upset persons are seldom found in important positions in business.

56	54	51	41	29	54	64

c. The insane laugh more than normals.

70	43	49	77	39	40	31

d. A child who daydreams a great deal should be discouraged from discussing them.

145	70	51	34	14	8	27

e. A person who has a nervous breakdown can recover faster if he is with his family.

67	45	53	84	47	28	25

f. Insanity is not contagious.

11	5	3	13	13	47	257

g. A child can be born feeble-minded as punishment for the mother's sins.

254	25	5	28	11	9	17

h. Mental patients are usually irritable and grouchy.

74	36	69	73	45	25	26

i. Few people could do the job of a psychiatrist even if they had the time and patience to talk with the mentally ill.

16	15	29	29	57	63	140

j. Aggressive people are usually more sure of themselves.

50	32	36	26	33	72	100

k. People who appear nervous and fidgety are the ones most likely to have a nervous breakdown.

46	41	56	65	54	40	47

l. If a person has little faith in psychiatrists, it will not help him to go to one.

24	23	42	31	63	79	87

m. A person returning from a mental hospital will usually have about the same attitudes toward the people that he has known.

35	38	55	59	56	57	48

n. Emotionally unstable people act nervous only when others are around.

80	73	52	43	38	36	26

o. Feeble-minded children are less obedient than normal children.

91	73	54	54	23	25	28

14

	Disagree						Agree
	1	2	3	4	5	6	7
a. A poor diet does not lead to feeble-mindedness.	22	21	41	25	40	52	148
b. The insane have little interest in sex.	83	76	47	77	26	29	11
c. People who live in the country are more likely to become insane than people who live in large cities.	188	74	43	22	9	3	10
d. Men take longer than women to recover from a nervous breakdown.	50	30	35	160	34	19	21
e. When a child gets very excited, such as at Christmas, he is likely to be upset for a few days.	46	32	40	27	69	58	75
f. A person can avoid worry by keeping busy.	10	15	14	15	83	102	110
g. Inferiority complexes often occur in people with high abilities.	29	24	35	35	52	75	99
h. Few of the people in mental hospitals are acting out the life of some great person, such as Napoleon.	24	18	22	44	59	80	102
i. Criminals have more nervous breakdowns than other people.	94	67	54	74	24	18	18
j. X-rays of the head will not tell whether a person is likely to develop insanity.	23	16	13	55	40	55	147
k. Hypnosis is often used by psychiatrists.	39	20	43	61	59	54	73
l. Worry over health brings on many emotional problems.	5	6	11	11	63	94	159
m. Most of the insanity cases are found in people over fifty years of age.	74	65	58	61	36	35	20
n. Most children could grow up to become doctors and scientists if they worked hard enough in school.	130	69	35	29	21	31	34
o. The highly intelligent mental patient is more easily treated by the psychiatrist.	59	42	41	73	43	43	48

	Disagree						Agree
15	1	2	3	4	5	6	7

a. If a child is "bossed" around a great deal, he is likely to boss everyone else around when he grows up.

37	44	46	55	45	64	58

b. Most of the hospital beds in the U.S. are occupied by mental patients.

113	50	43	53	33	24	33

c. Noisy children are more likely to become emotionally disordered adults than quiet ones.

149	84	37	36	18	11	14

d. A boy inherits his emotional disposition from his mother.

149	51	23	75	26	16	9

e. Most doctors can use psychiatric methods if a patient has a mental disorder.

83	46	35	46	42	45	52

f. A person becomes feeble-minded because his brain stops growing in early childhood.

153	45	28	42	23	28	30

g. People who are able to return from mental hospitals usually grow stronger and stronger like the recovery from other diseases.

37	37	55	69	43	48	60

h. Even though a person becomes insane, he still cares about what others think of him.

56	49	17	59	46	60	62

i. The eyes of the insane are glassy.

86	48	33	98	29	23	32

j. Psychiatrists try to teach mental patients to hold in their strong emotions.

89	47	40	80	34	24	35

k. More men than women have nervous breakdowns.

81	49	50	99	24	18	28

l. Most of the nervousness in children comes from seeing frightening movies.

117	76	53	37	31	20	15

m. Telling a child that you don't love him is usually more disturbing to him than giving him a spanking.

9	9	4	9	23	79	216

n. Few of the people who go to a psychiatrist do so primarily because of sex problems.

40	29	46	79	46	56	53

o. Offering rewards is a poor way to cure a child of thumb sucking.

28	19	24	31	35	62	150

	Disagree						Agree
16	1	2	3	4	5	6	7
a. A person's mental illness may come from having a spell cast on him by a fortune-teller.	267	32	13	14	14	4	5
b. Most people who "go crazy" try to kill themselves.	147	76	46	36	25	10	9
c. Parents encourage mental disorder if they severely threaten their children.	24	19	38	44	80	68	76
d. Women who have no children are less likely to develop emotional disorders.	131	76	60	38	15	13	16
e. We dislike people who show the qualities that we dislike in ourselves.	20	9	14	50	65	96	95
f. The main job of the psychiatrist is to explain to the patient the origin of his troubles.	40	26	22	34	51	71	105
g. A person in treatment by a psychiatrist needs to make several visits each week.	43	27	40	85	60	48	46
h. Girls are more likely to develop a mental disorder if they have no father rather than no mother.	80	58	58	90	36	12	15
i. Fathers have more influence than mothers on the emotional development of their children.	125	71	67	56	11	8	11
j. Most of the mentally ill have regular cycles of sanity and insanity.	37	33	37	94	57	38	53
k. Psychiatrists usually do not tell patients the seriousness of their emotional problems.	8	15	36	59	54	65	112
l. The insane are more likely to attack children rather than other adults.	71	52	49	84	36	30	27
m. People who do a variety of things in their work are more likely to have a nervous breakdown than those who do routine jobs.	159	83	39	27	14	13	14
n. Nervous breakdowns seldom occur among people in high-income groups.	172	85	50	15	12	5	10
o. Physical exhaustion does not lead to a nervous breakdown.	63	49	52	26	34	49	76

2

The Final 60-item Information

Questionnaire

THE MEASURE OF public information used in most of our studies of communication effectiveness was derived in three stages. First, 180 items from the 240-item preliminary form were factor analyzed; then, from this analysis the 50-item questionnaire was developed (see Ch. 2 for details). The 50-item form was used in surveying public opinion. Continued experience with and analysis of the 50-item form led to a final revised 60-item form. The number in the right-hand margin indicates the information factor most prominently related to each item. These numbers correspond to the factors listed and described in Chapter 2. Some of the items were completely unchanged from the original forms. Others were changed only in a trivial manner; for example, in one item, ". . . likely to develop insanity" was changed to ". . . likely to become insane." Still other items in the final form were considerably altered or developed especially for that form. The extent to which items were changed from the preliminary questionnaire to the final version is indicated by the factor number in the right-hand column. Items which were unchanged or only slightly altered carry the numbers 1, 2, and so on; those which underwent considerable change carry the numbers 1*, 2*, and so on. The last twenty items in the questionnaire presented here do not relate strongly to any of the ten information factors. These items were included in the revised form because they seemed to measure interesting ideas not directly included in the factors.

INSTRUCTIONS

You are being asked to participate in a study of mental health problems. Your participation will supply valuable information to those responsible for the nation's health.

On the following pages you will find a number of statements about health problems. We want to know how much you agree or disagree with each of the statements. To the right of each statement you can find a rating scale:

The points along the scale (1, 2, 3, . . . 7) can be interpreted as follows:

1. Completely disagree
2. Mostly disagree
3. Disagree more than agree
4. Neutral
5. Agree more than disagree
6. Mostly agree
7. Completely agree

The use of the scale can be illustrated with the following statement:

"Smoking causes lung cancer."

If you agreed completely with this statement, you would place a mark in column 7. If you agreed slightly with the statement, you would place a mark in column 5. If you mostly disagreed with the statement, you would place a mark in column 2. In this manner you can indicate the extent to which you agree or disagree with each of the statements on the following pages.

Like everyone else, you will probably feel that you do not know the answer to some of the statements. When this occurs please make the best guess that you can.

Please make your marks inside the agreement and disagreement boxes of the scales. Do it like this:

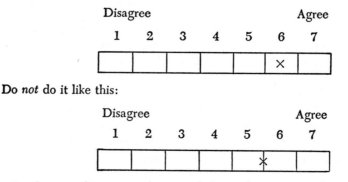

Please make sure that you make a mark for each statement. Leave none of the statements blank and make only one mark for each. You should not spend more than a few seconds marking each statement. If it is difficult for you to make up your mind, make the best guess that you can and go on to the next one.

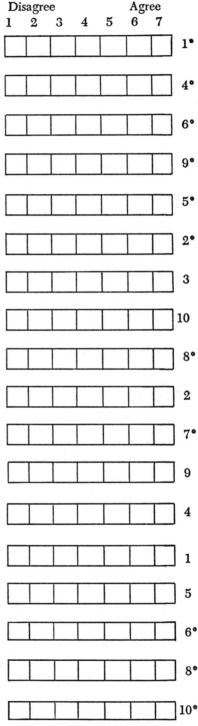

	Disagree					Agree	
	1	2	3	4	5	6	7

1. The mentally ill pay little attention to their personal appearance. — 1°

2. People who keep themselves occupied with pleasant thoughts seldom become mentally ill. — 4°

3. Few people who enter mental hospitals ever leave. — 6°

4. Older people have fewer emotional problems than younger people. — 9°

5. People cannot maintain good mental health without the support of strong persons in their environment. — 5°

6. Will power alone will not cure mental disorders. — 2°

7. Women have no more emotional problems than men do. — 3

8. X-rays of the head will not tell whether a person is likely to become insane. — 10

9. Emotional problems do little damage to the individual. — 8°

10. Psychiatrists try to teach mental patients to hold in their strong emotions. — 2

11. Mental illness can usually be helped by a vacation or change of scene. — 7°

12. Disappointments affect children as much as they do adults. — 9

13. The main job of the psychiatrist is to recommend hobbies and other ways for the mental patient to occupy his mind. — 4

14. The insane laugh more than normal people. — 1

15. Psychiatrists try to show the mental patient where his ideas are incorrect. — 5

16. Mental disorder is not a hopeless condition. — 6°

17. Mental health is one of the most important national problems. — 8°

18. Mental disorder is usually brought on by physical causes. — 10°

	Disagree					Agree	
	1	2	3	4	5	6	7

19. It is easier for women to get over emotional problems than it is for men. 3°

20. A change of climate seldom helps an emotional disorder. 7

21. The best way to mental health is by avoiding morbid thoughts. 4°

22. There is not much that can be done for a person who develops a mental disorder. 6

23. Mental disorder is one of the most damaging illnesses that a person can have. 8

24. Children sometimes have mental breakdowns as severe as those of adults. 9°

25. Nervous breakdowns seldom have a physical origin. 10°

26. Most of the people in mental hospitals speak in words that can be understood. 1

27. Mental health is largely a matter of trying hard to control the emotions. 2

28. If a person concentrates on happy memories, he will not be bothered by unpleasant things in the present. 4

29. The mentally ill have not received enough guidance from the important people in their lives. 5°

30. Women are as emotionally healthy as men. 3°

31. The seriousness of the mental-health problem in this country has been exaggerated. 8°

32. Helping the mentally ill person with his financial and social problems often improves his condition. 7

33. Mental patients usually make a good adjustment to society when they are released. 6°

34. The good psychiatrist acts like a father to his patients. 5

35. Early adulthood is more of a danger period for mental illness than later years. 9°

Disagree   Agree

1 2 3 4 5 6 7

36. Almost any disease that attacks the nervous system is likely to bring on insanity.   10

37. You can tell a person who is mentally ill from his appearance.   1°

38. People who become mentally ill have little will power.   2°

39. Women are more likely to develop mental disorders than men.   3

40. Most mental disturbances in adults can be traced to emotional experiences in childhood.   7°

41. People who have little sexual desire are more likely to have a "nervous breakdown" than are other people.

42. A person can avoid worry by keeping busy.

43. A poor diet often leads to feeble-mindedness.

44. Emotionally upset persons are often found in important positions in business.

45. Good emotional habits can be taught to children in school as easily as spelling can.

46. The eyes of the insane are glassy.

47. When a person is recovering from a mental illness, it is best not to discuss the treatment that he has had.

48. People who go from doctor to doctor with many complaints know that there is nothing really wrong with them.

49. A person cannot rid himself of unpleasant memories by trying hard to forget them.

50. The main job of the psychiatrist is to explain to the patient the origin of his troubles.

51. Most suicides occur because of rejection in love.

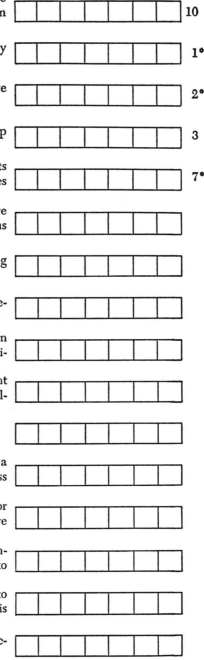

	Disagree					Agree
	1	2	3	4	5	6	7

52. People who are likely to have a nervous breakdown pay little attention to their personal appearance.

53. Most of the time psychiatrists have difficulty in telling whether or not a patient's mental disorder is curable.

54. Children usually do not forget about frightening experiences in a short time.

55. Books on "peace of mind" prevent many people from developing nervous breakdowns.

56. Most clergymen will encourage a person with a mental disorder to see a psychiatrist.

57. Physical exhaustion does not lead to a nervous breakdown.

58. The adult who needs a great deal of affection is likely to have had little affection in childhood.

59. Physical rest will not prevent a mental disorder.

60. Most of the people who seek psychiatric help need the treatment.

Now that you have completed the questionnaire would you please check to make sure that you have done the following things:

1. Rated your agreement or disagreement with every statement in the questionnaire. If you have failed to mark a single statement, we will be unable to use your questionnaire.
2. Made only one mark for each statement.

THANK YOU AGAIN FOR YOUR HELP IN THIS RESEARCH.

3

Instructions Used for the Study

of Experts

*F*OLLOWING ARE THE instructions used for the experts' information form (see Ch. 3).

MENTAL-HEALTH STUDY

This questionnaire concerns opinions and attitudes about mental-health problems. Each item in the questionnaire is an opinion that was found to be important in studies of the lay population. In order to formulate better programs of public information, it is necessary to make decisions as to what the public should be told. We are asking your help in making these decisions.

On the following pages you will find fifty opinions about mental-health problems. We want to know how you think each of these should be treated in the mass media of communication (radio, television, newspapers, pamphlets, and so on). We would like you to make a decision for each opinion as to whether it should be affirmed by the media, not mentioned, or disavowed. Our principal interest is in what you think should be communicated to the public and not in whether the opinions are true or false in any absolute sense. For example, you may find some statements which you think are true but which would not contribute to the public understanding; and you may find others which are false but which are of insufficient importance to be emphasized as incorrect by the media of communications. For each opinion you will be provided with a rating scale as follows:

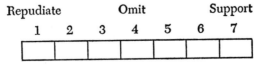

The points along the continuum (1 2, 3, . . . 7) are to be interpreted as follows:

1. Should be strongly repudiated in the media.
2. Should be repudiated to a moderate extent.
3. Should be repudiated but only with slight emphasis.
4. Should be omitted from discussion: not an important matter for public information efforts.
5. Should be supported but only with slight emphasis.
6. Should be supported to a moderate extent.
7. Should be strongly supported in the media.

The use of the scale can be illustrated with the following opinion:

> "Emotional problems in children can be treated more easily than those in adults."

If you thought that this opinion was one that should be strongly supported in the media, one that should be emphasized as correct to the public, you would make a mark in column 7. If you thought that the opinion had only slight merit for communication, you would make a mark in column 5. If you thought that the opinion was a very harmful one for the public to believe, you would make a mark in column 1, indicating that the media should strongly emphasize that the opinion is incorrect.

Please make your marks inside the boxes of the scales. Do it like this:

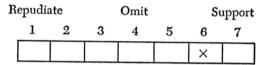

Do *not* do it like this:

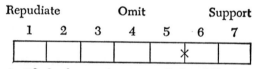

Because of your scientific background you may find it difficult to rate some of the opinions in the questionnaire. The language in which the opinions are expressed is most likely not that which you would want to use in discussing the problems. Also, you may find it difficult to give a judgment on statements of this level of simplicity: you might want to add qualifications. However, these are the things that people actually say, and it is about these opinions that the judgments of experts will have to be made. With these considerations in mind, try to make a judgment about each of the opinions in the questionnaire. Thank you for participating in the study.

[*The 50-item questionnaire followed.*]

4

Instructions and Sample Pages

from the Semantic Differential

FOLLOWING ARE THE instruction sheet and three sample pages of the Semantic Differential. The form is called "the word-association study" simply to provide an innocuous-sounding introduction for the subject. The Semantic Differential forms used in our studies usually employed from ten to twenty scales and twelve to fifteen concepts.

THE WORD-ASSOCIATION STUDY

You are being asked to participate in a study of word meanings. The object of the study is to find out how you like to describe different kinds of persons. On each of the following pages there is a different person for you to describe. Your description can be made by marking the list of words on the page. Take a look to see how this is done. Each pair of words forms a scale. By making a check mark along the scale you can indicate what you associate with the particular kind of person.

If you feel that the issue or person named at the top of the page is *highly related* with one end of the scale, you would place a check mark as follows:

fair_:_:_:_:_:_:✓unfair   OR   fair✓:_:_:_:_:_:_unfair

If you feel that the person or issue is *moderately related* to one or the other end of the scale, you would place your check as follows:

strong_:✓:_:_:_:_:_weak   OR   strong_:_:_:_:✓:_weak

If the issue or person seems *only slightly related* to one side as opposed to the other, you would check as follows:

active_:_:✓:_:_:_:_passive   OR   active_:_:_:_:✓:_:_passive

If you considered both sides equally related, you would check the middle space on the scale:

safe_:_:_:✓:_:_:_dangerous

Remember: *never put more than one check mark on any scale.* And also be sure to *check every item.* If you feel that a pair of adjectives does not apply, or if you are undecided, place the check mark in the center space. Do not leave the line blank.

Do not spend more than a few seconds marking each scale. Your first impression is what we would like to learn about. We have found you can work quicker if you first form a picture in your mind of the person mentioned at the top of each page, and after that check each scale rapidly.

We do not need your name on the questionnaire for this study. Thank you very much for your cooperation.

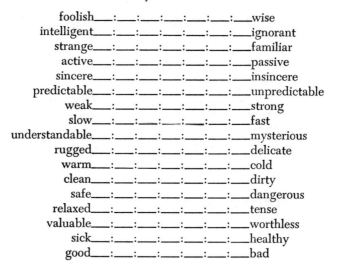

Psychiatrist

```
        foolish___:___:___:___:___:___:___wise
    intelligent___:___:___:___:___:___:___ignorant
        strange___:___:___:___:___:___:___familiar
         active___:___:___:___:___:___:___passive
        sincere___:___:___:___:___:___:___insincere
    predictable___:___:___:___:___:___:___unpredictable
           weak___:___:___:___:___:___:___strong
           slow___:___:___:___:___:___:___fast
 understandable___:___:___:___:___:___:___mysterious
        rugged___:___:___:___:___:___:___delicate
          warm___:___:___:___:___:___:___cold
         clean___:___:___:___:___:___:___dirty
          safe___:___:___:___:___:___:___dangerous
       relaxed___:___:___:___:___:___:___tense
      valuable___:___:___:___:___:___:___worthless
          sick___:___:___:___:___:___:___healthy
          good___:___:___:___:___:___:___bad
```

Mental Patient

```
        foolish___:___:___:___:___:___:___wise
    intelligent___:___:___:___:___:___:___ignorant
        strange___:___:___:___:___:___:___familiar
         active___:___:___:___:___:___:___passive
        sincere___:___:___:___:___:___:___insincere
    predictable___:___:___:___:___:___:___unpredictable
           weak___:___:___:___:___:___:___strong
           slow___:___:___:___:___:___:___fast
 understandable___:___:___:___:___:___:___mysterious
        rugged___:___:___:___:___:___:___delicate
          warm___:___:___:___:___:___:___cold
         clean___:___:___:___:___:___:___dirty
          safe___:___:___:___:___:___:___dangerous
       relaxed___:___:___:___:___:___:___tense
      valuable___:___:___:___:___:___:___worthless
          sick___:___:___:___:___:___:___healthy
          good___:___:___:___:___:___:___bad
```

Mental Hospital

foolish___:___:___:___:___:___:___wise
intelligent___:___:___:___:___:___:___ignorant
strange___:___:___:___:___:___:___familiar
active___:___:___:___:___:___:___passive
sincere___:___:___:___:___:___:___insincere
predictable___:___:___:___:___:___:___unpredictable
weak___:___:___:___:___:___:___strong
slow___:___:___:___:___:___:___fast
understandable___:___:___:___:___:___:___mysterious
rugged___:___:___:___:___:___:___delicate
warm___:___:___:___:___:___:___cold
clean___:___:___:___:___:___:___dirty
safe___:___:___:___:___:___:___dangerous
relaxed___:___:___:___:___:___:___tense
valuable___:___:___:___:___:___:___worthless
sick___:___:___:___:___:___:___healthy
good___:___:___:___:___:___:___bad

5

Mean* Semantic Differential Ratings of 74

and Mental Illness

Concepts	Scales					
	Foolish . . . Wise	Sad . . . Happy	Passive . . . Active	Insincere . . . Sincere	Ignorant . . . Intelligent	Unpre-dictable . . . Pre-dictable
1. Child	4.62	6.51	6.74	6.18	5.51	2.44
2. Someone who is ex-tremely withdrawn	2.89	1.98	1.78	3.98	4.11	2.98
3. Someone who is incap-able of making even un-important decisions	2.07	2.93	2.56	2.93	2.73	2.36
4. Someone who always feels lonely	2.64	1.44	2.04	4.07	3.98	3.40
5. A person with a brain tumor	3.69	2.18	2.71	4.04	4.02	2.82
6. A person who feels un-reasonably depressed	2.47	1.38	1.82	3.82	3.62	2.33
7. A person who is sick with jealousy	1.44	1.47	3.33	3.18	2.44	1.93
8. An alcoholic	1.42	2.22	2.76	2.47	2.60	1.68
9. Someone who is incapa-able of loving anyone but himself	1.42	2.11	3.07	2.47	2.78	2.82
10. Someone who is dying from cancer, but does not know it	4.16	3.36	3.40	4.80	4.13	3.98
11. Insane man	2.20	2.76	3.91	2.73	2.84	1.49
12. Someone who always bottles up his problems	1.73	1.71	2.56	3.42	3.40	3.00

* Each mean is based on the responses of 50 members of our opinion panel. For group there is an approximately equal division of men and women and a wide distri-to 7.00. A mean greater than 4.00 implies that the concept is like the adjective below;

Concepts Related to Mental Health

Scales

Weak . . . Strong	Slow . . . Fast	Delicate . . . Rugged	Cold . . . Warm	Dirty . . . Clean	Danger- ous . . . Safe	Tense . . . Relaxed	Worth- less . . . Valuable	Sick . . . Healthy	Bad . . . Good
4.67	5.53	4.84	6.18	4.22	5.09	5.62	6.62	5.71	5.89
3.04	2.89	3.22	2.49	4.51	3.87	1.87	4.16	3.47	4.40
1.82	1.78	3.13	3.71	4.09	3.33	2.42	3.09	3.18	3.96
2.67	3.11	3.02	2.93	4.40	4.31	2.24	3.96	3.20	4.38
2.71	2.76	2.22	3.82	4.38	3.24	2.27	3.91	1.31	4.38
2.36	2.47	3.04	2.87	4.09	2.78	1.58	3.53	2.13	3.78
1.82	3.49	3.51	3.62	4.02	2.16	1.56	3.24	2.22	3.04
1.31	2.44	3.38	3.78	2.62	1.76	2.49	2.71	1.51	2.76
2.18	3.33	3.69	2.07	4.16	3.07	2.49	3.20	2.76	3.11
2.73	2.93	2.38	3.96	4.67	4.18	3.07	4.11	1.13	4.29
3.02	3.76	3.91	3.33	3.58	1.40	1.82	2.69	1.44	3.04
3.36	3.33	3.80	2.91	4.31	3.53	1.93	3.71	3.07	4.13

this purpose four matched groups of 50 each were drawn from the panel. In each
bution of ages, and years of education. The means are restricted to the range of 1.00
a mean less than 4.00 implies that the concept is like the adjective above.

Concepts   *Scales*

	Foolish . . . Wise	Sad . . . Happy	Passive . . . Active	Insincere . . . Sincere	Ignorant . . . Intelligent	Unpre- dictable . . . Pre- dictable
13. A person who has re-current attacks of malaria	4.09	3.07	3.69	4.31	4.53	3.91
14. Someone who lives in constant fear because he thinks people are after him	1.40	1.38	3.51	3.33	2.49	1.91
15. A person with a character disorder	2.87	2.67	4.00	2.87	3.11	2.16
16. Someone who will fight even on an imagined provocation	1.58	2.93	5.53	3.27	2.51	2.29
17. A person with uncalled-for spells of laughter	2.11	4.40	4.31	3.33	3.31	2.16
18. A person who feels unwanted	2.51	1.56	2.24	3.84	3.64	2.67
19. Father	6.17	6.12	6.12	6.60	6.52	5.76
20. A person who suffers from many allergies	3.67	3.64	4.24	4.98	5.14	4.12
21. An anxious person	3.26	3.45	5.50	5.43	5.07	3.76
22. A person whose moods change in a second	2.50	3.29	5.12	3.55	4.14	2.07
23. An aggressive person	5.24	5.17	6.41	5.00	5.55	4.74
24. A leper	4.26	2.48	2.86	5.17	4.62	4.38
25. Someone who gets frustrated with the least little thing	1.57	2.31	4.26	3.86	3.50	2.21
26. A person who feels hopeless about life	1.41	1.33	1.88	3.52	2.86	2.48
27. A juvenile delinquent	2.10	2.60	5.45	2.57	3.38	2.02
28. Someone who always feels guilty	1.95	1.95	3.21	3.67	3.57	2.95
29. An emotionally sick person	3.24	1.93	2.60	4.29	4.26	2.12
30. A person who has all kinds of compulsions about little unimportant things	1.88	2.55	4.43	4.07	3.79	2.50
31. Someone who is emotionally unbalanced	2.86	2.43	3.19	3.83	3.79	1.79
32. A person with a broken leg	4.48	3.43	3.38	5.14	5.05	4.86
33. Neurotic woman	2.26	2.14	3.36	3.07	3.52	2.12
34. Someone who is convinced that he is vastly superior to the mass of humanity	1.60	3.74	5.41	3.48	3.00	3.07
35. An overprotective mother	2.36	3.21	4.81	5.26	4.05	4.00

Scales

Weak ... Strong	Slow ... Fast	Delicate ... Rugged	Cold ... Warm	Dirty ... Clean	Danger- ous ... Safe	Tense ... Relaxed	Worth- less ... Valuable	Sick ... Healthy	Bad ... Good
2.98	3.71	2.60	4.11	4.53	4.09	3.02	4.38	2.00	4.00
2.07	3.60	3.02	2.78	4.02	2.40	1.44	3.29	2.00	3.40
2.67	3.49	3.11	3.38	4.00	2.56	2.40	3.44	2.33	3.18
3.20	5.16	5.00	3.44	3.89	2.18	1.07	3.42	3.22	3.00
3.04	3.84	3.60	4.49	4.18	3.87	3.36	3.98	3.47	3.96
2.84	3.44	3.40	3.04	4.18	3.78	2.02	3.76	2.87	3.87
6.33	5.17	5.38	6.12	6.45	6.41	5.29	6.67	5.79	6.57
3.60	3.31	2.71	3.79	5.48	4.98	4.67	4.81	2.57	5.29
3.76	4.95	3.74	4.81	5.67	4.14	1.98	4.88	3.62	5.10
2.93	5.00	3.79	3.71	5.07	3.60	2.52	3.88	3.69	4.29
5.64	5.52	5.36	4.36	5.43	4.52	3.31	5.45	5.40	5.36
3.00	3.07	2.71	4.21	4.02	3.62	3.26	4.26	1.79	4.52
2.38	4.26	3.05	3.95	5.07	3.57	1.95	3.98	3.12	4.12
1.98	2.83	2.88	3.21	4.50	3.07	2.33	3.24	2.24	3.91
2.21	4.21	4.14	3.17	3.71	2.29	2.05	3.36	2.83	2.76
2.48	3.17	3.36	3.88	4.60	3.91	2.14	3.69	3.12	4.07
2.38	3.24	2.98	3.71	4.43	3.00	1.83	4.05	1.71	4.07
2.71	3.88	3.38	4.02	4.57	3.93	2.21	3.88	3.21	4.41
2.31	3.12	2.81	3.38	3.81	2.36	1.93	3.31	1.81	3.86
4.12	3.41	3.60	4.64	4.93	5.07	3.74	4.81	3.40	5.00
2.36	3.45	2.86	3.24	4.69	3.31	1.95	3.62	2.05	4.12
3.60	4.43	4.48	3.02	4.79	3.17	2.57	3.43	3.37	3.48
4.10	4.45	3.91	5.02	5.31	3.88	2.36	4.21	3.67	4.12

Concepts   *Scales*

	Foolish … Wise	Sad … Happy	Passive … Active	Insincere … Sincere	Ignorant … Intelligent	Unpredictable … Predictable
36. Someone who is convinced that he alone gets all the bad luck in the world	1.48	1.68	3.05	3.48	2.76	2.88
37. A criminal without any conscience whatsoever	1.57	3.24	4.93	2.17	1.91	1.67
38. Average woman	5.35	5.55	5.76	5.96	5.75	4.76
39. A person who has to do everything in a certain fixed way	3.14	3.76	4.94	5.39	4.55	4.76
40. Someone who is mean and cruel to animals	1.57	2.33	3.65	2.29	2.06	2.37
41. An unreasonably sensitive person	2.74	2.45	3.08	4.47	4.02	2.69
42. Someone who lost eyesight because he had a severe case of syphilis	2.27	1.80	2.74	3.49	2.65	3.25
43. An emotionally immature person	2.37	2.71	3.74	3.04	2.94	2.10
44. A person who is so shy that every time he has to meet with others he breaks out in a rash	2.63	2.18	2.71	4.31	3.74	3.06
45. A person who is overcome with despondent feelings	2.39	1.71	2.43	4.02	3.61	2.49
46. Someone who cannot relax	2.94	2.67	5.08	4.59	4.59	3.51
47. Someone who always seems to do the wrong thing when he is in a group	2.69	2.71	4.39	4.12	3.76	2.86
48. A person with a nervous breakdown	3.57	2.06	4.10	4.51	4.59	2.71
49. Someone who has spells when he does not say a word to anyone	2.57	2.20	3.37	3.80	3.88	2.63
50. A person with a stomach ulcer	3.80	3.00	4.94	5.14	5.00	4.33
51. An utterly irresponsible person	1.76	3.84	3.98	2.31	3.02	1.65
52. A person who is incapable of finishing anything	2.49	3.20	3.61	2.82	3.31	2.49
53. A person who lives in a phantasy world	1.92	4.39	2.86	3.59	3.37	2.37
54. Someone who was born blind	4.67	4.20	4.04	5.45	5.31	4.98
55. Neurotic man	2.51	2.30	3.57	2.84	3.53	2.22
56. Me	4.93	5.96	6.18	6.56	5.76	5.47

Scales

Weak . . . Strong	Slow . . . Fast	Delicate . . . Rugged	Cold . . . Warm	Dirty . . . Clean	Danger- ous . . . Safe	Tense . . . Relaxed	Worth- less . . . Valuable	Sick . . . Healthy	Bad . . . Good
2.02	3.05	3.21	3.38	4.52	3.86	2.62	3.64	2.98	3.79
2.41	4.12	4.50	2.00	2.88	1.36	2.21	1.95	2.31	1.71
4.92	4.88	4.20	5.22	6.20	5.45	4.41	6.12	5.45	6.10
4.27	3.16	4.25	3.37	5.37	4.96	2.49	4.67	4.02	4.71
2.39	3.59	4.78	2.06	3.31	2.10	2.00	2.90	3.16	2.27
2.51	3.45	2.83	4.20	5.06	4.12	1.82	4.04	3.26	4.35
2.37	3.12	3.53	3.86	2.88	2.94	2.45	3.29	2.29	3.39
2.35	3.20	3.16	3.80	4.43	2.94	2.49	3.41	3.06	3.82
2.43	2.90	2.82	3.96	2.59	4.22	1.53	3.74	2.98	4.33
2.20	2.90	2.84	3.55	4.57	3.29	2.04	3.45	2.61	4.06
3.57	5.06	3.82	4.02	4.92	4.02	1.43	4.10	3.24	4.18
3.22	3.86	3.92	3.92	4.12	3.43	2.33	3.71	4.00	3.94
2.61	4.16	2.78	4.12	4.76	3.22	1.57	3.69	1.96	4.16
2.96	3.51	3.35	3.16	4.55	3.63	2.22	3.67	3.10	3.86
3.76	4.63	3.41	4.33	4.86	4.67	2.08	4.65	2.22	4.49
2.31	3.59	3.74	3.74	3.84	2.43	3.71	2.51	3.37	2.94
2.55	3.00	3.74	3.94	4.08	3.55	3.31	2.80	3.65	3.67
2.51	2.86	2.90	4.31	4.53	3.51	4.00	2.98	3.26	4.10
4.55	3.37	3.57	5.00	5.06	5.14	4.14	4.84	4.02	4.98
2.47	3.45	3.39	3.14	4.25	2.88	2.10	3.16	2.47	3.41
5.11	4.98	5.49	6.02	6.47	6.51	4.22	5.91	5.96	5.96

Concepts   *Scales*

	Foolish . . . Wise	Sad . . . Happy	Passive . . . Active	Insincere . . . Sincere	Ignorant . . . Intelligent	Unpredictable . . . Predictable
57. A person who gets his feelings hurt easily	2.00	2.04	3.40	4.38	3.87	3.00
58. A person ridden with all kinds of fears	1.67	1.42	3.13	3.56	3.00	2.20
59. A person who does not care what happens to him or anyone around him	1.36	2.49	3.36	2.27	2.16	1.73
60. An adult who has never developed beyond adolescence	1.87	3.64	3.36	3.09	2.42	1.80
61. Someone who gets upset by even small changes in his daily routine	2.16	2.60	4.13	4.96	3.91	3.33
62. Someone who is so self-conscious that it makes his life very difficult	2.22	2.16	3.33	5.04	4.29	3.53
63. Insane woman	2.20	2.93	3.20	3.47	3.33	1.31
64. A person who has cancer of the lungs	4.00	2.13	2.62	4.87	4.60	4.02
65. A tense person	3.27	2.91	5.49	4.89	4.73	3.40
66. Average man	4.84	5.07	5.49	5.56	5.38	5.33
67. A person who does not like to be with others	2.38	2.33	2.51	3.64	3.69	3.44
68. A person who lost both eyes in an auto accident	4.44	2.87	3.60	5.31	4.93	4.89
69. A person who is convinced he is someone else	1.51	3.04	4.07	3.53	2.51	2.02
70. An overly excited person	2.60	3.82	5.91	4.56	4.44	2.16
71. Someone who feels a strong hatred for the world	1.58	1.58	3.18	2.84	2.00	1.82
72. Someone with tuberculosis	3.93	2.69	2.51	4.58	4.53	4.36
73. A person who cannot help hurting others	2.02	2.24	3.93	2.58	2.62	2.24
74. Someone who cannot pull himself out of a sad spell	2.38	1.56	2.24	3.53	3.20	2.63

Scales

Weak ... Strong	Slow ... Fast	Delicate ... Rugged	Cold ... Warm	Dirty ... Clean	Dangerous ... Safe	Tense ... Relaxed	Worthless ... Valuable	Sick ... Healthy	Bad ... Good
2.18	3.76	2.91	3.60	4.44	3.38	1.64	3.84	2.91	4.07
1.87	3.16	2.67	3.40	4.40	2.69	1.51	3.20	2.31	4.02
2.40	4.07	4.20	2.53	3.47	1.71	3.13	2.09	2.84	2.47
2.27	2.76	3.29	3.73	3.96	2.98	3.53	2.60	3.29	3.51
2.96	3.93	3.44	3.20	5.02	4.02	1.76	3.71	3.31	4.04
2.42	3.20	2.96	3.67	4.89	4.30	1.84	4.07	3.42	4.42
2.98	4.00	3.24	3.20	3.40	1.60	1.84	2.27	1.40	3.13
2.58	3.13	2.18	4.04	4.47	4.27	2.73	3.84	1.24	4.20
3.71	5.18	3.91	3.82	4.93	4.11	1.36	4.16	3.49	4.22
5.49	4.87	5.31	5.42	5.73	5.67	5.31	5.96	5.44	5.64
2.91	3.24	3.42	2.62	4.27	3.89	2.71	3.84	3.27	3.76
4.31	3.09	4.02	4.76	4.64	4.93	3.51	4.91	3.62	4.87
2.31	3.82	3.44	3.67	4.24	2.47	2.29	2.89	2.22	3.67
3.00	5.36	3.56	4.27	4.42	3.16	1.58	3.53	3.27	3.98
2.24	3.36	3.40	1.91	3.62	1.60	1.91	2.04	2.09	2.22
2.58	2.71	2.80	4.18	4.56	3.29	3.09	3.91	1.49	4.31
2.71	3.82	3.73	2.44	3.93	2.13	2.22	2.73	2.91	2.89
2.18	2.82	2.76	3.22	4.00	3.18	2.38	3.09	2.40	3.62

6

Mean Semantic Differential Ratings by

Scales						Concepts
		Neurotic man	Average man	Insane woman	Average woman	Old man
Foolish	(men)	3.05	5.01	2.47	4.93	5.15
	(women)	3.01	5.37	2.82	5.17	5.04
Ignorant	(men)	4.10	5.34	3.02	5.43	5.37
	(women)	4.16	5.66	3.69	5.51	5.25
Sad	(men)	2.76	5.62	2.72	5.61	4.79
	(women)	2.43	5.94	2.86	5.73	5.01
Passive	(men)	4.00	5.77	3.04	5.72	3.49
	(women)	3.78	6.06	3.24	5.99	3.67
Insincere	(men)	3.95	5.78	2.99	5.60	5.38
	(women)	3.75	5.88	3.29	5.96	5.77
Poor	(men)	3.83	3.84	3.49	3.88	4.01
	(women)	3.87	4.14	3.81	4.05	4.05
Unpredictable	(men)	2.82	5.21	1.75	4.40	4.17
	(women)	2.43	5.26	1.59	4.48	4.19
Weak	(men)	2.93	5.17	3.21	4.66	3.41
	(women)	2.75	5.54	3.24	5.02	3.43
Slow	(men)	3.93	4.88	3.67	4.69	2.42
	(women)	3.58	5.09	4.01	4.93	2.52
Delicate	(men)	3.40	5.25	3.66	3.98	3.59
	(women)	3.65	5.66	3.85	4.49	3.60
Cold	(men)	3.49	5.32	3.60	5.37	4.83
	(women)	3.66	5.55	3.84	5.48	4.85
Dirty	(men)	4.62	5.85	3.59	6.20	4.84
	(women)	4.66	5.84	4.18	6.21	4.77
Dangerous	(men)	3.25	5.96	2.04	5.97	5.51
	(women)	3.45	6.14	2.28	6.21	5.39
Tense	(men)	2.10	5.10	1.93	4.72	5.18
	(women)	1.79	5.51	2.00	4.95	5.21
Worthless	(men)	3.90	5.93	2.89	5.96	5.35
	(women)	4.01	5.95	3.43	6.02	5.49
Sick	(men)	2.38	5.55	1.81	5.31	3.85
	(women)	2.25	5.74	1.66	5.37	3.90
Bad	(men)	4.15	5.88	3.51	6.02	5.71
	(women)	4.29	5.81	4.06	6.02	5.69

* Two matched groups of 50 men in one and 50 women in the other were
If the mean is above 4.00, it indicates that the concept is like the adjective on the
the left. Means cannot be greater than 7.0 nor less than 1.0.

Men (above) and Women (below)

Psychi-atrist	Neurotic woman	Insane man	Child	Me	Mother	Father	
5.92	2.80	2.69	4.68	4.94	5.99	5.60	Wise
6.09	2.74	2.84	4.86	4.90	5.91	5.84	
6.31	3.92	3.13	5.25	5.53	6.06	5.83	Intelligent
6.53	4.20	3.58	5.61	5.52	5.97	5.80	
4.86	2.88	2.97	6.30	5.83	5.83	5.80	Happy
5.27	2.32	2.99	6.29	6.21	5.63	5.56	
5.65	4.05	3.66	6.45	6.03	6.08	5.88	Active
5.89	3.82	3.40	6.66	6.24	6.15	6.03	
5.87	3.74	2.92	5.52	6.19	6.40	6.13	Sincere
6.25	3.55	3.20	6.32	6.41	6.41	6.37	
4.97	3.83	3.55	3.94	3.61	3.99	3.92	Rich
5.04	4.02	3.88	4.20	3.90	4.20	4.07	
5.04	2.84	1.70	2.94	5.26	5.79	5.34	Predictable
5.54	2.26	1.75	2.97	5.25	5.73	5.55	
5.21	2.94	3.31	5.05	5.41	5.44	5.67	Strong
5.71	2.72	3.24	5.03	5.20	5.64	5.73	
4.76	3.89	3.66	5.46	4.87	4.89	4.91	Fast
4.77	3.85	3.78	5.71	5.29	5.17	5.07	
4.69	3.23	3.98	4.69	5.34	4.39	5.46	Rugged
4.98	3.17	4.08	4.00	4.83	4.55	5.46	
5.17	3.32	3.36	5.95	5.67	5.96	5.91	Warm
5.05	3.43	3.55	6.27	5.76	5.94	5.67	
6.06	4.74	3.50	4.88	6.30	6.41	6.28	Clean
6.30	4.92	3.80	5.18	6.48	6.48	6.17	
5.92	3.41	2.84	5.56	6.28	6.51	6.20	Safe
6.05	3.56	2.00	5.66	6.48	6.49	6.44	
5.31	2.12	2.08	4.91	4.83	4.47	5.05	Relaxed
5.58	1.81	1.93	5.57	4.69	4.87	5.23	
6.22	3.89	2.72	6.38	5.72	6.52	6.25	Valuable
6.32	4.12	3.34	6.54	5.59	6.52	6.46	
5.54	2.49	1.67	5.79	6.07	5.27	5.19	Healthy
5.80	2.26	1.59	5.87	5.80	5.32	5.49	
5.96	4.33	3.25	5.95	5.94	6.49	6.32	Good
5.90	4.25	3.69	6.05	5.82	6.45	6.31	

selected from our opinion sample. They were matched in terms of age and education. right; if the mean is below 4.00, it indicates that the concept is like the adjective on

APPENDIX

7

Mean* Semantic Differential Ratings for a

Age 16-39 (below)

Scales   *Concepts*

		Neurotic man	Average man	Insane woman	Average woman	Old man
Foolish	(50–79)	2.70	5.18	2.26	5.42	5.12
	(16–39)	2.93	5.22	2.92	5.08	4.89
Ignorant	(50–79)	3.98	5.52	3.32	5.72	5.44
	(16–39)	4.10	5.45	3.67	5.33	5.22
Sad	(50–79)	2.48	5.84	3.00	5.70	5.02
	(16–39)	2.70	5.75	2.73	5.75	4.73
Passive	(50–79)	3.48	6.10	3.54	5.92	4.00
	(16–39)	4.15	5.87	3.37	5.72	3.50
Insincere	(50–79)	3.62	5.68	3.02	5.84	5.52
	(16–39)	3.90	5.90	3.32	5.95	5.52
Poor	(50–79)	3.70	3.88	3.58	3.84	3.98
	(16–39)	3.97	3.93	3.88	3.98	4.00
Unpredictable	(50–79)	2.78	5.08	1.80	4.44	4.46
	(16–39)	2.68	5.22	1.83	4.55	4.15
Weak	(50–79)	2.86	5.22	3.42	5.30	3.68
	(16–39)	2.95	5.28	3.42	4.48	3.53
Slow	(50–79)	3.62	4.88	3.86	4.98	2.72
	(16–39)	3.77	4.82	4.10	4.65	2.42
Delicate	(50–79)	3.22	5.54	3.60	4.66	3.52
	(16–39)	3.60	5.18	4.03	3.92	3.48
Cold	(50–79)	3.44	5.26	3.68	5.52	4.76
	(16–39)	3.78	5.42	3.98	5.23	4.82
Dirty	(50–79)	4.42	5.52	3.70	6.14	5.00
	(16–39)	4.55	5.90	4.25	6.18	4.58
Dangerous	(50–79)	3.60	6.02	1.86	6.28	5.50
	(16–39)	3.32	5.92	2.40	5.88	4.98
Tense	(50–79)	2.24	5.40	1.90	5.00	5.10
	(16–39)	1.87	5.13	1.98	4.70	5.10
Worthless	(50–79)	3.86	5.94	2.98	6.22	5.52
	(16–39)	3.77	5.88	3.18	5.82	5.25
Sick	(50–79)	2.20	5.70	2.08	5.16	4.02
	(16–39)	2.27	5.47	1.88	5.33	3.75
Bad	(50–79)	4.20	5.50	3.84	6.00	5.76
	(16–39)	4.20	6.00	3.82	5.85	5.43

* There were 50 subjects in the older group and 60 subjects in the younger group.
of sex ratio and education.

Group Age 50-79 (above) and a Group

Scales

Psychi-atrist	Neurotic woman	Insane man	Child	Me	Mother	Father	
6.00	2.54	2.46	4.86	5.14	6.18	5.78	Wise
5.85	2.92	3.27	4.65	4.85	5.87	5.73	
6.38	4.10	3.34	5.52	5.78	6.26	5.74	Intelligent
6.33	4.07	3.42	5.35	5.25	5.87	5.83	
5.20	2.52	2.96	6.40	6.12	5.76	5.88	Happy
4.97	2.52	2.73	6.33	5.98	5.70	5.67	
5.88	3.76	3.76	6.56	6.06	6.10	6.16	Active
5.72	4.23	3.35	6.58	6.18	6.02	5.75	
5.90	3.72	2.78	6.20	6.34	6.42	6.10	Sincere
5.93	4.03	3.28	5.68	6.17	6.32	6.25	
4.48	3.94	3.68	4.02	3.76	4.02	4.06	Rich
5.08	3.87	3.98	4.08	3.50	4.17	3.87	
5.12	2.72	3.72	3.46	5.58	5.96	5.48	Predictable
5.25	2.88	1.88	3.05	5.30	5.42	5.50	
5.52	2.82	3.38	5.12	5.28	5.72	5.64	Strong
5.28	2.87	3.15	4.93	5.37	5.28	5.60	
4.62	3.94	3.78	5.56	5.04	4.80	4.80	Fast
4.73	3.83	3.83	5.50	5.10	5.07	5.15	
5.18	3.06	4.02	5.16	5.14	4.58	5.54	Rugged
4.50	3.20	3.75	4.43	5.05	4.10	5.40	
4.90	3.62	3.48	6.16	5.68	6.04	5.64	Warm
5.02	3.30	3.50	6.10	5.82	5.58	5.65	
6.00	4.70	3.42	5.12	6.26	6.46	6.10	Clean
6.03	4.82	3.93	5.30	6.43	6.58	6.22	
5.96	3.68	3.90	5.98	6.46	6.46	6.24	Safe
5.97	3.33	2.17	5.33	6.17	6.33	6.17	
5.28	4.20	2.00	5.34	5.44	5.06	5.36	Relaxed
5.32	1.93	2.13	5.55	4.47	4.37	4.83	
6.02	3.82	2.70	6.52	5.64	6.64	6.14	Valuable
6.27	3.97	3.28	6.33	5.65	6.28	6.38	
5.60	2.26	1.78	5.92	5.62	5.48	5.50	Healthy
5.52	2.42	1.78	5.82	6.00	5.27	5.35	
5.76	4.32	3.34	5.96	5.72	6.60	6.32	Good
5.97	4.23	3.72	5.98	5.88	6.28	6.23	

The two groups were taken from our opinion panel. They were matched on the basis

8

Some Semantic Differential Results from Studies of High-school Students in Psychology Courses

FOLLOWING ARE SOME Semantic Differential results from studies of high-school psychology courses. Students from two schools are represented: H-A symbolizes students ($N = 36$) in psychology courses in one high school, and H-B symbolizes students ($N = 67$) in psychology courses in another high school. Results are also shown for a control group composed of students ($N = 58$) who were not participating in psychology courses. Their results are symbolized as C-A. Semantic Differential forms were administered to the students participating in psychology courses on three occasions—at the beginning of the semester, at the end of the semester, and six months to one year later. The control group was tested at the beginning of the semester and at the end of the semester but was not tested subsequently.

Mean * Semantic Differential Ratings

Concepts

Scale		Me			Insane people			Neurotic people			My parents		
		First test	Second test	Third test	First test	Second test	Third test	First test	Second test	Third test	First test	Second test	Third test
Evaluation	H-A	6.33	6.46	6.31	3.91	4.00	4.24	4.08	4.44	4.89	6.68	6.71	6.66
	H-B	6.33	6.29	6.42	3.84	3.76	4.17	4.09	4.50	4.70	6.79	6.72	6.72
	C-A	6.07	6.36	—	3.56	3.97	—	3.81	4.31	—	6.35	6.40	6.40
Tense-relaxed	H-A	4.94	4.64	4.89	1.61	1.92	1.64	2.11	1.61	1.75	4.89	4.50	4.67
	H-B	4.75	4.99	4.66	2.00	2.13	1.96	1.78	1.88	1.79	5.09	5.06	4.81
	C-A	4.78	5.03	—	1.67	1.86	—	2.36	2.79	—	4.31	4.22	—
Understandability	H-A	4.92	4.75	5.44	1.56	1.75	1.81	2.00	2.33	2.31	5.53	5.64	5.25
	H-B	4.87	5.52	5.22	1.76	1.81	2.00	2.36	2.54	2.69	5.75	5.84	5.85
	C-A	4.52	4.97	—	1.86	2.07	—	2.69	2.57	—	4.53	4.74	—
Sick-healthy	H-A	6.22	6.17	6.36	1.97	1.81	1.75	2.67	2.42	2.78	6.00	5.97	5.97
	H-B	6.46	6.54	6.57	1.75	1.99	1.90	2.57	2.43	2.51	6.03	6.16	6.25
	C-A	6.28	6.50	—	1.95	1.93	—	2.41	2.69	—	5.97	5.90	—
Dangerous-safe	H-A	6.69	6.69	6.56	2.53	2.72	2.64	3.25	3.97	4.08	6.61	6.75	6.44
	H-B	6.43	6.48	6.58	2.73	2.84	3.10	3.75	4.34	4.08	6.79	6.66	6.78
	C-A	6.22	6.53	—	2.45	2.74	—	2.99	3.35	—	6.45	6.40	—

* Ratings were made on a seven-point scale. The means are arranged such that a large mean always indicates "good" ratings—high in evaluation and understandability, and highly relaxed, healthy, and safe.

Mean Semantic Differential Ratings (continued)

Concepts

Scale		Most people			Old man			Ex-mental patient			Psychotherapy			Mental hospital		
		First test	Second test	Third test	First test	Second test	Third test	First test	Second test	Third test	First test	Second test	Third test	First test	Second test	Third test
Evaluation	H-A	5.79	6.14	6.10	5.15	5.47	5.85	5.71	5.91	5.72	5.49	6.00	6.27	6.45	6.41	6.54
	H-B	5.89	5.91	6.03	5.56	5.58	5.63	5.61	5.77	5.72	5.65	6.03	6.26	5.96	6.19	6.26
	C-A	5.76	5.95	—	5.24	5.36	—	5.29	5.53	—	5.11	5.46	—	5.51	5.94	—
Tense-relaxed	H-A	4.72	4.92	4.78	4.28	4.44	4.72	3.75	3.97	3.56	4.14	4.69	5.08	3.06	4.19	4.33
	H-B	4.39	4.40	4.27	4.96	5.06	5.06	3.67	3.87	3.84	5.09	5.27	5.39	3.58	4.61	4.13
	C-A	4.83	4.62	—	4.67	4.57	—	3.93	4.07	—	4.50	4.57	—	3.66	3.81	—
Understandability	H-A	4.00	4.42	4.69	3.56	3.92	4.78	4.28	4.89	4.44	3.61	4.08	4.39	4.14	4.36	4.61
	H-B	4.46	4.61	4.76	3.82	4.16	4.19	4.31	4.42	4.40	4.06	4.54	4.64	4.15	4.45	4.91
	C-A	4.24	4.41	—	3.67	3.43	—	4.38	4.19	—	3.98	4.50	—	4.07	4.45	—
Sick-healthy	H-A	5.39	6.08	5.81	3.64	3.83	3.69	4.75	4.81	5.00	4.22	4.78	5.11	4.14	3.97	4.50
	H-B	5.54	5.75	5.63	3.30	4.05	4.15	5.21	5.28	5.12	4.54	4.85	5.30	3.08	3.73	4.34
	C-A	5.48	5.59	—	3.78	3.62	—	4.41	4.41	—	4.83	4.71	—	3.60	4.16	—
Dangerous-safe	H-A	5.61	6.28	6.03	5.08	5.69	5.94	5.06	5.23	5.31	5.50	6.00	6.22	5.67	5.53	5.58
	H-B	5.78	5.91	6.08	5.97	6.03	6.02	5.51	5.66	5.40	5.87	5.99	6.22	5.12	5.48	5.72
	C-A	5.45	5.86	—	5.55	5.53	—	4.95	4.85	—	5.09	5.31	—	5.03	5.33	—

9

The Multiple-choice Association

Questionnaire

FOLLOWING IS THE multiple-choice association test mentioned in Chapter 4. It was a pilot instrument which was applied to a pilot sample of respondents. If it had produced results contradictory to those found with the Semantic Differential, or if it had added materially to the results of the Semantic Differential, we would have improved the instrument and administered it to larger groups. However, the results obtained from the instrument were very much the same as those found in prior Semantic Differential studies, and the instrument added only a small amount of new information about public attitudes.

The sample consisted of 101 persons in Lafayette, Indiana. Following are some demographic characteristics of the sample:

> Mean education: 10.5 years
> Mean age: 33.7 years
> Mean income: $3,800
> Number of men: 42 Number of women: 59

The frequencies of response to each alternative are included on the form. Because of incomplete data, some of the item frequencies add up to less than 101. Because of the closeness of the N to 100, the frequencies can be interpreted, approximately, as percents.

MENTAL-HEALTH OPINION QUESTIONNAIRE

This questionnaire concerns some things that you might believe about mental health problems. There are twenty statements in the questionnaire. We want to know what you think about each one of these. Under each statement there will be six possible answers. Please pick the answer that is nearest to what

/ **285**

you believe. You can see how this way of answering works with the following statement:

> I believe that the best way of disciplining children is to
> a. spank children whenever they disobey _____
> b. offer rewards for being good _____
> c. let children have their own way __√__
> d. try to reason with children _____
> e. keep their minds off of mischief _____
> f. withhold privileges for being bad _____

If you thought that it is best to "let children have their own way," then you would make a mark opposite answer "c." If one of the other answers was closer to what you believe, you would mark that one instead. Please mark one answer for each statement even if it does not fit your belief exactly. Please do *not* mark more than one answer for each statement, even if you feel that more than one is right.

We are not interested in what you think other people believe. It is your private opinion that we want. You will help us most by being as frank as possible.

We would appreciate it if you would give us the following information about yourself:

1. Age at nearest birthday _____ 2. Male _____ Female _____
3. Please circle the number of the last year of education completed:

Elementary	High School	College	
1 2 3 4 5 6 7 8	9 10 11 12	13 14 15 16	17 18 19

4. What is your major occupation? _____
   If you are retired, please list your former occupation. If you are gainfully employed less than four hours a day, please write in the word, such as "student" or "housewife," that would apply to your case.
5. What is the occupation of the major wage earner in your household? _____
   If you are the major wage earner, your answer to this question will be the same as your answer to question 4.
6. If you do not mind, would you check the group in which your total household income fell in 1954 (income of husband, wife, children, and any other sources).

under $1,500 _____	$6,001–7,500 _____
$1,501–3,000 _____	$7,501–9,000 _____
$3,001–4,500 _____	$9,001–10,500 _____
$4,501–6,000 _____	over $10,500 _____

QUESTIONNAIRE

1. *When I imagine an "insane" person, I usually think of*

   a. an old man 23
   b. a young woman 3

c. an ignorant person 39

d. an old woman 17

e. an intelligent person 18

f. a young man 0

2. *The best way to guarantee the mental health of my child would be*

   a. to avoid marrying anyone with insanity in his or her family 12

   b. to give the child all the affection and attention that he wants 22

   c. to show him the right path and make sure that he follows it 22

   d. to make sure that he stays physically healthy 25

   e. to keep his mind off of unpleasant ideas 5

   f. to let him work things out for himself 14

3. *When I think of a neurotic person (a person who has a nervous break-down), I also think of*

   a. selfishness 7

   b. physical weakness 31

   c. fear of something 39

   d. wild sex life 1

   e. being lonesome and unloved 23

   f. paying for misdeeds 0

4. *If I, myself, or someone close to me needed advice on mental health problems, I would*

   a. go to a psychological clinic 16

   b. ask my parents about it 3

   c. talk to my family doctor 47

   d. go to a psychiatrist 28

   e. seek religious guidance 5

   f. handle it myself 2

5. *A person who has a "neurosis" or a nervous breakdown*

   a. has a good chance of recovering if treated by a specialist 84

   b. has a good chance of recovering without treatment 2

   c. has a near-equal chance of getting better or worse 14

   d. is likely to become completely insane 0

   e. is likely to get better for a while and then get worse again 1

   f. will most likely be a permanent loss to society 0

6. *If a man who had recently been released from a mental hospital came to me for a job, I would*

   a. hire him if possible 15

   b. treat him like anyone else 39

   c. put him on a job that would not strain him 18

   d. hire him, but not for a job where the safety of others was in-volved 16

   e. hire him, but keep a close watch on his behavior 10

   f. not hire him 0

7. *When I last heard about a "crazy" person, it was probably from a*

    a. television show 21

    b. magazine article 17

    c. newspaper 23

    d. book 4

    e. movie 5

    f. friend 28

8. *Mental illness in this country is equal in seriousness to*

    a. automobile accidents 25

    b. heart disease 41

    c. polio 2

    d. alcoholism 28

    e. the common cold 1

    f. corns 1

9. *When I think of good mental health, I think mostly of*

    a. self-control 42

    b. physical health 22

    c. good inheritance 3

    d. someone greater than myself to rely on 3

    e. a secure childhood 19

    f. no worries 12

10. *If I were to spend the day in the home of someone who is mentally ill, I would*

    a. try to get him to talk about his problems 6

    b. expect him to do unusual things 6

    c. humor him in every way possible 9

    d. act like I do with everyone else 77

    e. try to stay as far away from him as possible 2

    f. treat him as I would a child 1

11. *When I imagine myself going to a psychiatrist, I think of*

    a. talking freely about whatever comes to mind 22

    b. letting him straighten out my life 7

    c. having to face and work out my own problems with his help 58

    d. revealing my most intimate thoughts about sex 0

    e. putting my problems in the hands of someone wiser than myself .. 14

    f. being hypnotized 0

12. *If a person who had been treated for a nervous breakdown wanted to borrow money, I would*

    a. consider the loan with him in the same way that I would with anyone else 66

    b. not lend the money 1

    c. lend the money only if there were someone to guarantee repay-
ment 24

    d. lend him only part of the money 2

    e. lend him the money only if he could pay it back in a short time .. 0

    f. be more likely to lend it to him than to other persons 7

13. *If a close relative living in my home were a mental case, I would*

    a. feel embarrassed when friends came to call 1

    b. be glad that I was there to help 51

    c. be afraid that he would cause trouble 2

    d. get my friends to make my relative feel more at ease 36

    e. keep out of social life to avoid trouble 1

    f. warn friends not to discuss his problems with him 9

14. *If a mental patient has been treated and pronounced cured, there is the best chance of remaining well if the person is*

    a. a child 68

    b. an older person 7

    c. a college graduate 12

    d. a woman 6

    e. an uneducated person 4

    f. a man 2

15. *If I needed information about mental health and illness, I would expect to find it in*

    a. radio programs 1

    b. magazines 14

    c. books 81

    d. movies 0

    e. newspapers 2

    f. television 1

16. *When I imagine a neurotic person, I think of*

    a. an old man 12

    b. a young woman 16

    c. an ignorant person 12

    d. an old woman 27

    e. an intelligent person 24

    f. a young man 6

17. *If I were to become mentally ill myself, I would probably*

    a. lose interest in things around me 32

    b. come to hate my friends 0

    c. feel worried all of the time 37

    d. forget who and where I was 2

    e. think that everyone was unfair to me 12

    f. lose my self-control 16

18. *When I think of a mental hospital, I also think of*

a. filth 1

b. hope 59

c. despair 29

d. peace 5

e. danger 3

f. cleanliness 2

19. *I would estimate the odds of one of my friends becoming mentally ill as*

a. 50/50 18

b. 1 in 4 10

c. 1 in 20 17

d. 1 in 100 29

e. 1 in 1,000 20

f. 1 in 10,000 6

20. *A person who is at present in a mental hospital*

a. has very little chance of ever coming home 4

b. may get out for a while, but will probably have to return 10

c. may come home but will never be normal 6

d. will probably recover by himself if he is left alone 2

e. will probably recover if treated for a long time 41

f. will usually recover after being treated for about a year 37

10

Information Interest Survey

*F*OLLOWING IS THE measure of public interest in mental-health topics which was discussed in Chapter 9. Responses were obtained from 190 members of our opinion panel. The mean responses to the item alternatives are recorded on the form. The means are restricted to the range of 1.00 to 4.00. A mean rank of 2.50 implies "average interest" (compared to the other three topics in each item). The nearer the mean rank is to 1.00, the higher the interest; the nearer the mean rank to 4.00, the lower the interest.

INFORMATION INTEREST SURVEY

This questionnaire concerns the things that you like to read about, listen to on the radio, and see in movies and on television. Each of the questions on the following pages will present four different types of programs or articles. We want you to pick the one that you like most and write the number 1 in the space to its left. Then choose the program that you would like next most and write the number 2 to its left, and so forth for the programs that you like third and fourth. An example of the kinds of items in the questionnaire is as follows:

Which one of the following kinds of sports would you rather watch on television?

2 Baseball

1 Boxing

4 Wrestling

3 Tennis

The person who marked this item liked boxing on television most, baseball second, tennis third, and wrestling fourth. Another person marking the same item might have liked them in a different order.

Each one of the questions will be of the kind shown in the above example. It is important that you complete each question and that you write the numbers 1, 2, 3, and 4 to fill all of the spaces. We will not be able to use your replies if you leave any of the spaces blank, if you place more than one number in a space, or if you use the same number twice in any one question (for example, marking both baseball and boxing 1 in the sample question).

What you indicate here may eventually have some influence on the things that actually appear on programs or in pamphlets. Therefore we are not interested in what you think people in general like. It is your own personal likes and dislikes that we want to learn. Thank you for helping us with this research.

In this first section of questionnaire we would like to learn your interest in a number of general topics. Please write the numbers 1, 2, 3, and 4 in the spaces to the left to indicate your order of interest in the topics in each group.

1. 2.26 Mental health
   2.26 Planning a vacation
   2.28 Comedy
   3.20 Industrial accidents

2. 3.15 Training your dog
   2.78 How they climbed Mt. Everest
   1.72 What we know about cancer
   2.36 Emotional sickness

3. 3.24 The life of a detective
   2.65 What you should know about vitamins
   2.65 The beginning of a "nervous breakdown"
   1.46 News about local events

4. 2.94 Skin disorders
   2.40 Treatment for the mentally ill
   1.75 Planning a home
   2.90 Civil War stories

5. 2.19 "Nervous" problems
   2.66 A serial on the life of a judge
   2.59 The birds of North America
   2.56 Do you have an allergy?

6. 1.96 What's happening in politics?
   2.20 Does weight affect your health?

   2.76 "High-strung" people
   3.08 Fun at the circus

7. 3.35 Catching and training lions
   2.38 The mental hospital
   2.29 The family car in 1970
   1.98 The life of a surgeon

8. 1.96 How to live with heart trouble
   3.18 How to become a salesman
   2.69 "Nerve" drugs
   2.17 An adventure tale

9. 2.08 The psychiatrist at work
   2.68 Are toothaches necessary?
   2.74 Romantic stories
   2.50 Do you have enough insurance?

10. 2.56 Business and financial news
    2.94 Psychological treatment
    2.33 Preventing a cold
    2.17 Musical programs

11. 2.28 Mystery adventures
    2.68 How to make your own furniture
    2.60 Psychological tests
    2.44 Tobacco and lung cancer

12. 1.90 How polio is being beaten
    2.65 Animals that act like humans
    2.66 Traveling in Europe
    2.80 The dull child

13. <u>2.42</u> The cause of jealousy
    <u>3.10</u> How to go around the world on a bicycle
    <u>2.29</u> Sports events
    <u>2.19</u> The family doctor

14. <u>2.21</u> Weather forecasts
    <u>2.60</u> Life in the Old West

    <u>2.88</u> Diet and constipation
    <u>2.32</u> Holding your temper

15. <u>3.42</u> The story of an unfaithful wife
    <u>2.35</u> Operating on the human heart
    <u>2.18</u> Getting along in marriage
    <u>2.05</u> World news

INSTRUCTIONS

In this next section of the questionnaire we would like to learn your interest in various mental-health topics. Each question will contain four titles of proposed programs or articles. Looking at only these titles, we would like you to indicate how much you would like to learn about the topics. Some of the titles will sound much alike. This is because it is necessary to make decisions about the kinds of subjects which will be placed in articles and programs. Please write the numbers 1, 2, 3, and 4 in the spaces to the left of each group of topics to indicate your relative interest in the subjects.

1. <u>2.29</u> The cure for a "nervous disposition"
  <u>2.43</u> Family aid for the person who worries too much
  <u>2.38</u> What can be done to help the overly emotional person
  <u>2.89</u> What can be done for a "nervous breakdown"

2. <u>2.31</u> What churches can do for the person who worries too much
  <u>1.99</u> Knowing emotional disorders when you see them
  <u>2.42</u> Help for an emotional disorder
  <u>3.28</u> How a mental-hospital patient acts

3. <u>2.36</u> How the family can help the person who has had a nervous breakdown
  <u>2.00</u> How "nervous breakdowns" develop
  <u>1.97</u> What causes emotional disorders
  <u>3.68</u> Emotional problems in government service

4. <u>1.65</u> How to recognize mental illness
  <u>2.66</u> The appearance of a person who worries a great deal
  <u>3.41</u> The cost to society for the treatment of neurosis
  <u>2.28</u> What to expect from a person who has emotional problems

5. <u>2.30</u> A cure for emotional sickness
  <u>3.08</u> The obstacles for a person who has had an emotional disorder
  <u>2.64</u> Treating the neurotic person
  <u>1.98</u> How an individual becomes neurotic

6. <u>3.09</u> Nervous breakdowns in the armed forces
  <u>2.43</u> What friends can do for the returning mental patient

2.04 The signs of insanity
2.44 How insanity develops

7. 3.20 The effect of emotional disorder in industry
   1.99 How schools can help prevent mental disorder
   2.77 What causes an individual to believe that he is someone else
   2.04 What makes an individual "overly sensitive"

8. 2.77 Treatment of mental-hospital patients
   2.30 How a mental disorder can be helped
   2.46 The road to mental illness
   2.47 How a person gets to be constantly afraid

9. 2.23 How the recovered neurotic can move back into society
   3.39 The cost to the community of mental illness
   2.14 What can be done to help the insane
   2.24 How the mentally ill move back into community life

10. 1.95 Knowing mental illness when you see it
    2.33 How the family can help the person who is recovering from mental illness
    2.87 Recovering from an emotional sickness
    2.86 The backgrounds of mental-hospital patients

11. 2.74 How schools can help the emotionally sick
    2.49 What friends can do for the "high-strung" individual
    2.51 What a "nervous disposition" will do to a man's work
    2.26 The signs of a "nervous disposition"

12. 3.13 How the community can aid the "overly sensitive" person
    2.42 Is there a cure for mental illness?
    2.47 How the family can help the overly emotional person
    1.98 What causes a person to worry too much?

13. 2.80 How a neurotic person acts
    2.42 How a person develops a "nervous disposition"
    2.53 How emotional problems can be handled
    2.25 How emotional problems develop

14. 2.71 What society must do for the insane
    2.94 The crowded conditions in mental hospitals
    1.62 How to tell when a "nervous breakdown" is coming on
    2.73 The obstacles for the person who was once insane

15. 1.96 How to recognize emotional sickness
    2.33 The treatment for a person who worries too much
    2.64 How an overly emotional person behaves
    3.06 How people react to someone who recovers from an emotional problem

16. 2.67 Psychotherapy
    2.08 Psychological counseling
    2.37 Psychoanalysis
    2.88 Shock treatment

17. 2.32 Medicines that make you restful
    2.57 Brain surgery
    2.51 Drugs that keep you from being anxious
    2.60 Mental-health drugs

18. 2.18 Advice on personal problems
    2.66 Mental-health clinics
    2.46 Advice on child rearing
    2.71 Psychological tests

19. 2.41 Psychoanalysis
    2.74 Psychotherapy
    2.70 Brain surgery
    2.16 Psychological counseling

20. 2.64 Mental-health drugs
    2.34 Medicines that make you restful
    2.45 Psychological tests
    2.56 Drugs that keep you from being anxious

21. 2.31 Advice on child rearing
    3.04 Shock treatment
    2.57 Mental-health clinics
    2.06 Advice on personal problems

22. 2.32 Psychoanalysis
    2.18 Psychological counseling
    2.66 Brain surgery
    2.84 Mental-health drugs

23. 2.64 Drugs that keep you from being anxious
    2.44 Medicines that make you restful
    2.30 Psychological tests
    2.63 Mental-health clinics

24. 1.90 Advice on personal problems
    2.60 Psychotherapy
    3.02 Shock treatment
    2.48 Advice on child rearing

25. 2.13 Psychological counseling
    2.71 Mental-health drugs
    2.68 Brain surgery
    2.48 Medicines that make you restful

26. 2.05 Advice on personal problems
    2.67 Mental-health clinics
    2.79 Drugs which keep you from being anxious
    2.50 Psychological tests

27. 2.34 Advice on child rearing
    2.51 Psychotherapy
    3.03 Shock treatment
    2.09 Psychological counseling

11

Content Analysis of the World

of Confession Magazines[1]

*T*HE "WORLD" we are here talking about has been created by approximately two dozen magazines which the trade calls "confessions" and which, for the most part, carry either "confessions" or "romance" in their titles. They appear monthly or bimonthly and sell largely on news stands. They offer sexy pictures and sensational titles ("Slave of Desire," "Bride by Force"). Their stories are told in the first person and purport to be "true" narratives of actual occurrences. To enforce this illusion of reality the magazines go to great lengths. Thus, except on rare occasions, their stories are anonymous. The magazines say they have "of course" changed names and places in the narratives. They avoid literary niceties, humor and satire, and prefer deadly serious studies of life problems. Occasionally a well-known story from recent history (for example, the Gray-Snider murder case) is interspersed among the anonymous "confessions."

This pretense to reality is apparently impressive and attractive to readers, for many of these magazines have enormous circulations. These are the top six among the confession periodicals, as listed by the Audit Bureau of Circulation in 1954:

True Story	2,473,169
True Confessions	1,418,720
Modern Romances	913,865
My Romance—Life Romance	824,486
True Romance	676,838
Secrets	593,624

[1] The study reported in this section was designed and executed by Dr. Wilbur Schramm. This section was taken verbatim from a project report written earlier by Dr. Schramm.

External evidence indicates that mostly these readers are women. And the letters they write to the editors are typically grateful and interested. For example, here is one which appeared in *True Story* for March 1955:

> . . . I never found a better magazine than yours. Your stories are so beautiful and true to life, and so easy to understand. The only thing which is too bad is that it appears only once a month.

It seems probable, therefore, that the world of the confession magazines is an important part of the experience of millions of women. It is therefore a world worth exploring.

The writer has attempted to explore it by the simple expedient of purchasing all the confession magazines available on local newsstands on February 15 and March 15, 1955,[2] and reading through them at random until 100 stories had been read and analyzed. It proved unnecessary to read that many. The results stabilized by the time 30 had been read. Indeed, the consistency and sameness of these magazines is one of their outstanding characteristics. The following pages are a report of this analysis— a description of reality as those magazines see it, an analysis of the life problems they treat and of the code by which they solve those problems, and finally an attempt to reconstruct the psychological formula of this kind of story.

The world of the confession magazines is a woman's world, a young person's world, an urban middle-class world, characterized by violence, overpowering sex drives, and broken homes. It is ruled by a code of ideal justice which demands and accepts payment for all transgressions against the code of accepted behavior. Therefore, the spectre of punishment constantly hangs over these stories. Let us look at some of the signposts of reality in the world these magazines describe.

THE PEOPLE AND PLACES IN THE STORIES

In the first place, life is typically seen in these magazines through the eyes of women in their twenties. The mean age of the narrators, so far as it was stated or inferred in our sample, is about 24 years (with a standard deviation of 5.4 years). This was the distribution by decades of age:

Age of narrator	
10–19	23%
20–29	58
30–39	16
40–	3

[2] In addition to the six previously mentioned, the sample included *Revealing Romances, Daring Romances, Personal Romances, Romance Time, My Romance, My Confession, My Love Secret, Real Story, True Romance, Romance Confessions, Intimate Romances.*

Eighty-eight of the 100 stories were told by women. In an even higher percentage, the main characters were women.

In the confession magazines few people are either very rich or very poor. The world is largely middle class, with some "upper-lower." So far as occupations go, the largest number of characters are housewives. Excluding this group, there was the following distribution of occupations in our sample:

Business	48%
Professions and art	19
Government	12
Industry	9
Farming and ranching	8
Shady jobs (gamblers, prostitutes, etc.)	4

Let us make clear, however, that the business people who appear in these stories are, except in rare instances, not tycoons. They are rather on the level of gift-shop operators, clerks, bookkeepers, and stenographers. On the other hand, the laborers live pretty well and show signs of rising in the world. Social class, therefore, is not very important in the confessions.

It is interesting that in these confession stories, as in radio soap operas, there should be such a large proportion of professional men. The reason may be simply that problems such as those in confession stories *require* doctors and lawyers. Or it may be that these are specially admired groups. But it should be noted that not all the professional men are admirable characters. One doctor in our sample runs an abortion racket. Another is an extortionist adulterer, and murderer. One lawyer is a shady dealer.

Most of these people live in an urban setting. Although the setting is deliberately left vague in such stories as these, still it was clear that no more than nine stories out of 100 had a rural setting. Twelve stories took place in a metropolis; the other 79, in small towns or cities.

When the setting is specified, California is most likely to be the place—13 percent of all stories in our sample. Florida was mentioned in 5 percent, the South outside Florida in 5 percent, New York and Brooklyn in 4 percent, Chicago in 1 percent, and the Middle West outside Chicago in 5 percent.

THEIR GOALS AND DRIVES

It is rather surprising that religion should appear as seldom as it does in these stories, which are so centrally concerned with the problems of atoning for "mistakes" and achieving peace and happiness. In only 3 percent of the stories in our sample was religion referred to in any significant way—in each case, positively, as a help in trouble. But the chief goals and values stated were worldly rather than spiritual.

It is rather surprising, too, that so relatively little attention among the worldly goals should be paid to economic striving. This became significant in about 15 percent of our stories, and in nearly half of those some illegitimate means—swindling, stealing, gambling, murder—was used as a means to the end.

It is not the economic but rather the sex drive that seems to dominate these people. The stories are animated Kinsey tables. Thus, for example,

> 40 percent of the stories in our sample contained incidents of adultery;
> 32 percent described premarital relations;
> 8 percent described rape;
> 4 percent described prostitution.

Sex drives were typically described as "overwhelming" and "overpowering," and love scenes were usually described with gusto, even though covered over with later shame.

The most common problem of these stories is to get these drives in socially accepted channels. Thus it is not surprising that the most frequently and clearly stated goal in these stories is a happy and secure family life. As one story in our sample puts it, "The two most important things a woman needs are self-respect and the right man's love. . . . A good home and marital relationships are more to be desired than any other success."

We shall have to say more about this later when we talk about the "code" of the confessions. It will be sufficient here to note that the world of the confessions seems to operate under a stern code of justice which demands punishment for every transgression, but will accept repentance and reward it with peace. On the one hand, therefore, these stories describe (with some relish) "overpowering" sex drives, and, on the other hand, they portray a goal of self-respect and marital happiness which can only be attained by making peace with a puritanical judge, who is neither spiritual nor legal, but seems to operate through the structure of social relations. This is the most common dynamic of the stories.

THEIR SOCIAL RELATIONSHIPS

Family life in these confession stories is—to put it mildly—troubled. Broken homes played significant parts in the family history of 38 percent of the narrators, and 44 percent of them reported their own marriages, at some point in the story, on the verge of breaking up. Looking back over their childhood, 21 percent of the narrators remembered unpleasant scenes in the marital relationship of their parents. Recorded in the stories are:

> frequent severe family quarrels
> beatings of children
> slappings

a wife murdering her husband

a father trying to sell a child

a foster-father trying to rape his daughter

mothers jealous of their daughters and fathers of their sons

a mother kicking her daughter out of the house because the daughter interfered with the mother's current romance

These stories are not notable for characterization, and despite this about one out of five of the parents portrayed are clearly portrayed as strong authoritarian types.

Inside or outside the family, there is no monotony in social relationships, because violence is always around the corner. The amount of this violence is rather surprising in magazines which make such prominent use of the title "romance." In our sample:

One out of every *four* stories told of an *accident,* two thirds of the accidents being fatal.

One out of every *six* stories had a *fist fight.*

One out of every *seven* had a *murder.*

One out of every *eight* had a violent *quarrel* without bloodshed.

One out of every *twelve* had a *rape.*

Drunkenness occurred, on the average, in one of every six stories. Among the many other instances of violence were beatings, a man gored by a bull, an earthquake, a knifing, a prison riot, epileptic seizures, and four suicides.

Illness comes frequently to the confessions, also. One out of three of the stories in our sample carried some reference to illness. Heart disease was the most persistent complaint. Few of the writers ever "confess" run-of-the-mill illnesses, like head colds or influenza. Their confessions run to more spectacular ailments: tuberculosis, surgical operations, death of a baby, an overdose of sleeping pills, epilepsy, an abortion, and death in childbirth.

One out of every five stories contains some reference to mental illness. The most frequent trouble is hysteria, but there is also senility, amnesia, a sexual psychopath, and what appears to be a case of schizophrenia described in considerable detail with many scenes inside a mental hospital.

In general the private services—such as hospitals—appear in a somewhat whiter light than the public services. While the majority of the policemen are businesslike and apparently kind, some are clearly crooked. A mayor is in cahoots with the local vice ring. A social worker is a "well-meaning nuisance." Judges, for the most part, are wise and well meaning. The government itself appears in terms of persons and services—police courts, old people's homes, asylums, sanitariums, and so forth—rather than in terms of elections and political issues.

These are a few of the external characteristics of the world of confession magazines. Now let us look at something which may tell us rather more about what kind of world it is—the kind of problems these magazines face up to.

THEIR PROBLEMS

When one reads a number of these stories consecutively, as the writer did, one gets the sensation of eavesdropping on a marriage clinic. Making and maintaining a happy marriage appears to be the center in the world of the confession magazines. In one way or another, practically all the stories deal with this value and the problem of achieving it.

By way of illustration, here is a list of central problems in our sample of stories. Because stories often deal with more than one problem, it is difficult to be quantitative with this list. However, the classes of problems in the table below are numbered roughly in the order of frequency of occurrence, class 1 being the most frequent. Under each class there are a few illustrative examples taken from the sample.

1. *The problem of controlling sex*

   What should a married woman do when she feels an overpowering passion for a man who is not her husband?

   How can a woman defend herself against sexual urges which she feels will ruin her life?

   How can one avoid being a slave to sex?

   Can love be bought?

   Will a "good-time" philosophy make for a happy marriage?

   Can sex rightly and effectively be used for business advancement?

2. *The problem of a past*

   Is it ever good to hide one's "past"? (A frequently recurring problem)

   How can a "blot on the family escutcheon" be kept from ruining a child's life?

   What should a woman do when she discovers that a former affair of her husband had resulted in an illegitimate child?

   How can a wife forget "the other woman"?

3. *The problem of adjustment*

   How can jealousy in a family be overcome?

   How can desirable relations be built up between child and foster-parent?

   How can a woman keep her individuality and still blend into a harmonious family relationship?

   How can hostility and jealousy between father and son be overcome?

4. *The problem of divorce and remarriage*

   What is the effect of divorce on children?

   How can a marriage be saved when it seems to be turning sour?

   How can one learn to be a good foster-parent?

   When should a woman take back her divorced husband?

5. *The problem of understanding*
   How can a girl make her father understand that he should not try to dominate her love life?
   What can a girl do when her mother doesn't let the girl have dates?
   Where can a girl who has lost her mother get the affection and attention she deserves?
6. *The problem of mismatching*
   What can a wife do about an unromantic second husband?
   What happens when a wife wants to have fun, but her husband wants to stay home?
   Can a prim girl and a wild boy make a happy marriage?
7. *The problem of philandering*
   Should a woman forgive her husband's philandering in order to hold the home together?
8. *The problem of illness*
   What does a case of mental illness do to a marriage?
   What does a case of tuberculosis do to a marriage?
9. *The problem of belongingness*
   How can a woman manage to feel needed, after her husband is dead and her children are married?
10. *The problem of a jilting*
    What effect does a jilting have on a woman's life?

Let us say again that the illustrative problems under each class in the preceding table are, in one or more cases each, the central problems of a confession story. They are quite explicitly stated, and never left unsolved. Indeed, as one reads through these magazines, one becomes aware of a sort of code by which the answers are given. Let us now turn our attention to this code.

THEIR CODE

Two characteristics of the confession magazines are quickly noted. One of these we have already suggested: the stern, fixed quality of the code by which justice is meted out and problems are solved. The other is the almost eighteenth-century willingness of these writers to moralize in print. It is possible, in fact, to complete a reasonable facsimile of the confession code by direct quotes from the stories in our sample:

The two most important things a woman needs are self-respect and the right man's love. . . . A good home and marital relationships are worth more than any other success.

These two sentiments are from different stories, and might be echoed from many others. They illustrate what we have already suggested as the central value of this confessional world: a happy, secure married life.

Life always exacts payment for a wrong. . . . But, the worst mistake can be changed into something fine.

This is the central dynamic of the confessions: you never "get by" with anything; you always pay for a mistake. But on the other hand, you *can* pay for it. You can expiate a sin. By doing the right thing, you can make a good life out of a sordid one, a happy marriage out of an unhappy beginning. Expiation and forgiveness walk side by side.

In other words, a code of ideal justice operates in the world of the confessions. Who administers the code? Who is the judge? There is very little reference to an ultimate source of wisdom; as we have already noted, very little reference to religion. Rather, the impression is given that this is the pattern of a behavioristic universe; this is how society works; this is the law of human behavior.

Patience, sacrifice, and compromise are ingredients of a happy marriage.

Almost like marriage counselors, these stories drum on the theme that a successful marriage has to be *made* successful. The magazines are full of accounts of marriages that started out most unpromisingly and still were salvaged. Thus, for example, a competent but not very pretty girl found the way to her husband's heart. A patient, understanding mother found the way to make both her son and his stepfather happy. Et cetera.

Once desire blots out honor, all is lost. . . . Once the devil has the soul of a woman, only violence and death can set her free.

These florid statements are direct quotes, and from different stories. A number of these writers profess to be considerably worried over the power of the sex drive. A number of the stories show the final sad plight of individuals who take their sex outside the code. Thus, for example, a wife who falls victim to an overpowering passion for a married man not her husband drives her own husband to commit murder, and herself goes to prison—although with the expressed intention of "paying her debt" and still making something good of her life. A big mistake like that can be atoned for only by complete repentance and major punishment. On the other hand, a small mistake can be atoned for on a lesser level. A husband infatuated with his secretary (in one of these stories) can be welcomed back to the family circle after he "comes to his senses" and cools his heels for a while at the front door. Even a real philanderer can, under the proper circumstances of repentance, be forgiven and taken back. On the other hand, adultery is invariably punished severely in these stories, and premarital relations, as we shall see in a moment, are regarded as highly dangerous to future happiness.

You are taking a terrible chance when you indulge in premarital relationships.

This kind of behavior seems to be at least as frequent in the confessions as in the Kinsey tables. It is apparently regarded as a lesser mistake than adultery, but still a highly dangerous one. In these stories it is usually atoned for by violence, too early marriage, miscarriages, loss of the right man, loss of respect, and so forth.

A man who has got a girl in trouble sticks by her.

Mistake or not, it is part of the code that a man does the right thing by a girl he has helped to get pregnant.

There is danger in shallow dreams. Love a man for what he is. . . . Value a faithful husband, even if he is stodgy.

The atmosphere of these stories is essentially realistic. The young girls can dream of Lochinvar, but when the chips are down they are advised by these stories to settle for a secure home and a husband who loves them even if he does not make love or dance or look like a movie star. It is very interesting to see how these "romance" magazines basically advise young women to shake the dew out of their eyes and the dreams out of their heads.

Talk out your troubles and your past; don't hide them. . . . But, sometimes it is better not to confess your past.

This is not an essential conflict. It is merely a behavioristic look at the situation. Usually it is better to talk things out frankly. Thus, by hiding her epilepsy, the heroine of one of these stories lost her fiance. On the other hand, there are conditions when one is only endangering family bonds by revealing a past. When a mistake has been atoned for, it is possible in some circumstances to lock it up tightly and say nothing. Several heroines in these confessions found it possible to "make a new start." And in perhaps the only instance within these confessions where adultery was not severely punished, a wife hid her indiscretion in order to make her impotent husband think he was not impotent. This was a case in which the husband had lost his potency when gored by a bull. The marriage was going on the rocks, when the wife had a brief *Walpurgisnacht* affair with a visiting artist and became pregnant. In this case, her atonement was in self-blame and fear of discovery. But a kindly family doctor kept her secret, the husband was saved from a bad psychological state, and the marriage went on happily.

You can't buy love.

Love has to be earned, and within the code.

Perhaps this will be sufficient to illustrate the general dimensions of the code.

THE FORMULA OF THE CONFESSIONS

It is always risky to try to deduce a communication formula without knowing either how the communicator intended it or the audience perceives it. It would be very interesting to know more about how readers use these magazines. Nevertheless, the confession formula is more apparent than most, and we can hazard an analysis of it which can and should be checked against later audience research.

Basic to the formula, of course, is the deliberately induced sense of reality—the hiding of the author's name, the first-person narration, the ostentatious covering up of names and places. In effect, then, the reader of one of these stories is being invited to eavesdrop or peep on a very personal scene which would otherwise be hidden from him. He is invited not only to enjoy the skilled narrative and safely vicarious satisfactions which he gets from fiction, but also to enjoy the specially favored status of being allowed to look in on someone else's "real-life" problem.

As far as problems go, this world of confession magazines revolves around the central problem of most women's lives: making a success of love and marriage. A woman can therefore turn to these magazines for reassurance that other people also have problems like hers—in fact, many of them have much more severe problems of the same kind. Furthermore, a reader can turn to these magazines for good advice on some of the problems. Ought she confess that episode out of her past? How can she handle a husband who always wants to sit at home in the evenings? And so forth. And still more important, the reader can get from these magazines a comforting sense that this is not a world of chance or caprice, but rather of order and justice. If she makes a mistake, she can do something to rectify it. Her neighbor, who seems to be getting by with murder, will be caught up with in good time; nobody is "getting by" with anything. But neither is anyone foredoomed to unhappiness, providing he is willing to do something about it. It is a comforting pattern of justice and free will.

So far, so good. But this does not yet explain the sexy pictures and the headlines, the youthfulness of most of the narrators, or the luscious descriptions of sexual relationships—many of them outside the code. Let us consider those circumstances.

It is clear that the formula tries to encourage the reader to identify with the narrator. If, therefore, the narrator can be made attractive and "sexy," so much the more complimentary to the reader. If the narrator can be put through love experiences which the reader may desire but cannot, for one reason or another, undertake, then perhaps the reader can reduce some drives vicariously. The reader can eat the cake and have it, too. Why are the narrators so young? Because, for one thing, this is the time of life when the stormiest experiences—and hence the most exciting stories—may be expected. Furthermore, an older reader can flatter herself by identifying with a girl in her twenties because the girl of that age is so young and attractive and full of energy, whereas a teen-age reader can also flatter herself by identifying with a narrator in her twenties because a girl of that age will be comparatively so "experienced."

The luscious descriptions of sex relationships in terms of "ecstasy," buckling knees, crumbling resistance, overpowering attractiveness, and so forth are apparently only an extra flavor in the drink. These incidents can be described safely because the inexorable code deals with them. On the other hand, they must represent a good deal of the vicarious satisfaction for many readers. It is almost as though these magazines were saying that such sexual deviations are reprehensible, but weren't they fun? Or, how desirable the straight-laced secure married life is, but how interesting to look back to a few scarlet chapters in the past!

Why so much moralizing? Why such a puritanical outlook on retribution? Unquestionably, these elements fill a void in our twentieth-century social structure. Things were safer, if duller, during the Victorian period when every young lady knew what was proper. Now the rules are more difficult to discern. The strong emphasis on punishment in these stories is a necessary rein on the desires the stories must arouse. It is hard to see how this cycle of arousal and repression could result in anything but tension in readers. That is another reason why it would be extremely interesting to know more about the readers and what use they make of these magazines.

References

Carroll, J. B. *A factor analysis of literary style*, Parts 1 and 2 (privately circulated mimeographed report), 1958.

Gray, W. S., and B. E. Leary. *What makes a book readable*. Chicago: University of Chicgo Press, 1935.

Hovland, C., I. Janis, and H. Kelley. *Communication and persuasion*. New Haven, Conn.: Yale University Press, 1953.

Nunnally, J. C. The communication of mental health information: A comparison of the opinions of experts and the public with mass media presentations. *Behav. Sci.* (1957), 2, 222–230.

———. Opinions of psychologists and psychiatrists about mental health problems. *J. consult. Psychol.* (1958), 22, 178–182.

———, and H. M. Bobren. Attitude change with false information. *Publ. Opin. Quart.* (1959), 23, 260–266.

———, and H. M. Bobren. Variables governing the willingness to receive communications on mental health. *J. Pers.* (1959), 27, 38–46.

———, and T. R. Husek. The phony language examination: An approach to the measurement of response bias. *Educ. psychol. Measmt.* (1958, a), 18, 275–282.

———, and T. R. Husek. "Semantic clarity": One standard for factored tests. *Educ. psychol. Measmt.* (1958, b), 18, 761–767.

———, and J. M. Kittross. Public attitudes toward mental health professions. *Amer. Psychologist* (1958), 13, 589–594.

Osgood, C. E., G. J. Suci, and P. H. Tannenbaum. *The measurement of meaning*. Urbana, Ill.: University of Illinois Press, 1957.

Stolurow, L. M., and J. R. Newman. A factorial analysis of objective features of printed language presumably related to reading difficulty. *J. Educ. Res.* (1959), 52, No. 7.

Survey Research Center. *A study of public attitudes toward mental health problems*. Vol. 1. *Causes of problems and means of solution* (mimeographed material). Ann Arbor, Mich.: University of Michigan, Sept. 1950.

Taylor, W. L. Gauging the mental health content of the mass media. *Journ. Quart.* (1957), 34, 191–201.

Walker, Helen M., and J. Lev. *Statistical inference*. New York: Holt, Rinehart and Winston, 1953.

Index

49450

RC Popular conceptions of
455 mental health, their
N8 development and change.
Nunnally, Jum C.